Red Dust Rising

For
Frederick Augustus and Maria Fryer -1864
and Ivor and Mary Jacobson - 1871,
The first arrivals.

Edward and Katherine Fryer
The pioneers- 1914.

Timothy, John, Scot and Fiona;
Katherine and John;
Samuel and Anna
Their descendants.

And,
Very especially,
Alexandra Mary Fryer,

8th August 1991 – 16th August 1999

Remembered with love.

Red Dust Rising

The Story of Ray Fryer of Urapunga

Marion Houldsworth

First published in 2004 by Central Queensland University Press

Published in 2011 by
Boolarong Press
PO Box 308
Moorooka QLd 4105

National Library of Australia Cataloguing-in-Publication entry

Author: Houldsworth, Marion.

Title: Red dust rising / Marion Houldsworth.

ISBN: 9781921920165 (pbk.)
ISBN: 9781921920172 (ebook)

Subjects: Fryer, Ray.
Cattle breeders--Northern Territory--Roper River Region--Biography.
Ranch life--Northern Territory--Roper River Region--Biography.
Roper River Region (N.T.)--Biography.

Dewey Number: 636.213092

Typeset in Berkeley Book 11pt

Cover design and typesetting by Jane Dorrington.
Cover photograph by Mick Swain (www.stephographics.com.au)
Images courtesy Professor Harry Messel were taken from his 13 volume monograph titled: *Surveys of Tidal River Systems in the Northern Territory of Australia and Their Crocodile Populations*, Pergamon Press, Sydney 1980

Printed by Boolarong Press, Salisbury Qld 4107

ACKNOWLEDGEMENTS

Where would any of us be without family and friends? Without a son like Michael, spot-on at proof-reading; without sons-in-law like Kristian and Nick, to subdue the snarls of subversive lap-tops; without daughters like Elizabeth and Airlie, to give sympathetic ear when the going gets rough? Our families are surely the source of the courage, inspiration and getting-on-with-it that make achievement of any sort not only possible, but worth while, for any of us.

And friends! The 'icing on the damper' of life! Nic and Brenda Wilson, with whom I once had the unforgetable experience of climbing Central Mount Stuart, acted as consultants on the history of the Overland Telegraph Line, in which Nic has had a lifelong interst, while Brenda, who worked with noted leprosy specialist, Dr. John Hargraves, gave me invaluable advice on the subject.

Louise and Michael Michie of Darwin, the parents of my godson Rhys, not only tracked down information on crocodile attacks in the Northern Territory but discovered that Rodney Ansell, upon whom the film character Crocodile Dundee was based, had worked on Urapunga station, been declared Territorian of the Year for 1988, been convicted of cattle duffing and was killed in a police shoot-out in 1999. That's the Northern Territory!

Warmest thanks to lifelong friends, Beryl and Ron Quelch of Townsville, Pearl Mahony of Brisbane, Graham and Joan Greenleaf of the Gold Coast and Marion and Charles Jaggers of Sydney for home-away-from home hospitality in the passenger pigeon lifestyle entailed in gathering material for a this type of book. Also to talented young friend, Melinda McKerney for her graphic designs, and Charles Jaggers for maps.

Very special thanks are due to Professor Harry Messel for permission to use photographs from Sydney University's ground-breaking Surveys of Tidal River Systems in the Northern Territory of Australia and Their Crocodile Populations.The work of Professor Messel and his team has done much towards arresting the decline in crocodile and barramundi populations in Australia's northern waters. Thanks also to Professor Gordon Grigg for use of photographs from his personal collection, and to Brother Robin, B.S.D, archivist of All Souls St Gabriels School Charters Towers, for photographs of All Souls during World War Two.

People imagine an editor to be a remote person sitting in judgement upon struggling authors. Not so Professor David Myers, of Central Queensland University's Outback Books. In his office, phones ring continually; emails pour in. Yet, should someone call needing help his voice remains calm and unflappable and he has all the time in the world to sort out the problem. No mere 'verandah-boss',

David Myers, 'Old Silvertail' of Outback Books, makes each person feel they really matter. At helping to preserve the spirit of the outback in its written history and stories there can be none better.

I would also like to pay tribute to the inspiration I have derived from the undaunted courage and determination of Gail Shann, who, though grievously injured in a fencing accident while working with her husband, Mac, on their property, Cantaur Park near Clermont, still faces the future with a lovely smile and a cheerful heart. There can be no-one who is not bettered by Gail's 'Never give in! Never give up!' indomitable spirit. Her courage sets the standard for us all.

CONTENTS

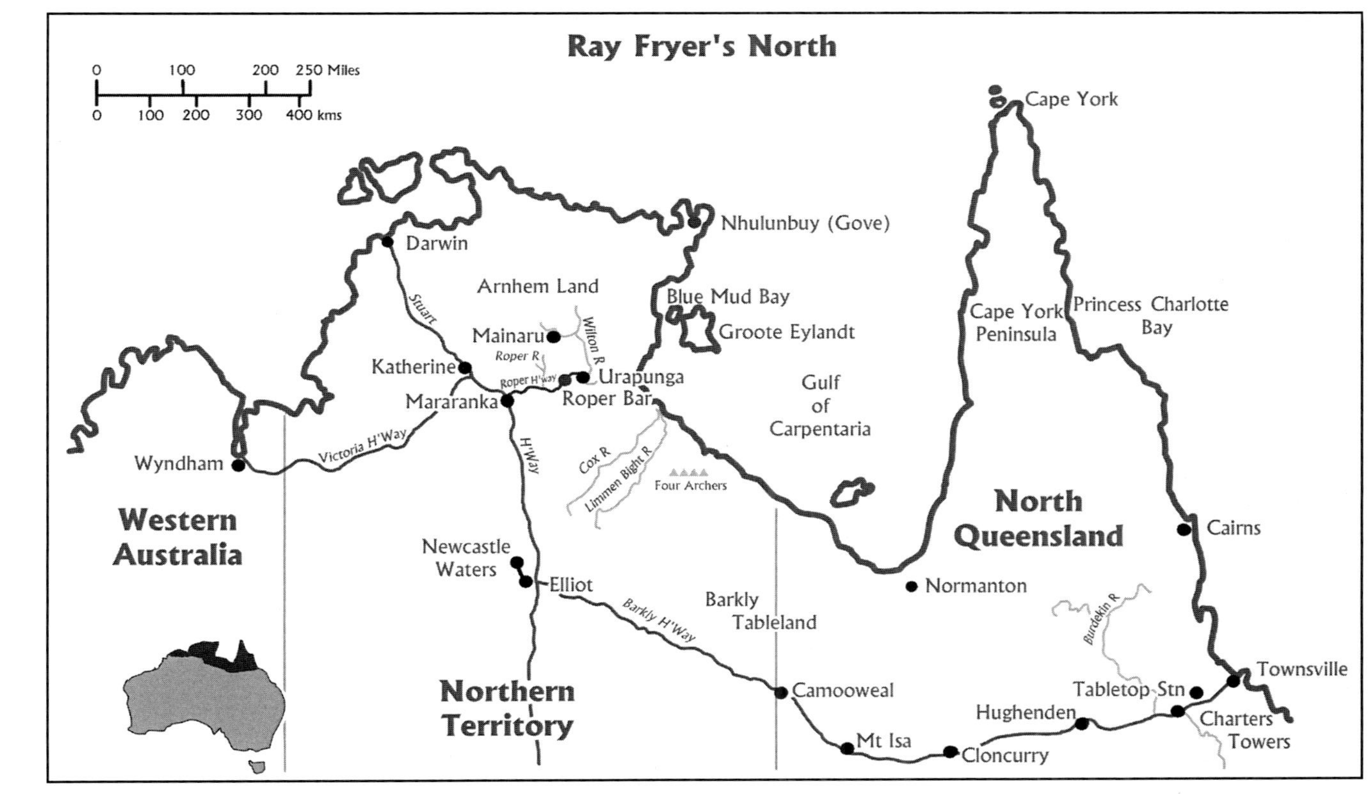

Ray Fryer's North
0 100 200 250 Miles
0 100 200 300 400 kms
Cape York
Nhulunbuy (Gove)
Darwin
Arnhem Land
Blue Mud Bay
Groote Eylandt
Cape York Peninsula
Princess Charlotte Bay
Mainaru
Wilton R
Roper R
Katherine
Roper H'way
Urapunga
Roper Bar
Mararanka
Gulf of Carpentaria
Stuart
Victoria H'Way
Wyndham
H'Way
Cox R
Limmen Bight R
Four Archers
North Queensland
Cairns
Western Australia
Newcastle Waters
Elliot
Normanton
Barkly Tableland
Barkly H'Way
Burdekin R
Townsville
Northern Territory
Camooweal
Tabletop Stn
Hughenden
Charters Towers
Mt Isa
Cloncurry

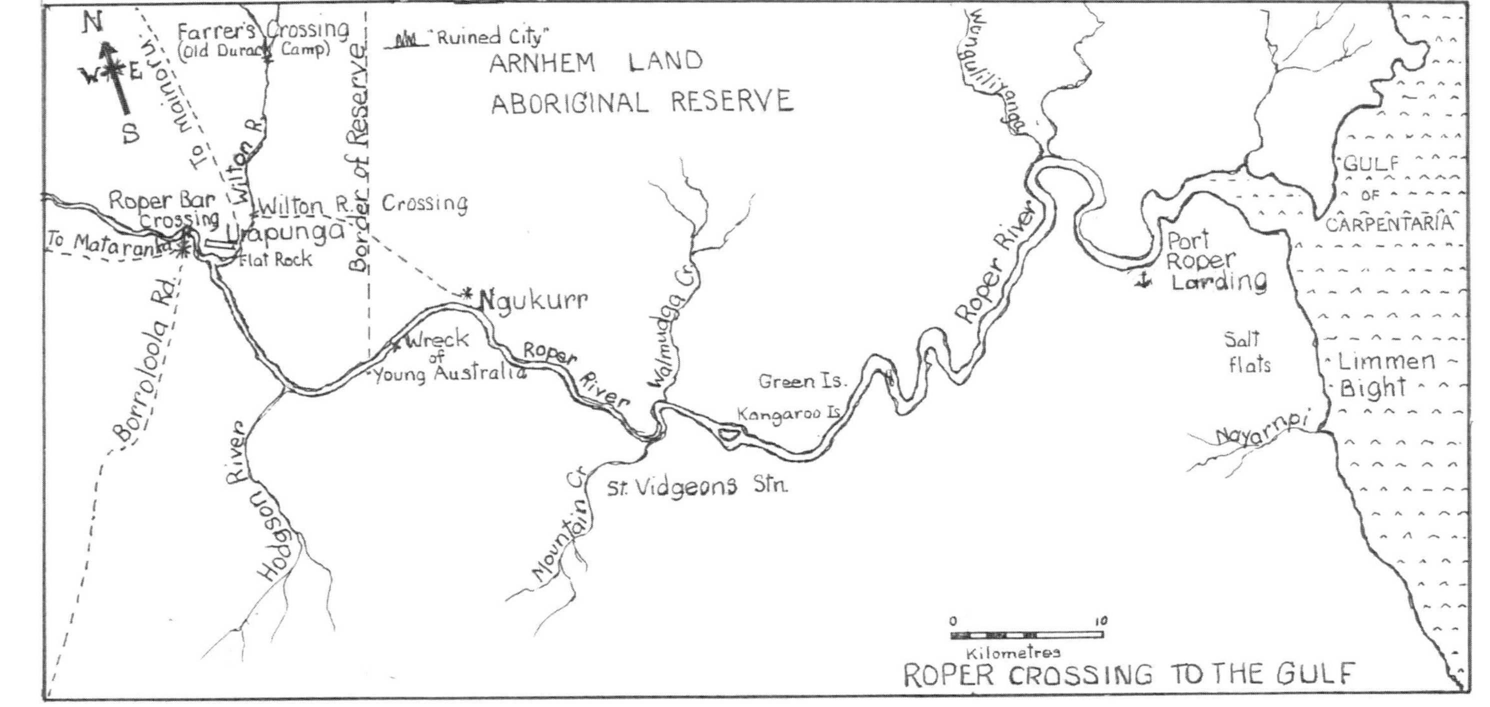

A 'mud-map' of the navigable course of the Roper from Roper Bar Crossing to the Gulf, based on information supplied by Capt. 'Bunny' Warren of the Sydney University Crocodile Research vessel *The Harry Messel*.

FOREWORD

When asked to write a foreword to *Red Dust Rising: The Story of Ray Fryer of Urapunga*, I saw it as a great opportunity to sing the praises of the Roper River as well as Urapunga and Ray Fryer himself. Digging back through my archives I found a short story that I had put together some twenty years ago, dealing both with Ray and Urapunga, penned back in 1988, in many ways making it even more relevant. I had called it:

URAPUNGA

"The words 'Ray Fryer' and 'Urapunga' go together like hand and glove. The two have been mixed up with each other for over a quarter of a century now, but I came across the pair of them in more recent times, about fifteen years ago. Urapunga Station was little more than a bark hut when Ray took it on, but like the man himself, the property was large. Ray is a big bloke physically, and pretty big hearted to go with it.

The first time I met him was late one morning. I'd been on the road for a month or two and simply drifted into the homestead. No longer a simple bark hut, Ray had created an oasis; slate-floored homestead, surrounded by mobs of green grass, big shade trees and lawn sprinklers. Peacocks perched on the roof of the house and in the branches of the trees. At the time, Ray was sitting at the kitchen table having a cup of tea, a big pannikin clasped in his paw-like mitt of a hand. It was a scene I became used to over the years. Ray's hospitality was the thing I remember most. As it said on the property signpost, "Urapunga - Home of Outback Hospitality". A true statement if ever there was one.

I stayed a day or two before moving on up into Arnhem Land, a youngish Army Captain in an old Army Land Rover, conscientiously chasing Bush Tucker. The years rolled by and I kept coming back and Urapunga became the place to stop for awhile, a place to recharge the batteries after months of battling the bush. Ray was one of the older, more-experienced cattle men, Queensland born and bred. He had his ideas about Aborigines and I had mine. They were not exactly the same, but the strange thing is I can't ever remember us ever arguing about it. That was the last thing either of us would have wanted and it never happened.

But Ray was a funny bloke. Every time I arrived at Urapunga he was quick to provide the cup of tea, pull up a stump on the cool verandah and have a yarn. Eventually the conversation always seemed to get around to Aborigines, and Ray used to go hammer and tongs on the subject. I'm sure he used to save up these stories for when I turned up again, because every time he had a fresh batch to tell. The Aboriginal population at Urapunga had grown from almost nothing to well over a hundred or so, and a primary school was set up at the station by the Northern Territory government. The kids were allowed pretty much free run of the shady garden and virtually used it as their own school yard.

Over the years I saw Ray's attitude mellow a bit; perhaps age was making its mark. He seemed to spend more time on the verandah than he used to, and the pace of the property was slowing down. The Aboriginals still camped out the back, if something went badly wrong like sickness, lack of food or even a death, it was still Ray they immediately turned to for help. And Ray's help was always forthcoming.

In 1987 for a variety of reasons, Ray found himself forced to put Urapunga up for auction. It had been his whole life for over three decades but there was no alternative. Ray Fryer and Urapunga parted company for the first time. He's probably a bit lost without his cups of tea and wide verandahs.

I drove past Urapunga the other day but didn't bother to call in. What would be the point! It's not the same place without Ray Fryer. Down the road a bit were some Aborigines beside their broken down car. They were from Urapunga and they said something which surprised me. 'Ray Fryer was a good bloke, might be he come back one day?' Might be indeed, because in this country.........anything can happen!

Les Hiddins
TOWNSVILLE.

INTRODUCTION

To enjoy Ray Fryer's story you should imagine yourself on the wide front verandah of the homestead at Tabletop, the family property on Hervey's Range, west of Townsville where the Fryers have lived since the early years of last century. The homestead is surrounded by lawns, gardens and shady trees. An avenue of venerable pines leads across the home paddock from the red-dust road, 'two cattle-grids', from the road to Greenvale and the Gulf.

Visitors come and go, for Ray and Betty Fryer keep open house. Most of their entertaining is done around the generously large table on the front verandah where an over-size enamel teapot makes continual trips to the kitchen for refills.

Most of the stories told by Ray on the tape-recordings which went to make this book were told around this table. Others however, were gathered round the campfire at the Outback Celebrations, 2002, in Charters Towers, which Ray, with his inexhaustible energy and enthusiasm, helped to organize, by fund-raising round the Gulf. In the background as the tape-recorder winds slowly, catching something of the lively yarns swapped backwards and forwards across the verandah, are the screeches of Ray's wandering peacocks, the chinkling of wind-chimes in the cool breeze – for Tabletop is degrees cooler than Townsville's coastal humidity – the hoo-hahing of kookaburras, or the occasional shout of 'Ray! The horses are in the garden!' It was drought time and they were after green pickings.

Ray Fryer could be called the quintessential Australian cattleman; quiet, understated, of tremendous drive and energy, down to earth, no nonsense – if brumbies have to be shot they have to be shot, for from the mountainous country backing on to Tabletop small herds frequently move into the station horse paddocks. Decisive, honest as the day, Ray would never do a bad turn for anyone and is first off the mark to do a good one. He possesses an amazing capacity for lateral thinking and the practicality to make his ideas work; adapting the principle of the drip-cooled Coolgardie safes of his boyhood to cooling the homestead at Urapunga with roof-top sprinklers being one striking example.

Ray's account of building up Urapunga almost from scratch; of carting rails for fences, of catching scrub bulls, of camping out for weeks at a time mustering yet still cooking for the camp, 'knocking up the dampers' at night, of spending the Wet making bricks for the homestead, makes the reader feel exhausted in the imagining. But there is something in Ray's story, of starting off from scratch – 'reaching up to touch bottom' as he calls it – and over the years building up a beautiful property, that stirs the pioneer spirit still deep within the Australian psyche. Something in us yearns to be fencing paddocks, pacing out the ground for a homestead, laying out lawns and gardens, planting fruit trees, building a chook run. We also recognize, ruefully, that few of us have the courage, the skill, the stamina and the sheer guts required. But as Ray, in his inimitable way tells his story, we can enjoy the dream at one remove, and revel in the thought that, Yes, this is what we Aussies can do if we set our minds to it, and be proud.

The reader should not be offended by Ray's swearing. It is simply part of the rhythm of his speech, always laconic and understated, never offensive or abusive. Similarly, his use of the terms 'gin' and 'blackfella'; never used in any derogatory sense, and usually with a great deal of affection – often admiration. Ray made a point of getting on well with the Aborigines of Urapunga, not only because they were valued members of his work-force but because he was deeply interested in their culture and their bush-skillls. He admired the artless courage with which they undertook the demanding and dangerous work involved in the northern cattle-industry especially their feats of bull-dogging, comparable, he felt, to the bull-vaulting skills of the youth of ancient Crete.

It was like pulling teeth to get Ray to make any admission of achievement on his own part, or even of emotional involvement. For example, in his recounting of the crash of the helicopter, I said, 'Yes, but how did you FEEL at that moment?' In response, all Ray could come up with was the recall of the pilot's comment, 'Shut up! Who's flying this thing!' Any fear he felt of imminent death it is forgotten. The only fear Ray does admit to is of the ever-present crocodiles in the rivers and lagoons of the Top End, and what sensible person wouldn't! Rays sincerest expression of emotion was in the recounting of the death of the old station saddler, Stan Norgren. The digging of the grave and the bush burial are in the best tradition of Bush Mateship. Henry Lawson would have looked on with approval.

Ray is uncompromisingly stubborn. He says of himself, 'My Dad taught us, if you know a thing is right, then stick to it!' His life-story demonstrates that he never knowingly deviated from what he believed to be 'the right thing'. Undeterred by the hostility of high government officialdom, wealthy but unscrupulous businessmen, and local hostility, he had Urapunga legally declared an Alcohol Free Zone, the first of its kind in the Northern Territory.

The book-shelves at Tabletop hold nearly every book on the outback ever published. Ray has an almost encyclopaedic knowledge of the cattle industry. If you ask a question, nine times out of ten he will know the answer. If he doesn't he will have an appropriate reference book at hand, or 'an old mate who will know'. Ray phones and, invariably, the 'old mate' does 'know'. They are a fraternity, the cattle men of the North. Their shared knowledge would fill volumes. Their experiences even more. They are a living part of the Australian legend. We honour them as such.

Ray's other great love is the history of Australia in two world wars. He says of himself, 'If there's a new war book out, I have to have it.' He has visited many of the War Cemeteries in Europe and the Middle East where Australians fought and died.

Ray's capacity for friendship is in the great Australian tradition of mateship. All that is necessary to be made welcome at Tabletop is genuineness of heart and a capacity for taking pleasure in the shared memories of the outback way of life. All are made welcome, from University academics, who, to their surprise, might find themselves chopping up an ironbark pumpkin for dinner while they talk, to television celebrities, down-to-earth bush-workers, truckies and drovers. Ray's most sincere commendation of a man is that he is 'a mate of mine. A very decent bloke,' or, more eloquently, 'a fine man'. What better tribute can any man ask? The outcome of any biography should be to increase respect for the subject. Ray's story, told in his own inimitable fashion, enhances our understanding and respect for all the mates, men and women, who, like himself, have 'put their backs' into the task of making the outback a better place for their having given their lives to it.

Methodology

I find the best method of getting a story on tape is simply to leave the tape-recorder playing on the table while people are talking. The rattling of tea-cups and spoons in the background serves to liven the proceedings. Ray and I between us may have originated a new method of doing oral history. Time ran out for me to record all the stories I needed to make this book. A much-loved daughter in England has four small boys, including twins, so it was Qantas, and away. But what is a problem but something to be solved! Of finding another way around difficulties? Ray bought a tape-recorder compatible with mine. I outlined problems and questions by phone; Ray recorded his responses and posted them; Presto! Long-distance interviewing! We did not use expensive equipment. Pocket-sized Sony micro-cassettes did splendidly.

My pleasure in doing so has been immeasurable. To catch something of a way of life which is now fading from memory, and to record some of the forgotten technologies that were part of everyday life – how to make a greenhide bed, how to preserve sacks of flour over the wet season (you sink them in a tank of water, of course!) is deeply satisfying. I especially loved writing the chapter about Tabletop station in the early days and of Ray's large family growing up, hardy, resilient, yet courteously concerned not only for one another but for neighbours and passing strangers. Understanding something of our past as personified by this exemplary North Queensland family enriches our own experience enormously. To me, Ray's story seems to embody all that is fine, manly and worthwhile about the Australian way of life. I hope that readers will similarly identify with his experiences of 'making a go of things' and that they, too, will take pride and pleasure in sharing them.

Prologue...

'RESUMED FOR ARMY EXERCISES...'

A cloud of dust was coming down the road. I was working at the homestead that day, loading the truck with gear to go brumby shooting. They were coming down out of the mountains and the stallion was getting into our mares. We wanted to get rid of them. I stopped work and waited to see who it was coming. The car drove in over the grid and this fellow in a town suit, with a brief-case in his hand, got out. I thought, 'I don't like the look of this. Who the hell is it?' But I went over and said, 'G'day', and shook hands.

He introduced himself and then he said, 'I'm from the Taxation Department. I'm the valuer.' Straight away alarm bells started to ring. I thought, 'Bloody hell! What's going on! What are they after?' He gave it to me straight. He said, 'They are going to be taking all that high country off you. It's being resumed. The army wants it for a training area.' He might as well have landed me one over the head with a shovel. My Dad had opened up Tabletop back in the early 1900s. Cleared it by hand. Now the government was going to resume it; just like that! I said, 'Christ! Can't they go somewhere else!' He said, 'No! This is where they've decided on. It's got the terrain, mountains, creeks, open areas, scrub; the lot. Ideal for army exercises. And it's close enough to Townsville to be ideal. They've got to have it.'

And so it was decided for us. The army would take all the high range country. We could keep most of the open tableland area, have access to the high country and under certain conditions we would still be able to graze a limited number of stock there. So things weren't as bad as they seemed at first.

But all the same I decided it was time to do something I had always wanted to do, and that was get out and go up to the Territory. Since Dad's death in 1948 my brother Fred and I had been running the place for Mother. I knew Fred could take over and handle it by himself. He'd always managed pretty well. And I'd always wanted get a place of my own. Now was the time.

I've always admired those old-time pioneers like the Duracks and the Buchanans who took cattle right across the north and opened up new country. I'd always wanted to have a go at something like that; something with a bit of challenge; where you could decide for yourself that when you got a few bob whether you would fence across a certain valley, or build a set of yards, or put up a shed. I wanted to breed up a herd from scratch. So I thought, Right! I'll poke on up to the Top End and have a bit of a look around. So, that's what I did. I threw my swag and my saddle and a bit of gear on to my truck and headed off.

And, Hell! Some of the places the agents told me to have a look at! Weren't they rough!

The first place they sent me to see was a place called Coniston[1], north west of the Alice, owned by a decent old chap by the name of Brian Bowman. He was brother-in-law to that chap who was killed in the Sundown murders in the '50s; the whole family were shot by a mongrel fellow while they were camped for the night. He even shot the dog. They caught up with him eventually in the Isa and he was the last person ever to be hanged in South Australia. Anyhow, this Brian Bowman was a decent stamp of old bloke. He also owned Glen Helen. He said to me, 'If you're looking around for a place to buy you'd better come out to Coniston and have a look round. See what you think of it.'

The manager of Dalgety's said to me on the quiet, 'Have you got your swag?' I said to him, 'Yes. I always carry my swag. I never travel without it.' He said, 'That's alright then, because don't go expecting the Hilton Hotel when you get out there.' I picked up from that that there might have been a bit of a galvanized-iron shed when we got there, or something along those lines.

But, God! This old fellow was a card! A couple of hundred miles north-west of Alice, way out on the edge of the Tanami country, and we get to this bit of a bough-shelter-looking place; there's a few gins sitting about. I'm thinking it's a bit of a mustering camp or something like that. But, no! That was the homestead! All there was were two old busted-up caravans with a bit of a bough shed over them and a thirty-thousand gallon water-tank. That was it!

He said to me, 'Just hang around for a bit and we'll get a cup of tea and we'll go out and check the waters. He calls out to this old gin, 'Put the billy on!' There's this old enamel mug lying out in the sand. She strolls over and picks it up and gives it a bit of a shake under the tap. I thought to myself, 'Oh, well. The tea's been boiled so that's OK.'

So we had a cup of tea and Brian says, 'I want to go up and see some of me cattle.' He says to the women, 'Hey! Get a bit of tucker on, will you! A man's got to have a feed, hasn't he!'

And this old gin, she gets up and she saunters over to this shoulder-blade of beef; it's been hanging up there in a bit of shade under this bough-shelter for God knows how long! Covered in flies! And she gets an axe, and, bang, she hits it about ten times till it will bend up enough. And there's this old drum lying out there in the dirt. She throws this shoulder in and chucks a bit of water in on top of it. And Brian, he yells out, 'You'll find a bag of spuds and onions and a pumpkin in the back of the truck!' So she gets them, and, bang, she chops them up with the axe. Made short work of the pumpkin! No knives or anything. And chucks them into the drum along with the meat and she sticks the whole thing on this smoky old fire they've got going.

And Brian, he says to me, 'Come on. I'll show you round the watering points while dinner's cooking, and you can get a look at me cattle.' So it's hours later when we get back. The fire's out. Gins all just sitting about. Flies everywhere! 'I dunno!' says Brian, 'You can't trust these bloody women to even get a feed going for a man!' So he stirs them up a bit. And I'm thinking to myself, 'Christ! How the hell am I going to get out of this one!' So I took my swag and went round behind the tank in a bit of shade and threw it down. And I'm lying down and after a bit Brian comes round to get me. 'Dinner's ready!' he says. And I tell him, 'I don't know, Brian. I'm a bit crook or something. I'll just have a bit of a camp, and I reckon I'll be all right.'

Brian says, 'Crook in the guts, eh? Poor bugger! Yeah! You know what it is. It's that bloody water back in the Alice! If you're not used to it it'll get you in the guts! Something wrong with the bore they've got in there, I reckon. But you sure you don't want something to eat? There's plenty here!'

And that night a big storm came up. Old Brian says, 'I don't like the look of them clouds. You can be caught in here for a few days if these rivers come down!' 'Jesus!' I thought, 'That's all I need!'

Brian came over to me about eight o'clock and he said, 'How yer feeling?' I said, 'Oh, I'll be pretty right when I've had a bit of a camp.' He said, 'I reckon we'd better go. This storm looks as though it could come. We don't want to get caught.'

Oh, wasn't that the best news I ever heard! So we hop in the truck and away we go! And we drive half the night through to Pine Hill, a lovely place, nice homestead, lawns all round, just out from Aileron, owned by a chap named Joe Dowling. His wife, she was English; a lovely lady. She said, 'Would you care for some breakfast?' I said, 'Oh, I don't want to put you to any trouble. We'll be in the Alice shortly.' She said, 'Oh, No! No! You must have something to eat. I've got some scones here. I've just taken them out of the oven.'

So we had these scones, and I must have made a hog of myself, because old Brian says, 'Well, he must be feeling better now! He couldn't eat last night!' And then he says, 'Yer know. That storm didn't come after all!' I thought, 'Jesus! I hope to Christ he doesn't want to turn around and go back!'

You know; I don't mind living a bit rough. I can throw my swag down anywhere; get a bit of a fire going, and I'm instantly at home. Sleep out under the stars, anywhere. I always reckon the best sort of motel is the Starlight Motel! But, God, there's got to be cleanliness! The man doing the cooking is the most important man in the camp. If the tucker's good then everyone is happy and they work better for it. There's no worse thing than a greasy cook!

So, anyway, I went to New Zealand Loan in Darwin and they gave me a list of places that were on the market in the Top End. And one, Urapunga, looked like being the only place that I could raise enough money to get into. They showed me the details; situated on the Roper River, 729 square miles that joined Arnhem Land on the east, and 23 miles of frontage on to the Roper, so plenty of water. On the south was Roper River Mission, with about a thousand blacks. And on the western side, Roper River Valley and Elsey. To the north were Mainoru and Mountain Valley, and to the south, Nutwood Downs and Hodgson Downs. It sounded the sort of place I was after so I thought I'd drive out and have a look at it.

I drove down to Mataranka, which wasn't much of a place in those days; just a roadside store and a couple of houses. They used to reckon there were two Shirleys in Mataranka – Sister Shirley and Shaggin' Shirley! From there out to the Roper there was only a two-wheel bush track – half the time you had to find it – a couple of hundred miles; that's dry-weather time, from May to October. You would never get through in the Wet, with all the creeks and jump-ups. One of them was the Elsey, where a big spring comes out of a volcanic crater called the Punchbowl.The Aboriginal name is something like Potchupul. There are big stands of palms and the water is very deep and very clear. Another bad crossing was the Strangways; all flat country that would bog a duck.You had to go miles up-river to find a crossing. Even after the road was built in later years the Strangways would always hold you up during the Wet. And all through that country you get a tree called kullawan along creeks or gullies, anywhere wet, a type of melaleuca, and, God! You've never smelt such a horrible smell! Just like flying-fox camp! Anyway, I finally got through to Roper Bar, on the western boundary of Urapunga. There was a Police Reserve with a policeman stationed there, nothing else. I crossed the river at the big rock bar, Leichhardt's Bar, discovered by Leichhardt on his trip north in 1845. I didn't know much about crocodiles in those days or I'd have been a bit more wary! There were plenty there.

When at last I got to Urapunga to where the homestead was, well! It consisted of a bark hut! Just a bit of a humpy made out of paper-bark and a few sheets of iron. There were some people there, a man named Ray Arven and his wife, a part-Aboriginal woman, and about four or five kids. They weren't too pleased to see me. The man gave me to understand that they had a part share in the place. I told them I had come to have a look around because I believed it was on the market. They bailed up on me. They didn't want to show me around at all.

So I drove back over Roper Bar to the police-station and managed to get a telegram through on the two-way radio with a message to the agent in Darwin. He told me I was within my rights to just go ahead. So I went back to this bit of a hut and told the fellow that was there that I had the OK, that the place was on the market. He agreed to let me use some of their horses. I had my own saddles and gear with me. There was an old blackfella there, Duncan Yappanala, head of the Rittarangu tribe, who in the years to come turned out to be a very loyal man to me. He said he would show me round the place, and he and I rode around and he showed me where all the waters were. As well as the Roper there was another big stream, the Wilton, as well as plenty of creeks and permanent waterholes and lagoons, well-grassed river-flats, lightly timbered country – I'm not much of a one for that open downs country; I like to see a few hills and ranges.

After a few days of this we pulled up on the top of a bit of a ridge and I looked at the Roper River heading away towards the Gulf, eighty-four miles away, and the big, wide open valleys of the place – the Wilton Valley, thirty miles to the ranges of the Arnhem Land border. I knew there would be a hell of a lot of work. There were no decent yards; no fencing; clapped-out looking cattle; mongrel horses; but I knew it was just what I had always wanted to take on, a decent sort of a challenge, somewhere I could build up from scratch. So I looked around me, and I looked at

Old Duncan and he gave me a bit of a grin, like an old mate would, and I thought to myself, 'By God! Yes! This is it!'

I went back up to Darwin to finalize buying the place, but not without a lot of problems caused by the people that were there. They had the idea they were there for the duration, even though it turned out they were just caretakers. They didn't give up without a fight. They refused to sign the papers. But in the end the agent got things settled and that was how I got started at Urapunga. It would have been somewhere in the early 'sixties.

1 Scene of the 1928 massacre of a number of Aborigines during a reprisal raid under Constble Murray from Alice Springs to avenge the spearing of a prospector Frederick Brooks who had been enticing the local Aboriginal women to his camp.

one...

'A BIT OF A CHALLENGE'

Tabletop Station in the Early Days

But to back-track a bit. I think any man is pretty-much the product of the family he comes from. And I want to pay tribute to my mother and father. They gave me – gave all eight of us kids – a pretty good start in life. And I'm not talking about finances. Dad didn't believe in that. He thought every man should make his own way in life – get out and work under a boss; learn to take orders before he starts giving them himself; and to stand on his own two feet.

What I mean by a good start is that Dad and Mother taught us good principles – good attitudes; that you had to pitch into things and pull your weight; always do the right thing; stand up for what you know to be right; and always to consider other people as well as yourself. Everything I have achieved in my life I owe to the way Mother and Dad brought us kids up. I take my hat off to them in every respect.

"Two cattle-grids in off the main road you'll come to our turn-off," we tell visitors to Tabletop, our family place, about thirty miles west of Townsville on Hervey's Range. There's an all-weather road up the range now, but when my parents took up the place in 1914, the only access was the old bullock-wagon track. It was so steep that the teamsters used to have to double-hitch their wagons to get up before they headed off inland, south across Fanning River to Charters Towers or north across the Upper Burdekin to Einasleigh and Georgetown and the Gulf.

Dad had worked for Dotswood station to the north, so when he drew the block in 1914, he had a fair idea of the the country, and he rode around looking it over. He wanted to build the homestead and yards as close as possible to where the old bullock-wagon track came up over the range so that he would have access to the meatworks on the coast. To fulfil the Lands Department agreement he had to put in improvements such as fences and a dwelling worth two thousand pounds within two years. First he wanted to make sure of there would be a decent water supply, so he and Mother's brother, Joe, sank a well. They struck water at thirty feet and Dad decided, that was it! That was where he would build the homestead. They logged in the well and later Dad put a Southern Cross mill on it.

The old homestead at Tabletop, on which Edward Fryer began work in 1914, adding rooms as the family grew.

Dad built the homestead, section by section. There was no such thing as sawn timber so everything was cut by hand out of the bush and brought in by horse and dray. Each slab of timber was hand-adzed, drilled with a one-inch auger and pegged into place with hand-made wooden pegs. The land was well-timbered with ironbark, blue gum and swamp mahogany. Some of those trees were so big around the girth that a man couldn't get his arms around them. Swamp mahogany is a good timber to work with, but no good in the ground. It was a good, soft timber for adzing so Dad used that for the walls and ceilings. Ironbark and blue-gum that could go straight into the ground were used for the out-buildings. The stumps for the house were ironbark.

Dad did all the work himself, as the older boys, Chris and Gulliver, were still only little fellows, five and six, when they took up Tabletop. Mother used to say that in the early years when Dad was burning-off, Chris and Gulliver used to get so black, that at night she would put a bag on the ground near the well, scrub them down and tell them, 'Now, don't you move!' until she got them clean enough to put to bed.

Sometimes Dad would have one or two itinerant workers passing through, as they did in those days after the war, when there was no dole, who gave him a bit of a hand. That bullock-wagon road up over the range was the road to the tin-fields in the north, so there were a lot of old tin-scratchers foot-walking up to Georgetown. They would call in and maybe help Dad grub a few trees in exchange for rations. There were also returned servicemen after the First World War looking for work. And when they were off on their way again Mother would fill their tucker-bags with corned-beef and sweet-potatoes and bread and, always, a brownie. Mother was a wonderful woman. She knew the hardships of their life.

Slab-built sheds on Tabletop station, the timber for which was felled on the property and hand-adzed by Edward Fryer about 1915. The slabs were drilled with a one inch auger and pegged into position with handmade wooden pegs.

There were good natural waters on the property, the Star River, Keelbottom Creek and the Upper Burdekin. To be on the safe side Dad also sank wells, sufficient to keep the water up to the stock in bad times. Drought years were tough. They just got through as best they could. After the First World War was over Dad was able to put in more improvements, yards and fencing and sheds and gardens and gradually began to build the property up.

Ticks were a problem right from the start. Dipping was done with arsenical dip; arsenic and caustic soda mixed at a rate of seven pounds of arsenic to every four hundred gallons of water. The mixture was boiled up and poured into the dip. You had to be very careful that you didn't make it over-strength or it would pull the hair off the beasts and kill the calves. There was no other means of tick control and that was what everyone had to do. Ticks were so bad Dad had to dip about every three weeks. He would just seem to be finished when he would have to start again.

Our brand was ULO. Cattle ready for the market were sold to the meatworks in Townsville; Dad and the older boys walked them down the wagon-road through to Townsville meatworks for slaughter. As I got on a bit, I would go with them. I thought it was great, getting out of the school-room. Dad would have been getting about two pounds or two pounds ten a head for cattle at the time. That was the average price right up till the war years. Then about 1939, Paddy Kelly, an old saddler who used to work his way round doing a bit of saddlery from station to station, called in on his way through, and he said to Mother and Dad 'Did you hear what Tom Salmon from Burdekin Downs got for his bullocks! Five pound a head!' That was regarded as phenomenal! Mother said, 'Five pounds ! Never! Who would ever think to hear it!' It seemed impossible to believe. In those days the price of a bullock was about the same as the price of a good working saddle. You would get a very fancy saddle for five pounds! But once war broke out the Department of Defence got into the act and all bullocks were put through the meatworks at a set price. After the war someone said, 'It won't be long till bullocks come twenty pounds a head!' But everyone agreed it would never come to that.

Once when Old Paddy was leaving Mother called out to him, 'Well, look after yourself, Paddy!' He called back, 'Yes! It's no good gettin' crook! Once you're dead you're buggered!' Mother had a wonderful way of always seeing the best in people. She believed every person was good until they proved themselves otherwise, and she instilled into us that you treat everyone the way you would like to be treated yourself.

My father was a man who never smoked, drank or swore and he must have been one of the gentlest, best-natured men that ever lived. He was a cousin of the Bishop of North Queensland, Bishop John Feetham, who used to come and visit Tabletop when we were kids. Maybe he thought he was going to straighten us all out! He used to get my elder brothers to make him a bit of a bough shed down the creek. A funny man! Mother would have a room and everything ready for him but he used to say to her, 'Oh, No. I like the fresh air and the open!' [1]

Dad's father had been a colonel in the Indian Army. He was the first Governor of Burma. Then he came to Australia and set up in partnership in an exporting and importing firm, Carter and Fryer, in the very early days of Townsville. At one stage he had some sort of a business partnership with Robert Towns who Townsville is named after. Grandfather built a weatherboard house with verandahs, called 'Eagles Nest' on Melton Hill right above where the waterfall is today. He probably thought he was a cut above the rest because one of his ancestors, Sir John Fryer, was Lord Mayor of London in 1720. Melton Hill in those days extended into the sea and people could only get around it in their sulkies at certain times of the tide. Then they blasted it away for stone for the first breakwater in the 1870s. Grandfather used to park his sulky at the foot of the hill about opposite St. Joseph's School, which is how Fryer Street got its name. Later he had a property on the Upper Ross called Five Head Creek, the three rock pinnacles you can see in the range west of Townsville were named Frederick's Peak after him.

Of course, being English, he had the homestead built on the river's edge because it was picturesque. He didn't wake up to the fact that rivers in Australia rise quickly after rain. So when a big flood came down he looked out and saw the river running a banker and he exclaimed, 'My God! Unless we move we are all going to be drowned!' He tied a rope from the house to a tree on the hillside and carried Grandma and the children to safety one by one.

Grandma had left a hurricane lamp on the kitchen table and they watched it all through the night. Then suddenly the lamp started to move and was gone. They knew then that the homestead had been washed away. They were marooned on that hillside for several days and Grandma told my mother that there is no worse sound in the world for a mother to hear than her little children crying with hunger when she has no food to give them. On the second day an old cow swam up on to the same hill so they caught her and milked her and survived on her milk until the flood receded. Grandmother had a courageous heart. When the flood went down sufficiently she set off into town on a horse to get help from her father, who owned the Queen's Hotel. She took Father, who must have been about ten at the time, to accompany her. She couldn't swim so when they came to the river she had to slip off and catch hold of the horse's tail and let it pull her across while father swam beside the saddle and guided it to the opposite bank.

My grandfather died when he was fifty-two. They say he must have had a very happy death. He used to drink a fair bit and he was just walking through the house when he dropped dead. So Grandmother's family set her up in the Royal Oak Hotel at Aitkenvale. Dad said he saw so much drunkenness around the hotel when he was growing up that it made him determined never to have anything to do with drink in his life, and he never did.

Grandmother had a woman working for her at the Royal Oak who had a baby with a turned eye. An old Chinaman used to come with vegetables and one day he looked at this baby and told Grandmother to get the woman to tie a piece of red rag on the opposite side of the cot, and that by looking to see it blowing in the breeze the child would exercise the eye and it would be cured. So the woman did this and it worked. Grandma would never hear a bad word about the old Chinamen around Townsville.

Grandma's cow-paddock extended all the way to Rising Sun. Their house was named 'Lytchette' after the family estate in Dorset. Grandmother donated the land where St. Matthew's Mundingburra stands today and she had St. Matthew's Hall built.

There were no schools in Townsville when Father was born and they were going to send him to England to be educated but he must have bailed up. He was one of the first pupils enrolled on the day Mundingburra School opened in 1884. He was also one of the first enrolled at the new Townsville Grammar School.

After Father left school he went as a jackeroo to the Right Honorable Aplin, the Member for Kennedy, who owned Southwick station north-west of Charters Towers. Aplin's Weir on the Ross is named after him. Later he got involved with James Simpson Love, a well-known exporter of horses for the Indian Army. Father

Edward Fryer with the McConachie children, Joan, Jimmy and Betty, on the verandah of the Eureka Hotel at Hervey's Range about 1930. It was little Jimmy who whispered "Did you forget about the lollies this time, Mr Fryer?"

worked for him for many years, going out to stations all over the north to buy horses.

It was when he was returning from one of these trips that he met my mother. He was at Townsville railway station waiting to take delivery of a stallion. Mother was waiting to catch the train to go up to Charters Towers. To fill in the time he offered to take her for a drive around Townsville to show her the sights. It must have been a case of love at first sight. After they were married they lived with his mother at Five Head Creek.

I was born in February, 1930, the youngest of nine. I was lucky to be born at all because Mother was driving herself to hospital in the sulky when the britchen – the strap holding the harness to the mare's back – broke. The sulky rolled back into the creek. Mother managed to get out of the overturned sulky and walk back for assistance. It can't have been much help that I turned out to be a fourteen pound baby.

Mother and Dad lost their first little girl, Elizabeth Florence. She was born prematurely because Mother had been out in the paddock bringing in the goats and she slipped and fell. The doctor told Mother she could try to keep the baby alive but that she would not live because her skin had not formed properly. Mother kept her in cotton wool moistened with olive oil in a shoe-box for a cot. She lived a fortnight. This was when Mother and Dad were still at Five Head Creek on the Ross. Her grave is covered by the waters of the Ross Dam now. Then they had Edward, who was always known as Gulliver, and Chris and Olive – she was Olive Allen, after the Samuel Allen side of things[2]; they also gave the Allen to me, I'm Ray Allen. Then came Florence, Elizabeth – always known as Betty, and Frederick Augustus – that's the English side of things, after the grandfather, the first one to come to the north. Then there was Mabel; but don't call her Mabel! She was always Mabbs! Then Norma, and last of all me. They said I was the shakings of the sack.

We never called our mother 'Mum'. Always 'Mother'. She told us 'If you call me 'Mum' I will think you are speaking to someone else. I am your Mother!' Mother's parents, Ivor and Mary Jacobson, were Norwegian. They came out in a ship called the *Lammershagen* in 1871. They landed at Port Keppel and came by bullock-wagon to Charters Towers to the gold fields. Kitty Jacobson died in childbirth when our Mother was very young. After she died her father called the children together and said to them, 'Well, now your mother is gone you will all have to do a few things to help keep the family going.' They had a dairy farm and he was also working in the mines. And one night the children thought they would make supper for him coming home from the mine tired. And they measured out six cups of rice. They must have thought well, there's six of us, so a cup each, and they put the pot on to boil. And, of course, it boiled, and up it comes and starts to boil over. So they take a dipperful out and race it out to the gate and chuck it over. And then it's still boiling over, so they take another dipperful out and race it out and chuck it over. And this goes on! And all the goats in Charters Towers think this is Christmas! They're all out the front hopping in for their cut! So being 'Mother' was important to our mother. She knew what it was like not to have one.

The homestead at Tabletop had a detached kitchen with a cement hearth with an open fire and a big old stone fire-place. Mother used to bath all of us in a big old galvanized-iron tub in front of the fire. One night a draught came down the chimney and sparks flew out and Florence's hair caught fire. Olive beat the flame out with her bare hands. She was the eldest girl in the family and had a very responsible way with her.

Dad used to get logs out bush and he'd cut them up with a cross-cut saw and bring them in for firewood. In the winter time us kids would be sitting round the fire, nice and warm, making toast. And one evening out of one of these logs comes this big old carpet-snake. Talk about scatter! There were kids going in all directions!

Mother was an excellent bread-maker. She had a large brown earthenware bottle that she made the yeast in; potato yeast. That bottle never had to be washed out. Some of the old yeast had to be put back into it to kick the next batch off. It was pretty powerful stuff. There was a cork which had to be tied into the neck of the bottle with string, otherwise it would build up so much pressure she would blow! Some nights it happened that there would be this great bang! And we would wake up and think, 'Oh! It's the yeast bottle! The cork's blown!' And we would all rush out to help save the yeast; it's frothing out everywhere. No lights, of course; only kerosene lamps. And Mother and Dad and us kids, we'd all be there, hunting round all over the kitchen for this cork! One of us had to stand there with our finger in the bottle to stop the yeast escaping or there would be no bread! Bread was made every second day. The dough was set at night near the fire to keep it warm. It rose to the top by the morning and was kneaded again and cut into loaves. After the second rising the loaves were baked in the oven.

There wasn't much of a road down the range, just the stock route, and to preserve the flour to see us through the rainy season, each sack was wrapped round with wire-netting. Then it was sunk in a galvanized-iron tank full of water. The wire-mesh is to hold the whole thing together for when you lift it out, in case the bag has rotted, which it usually did. Of course, you lose about an inch of flour around the outside. That gets wet and sets like a shell. And after you lifted it out of the water, you leave it in the sun for a day and let it dry. Then you knock a hole in the shell and scoop the flour out. It would be perfectly fresh. No weevils, or anything. They were still using this method when I was a boy. If Mum said she needed more flour, we'd go and lift a sack out of the tank and leave it to dry. If people were hard up and didn't have a galvanized-iron tank they would sink their sacks in a turkey-nest dam, but then the yabbies burrow into them and that mucks up a whole lot of the flour.

When the storm rains came each year – after a couple of good falls; a couple of inches or so – you might get a few sunny days, and all around the stockyards and troughs mushrooms would come up! We looked forward to this every year; going out hunting mushrooms. We would gather buckets of them. Then we would sit down around the big table with Mother, cleaning the grass and bits of dirt off. Mother would cook up big pans of them; mushrooms on toast, steak and mushrooms, mushroom stew, mushrooms with everything until they cut out. Another thing we would gather after a good wet season was bush spinach which has a leaf similar to proper spinach but is more of a brownie colour. When they were about a foot high we would cut them and mother would wash it and cook it just like ordinary spinach.

Mother was very good at making preserves and jams. We would go down the creeks and collect pie-melons and she would chop them up and make melon-and-lemon jam and pies. We also used to gather rosellas and we would sit around the table and husk the pods. During the war there were always soldiers in the area, training, and mother was very good to them. If a section came along and they weren't in a hurry she would make scones for them. One time this soldier said, 'Gee! This's nice jam! What is it?' Mother said, 'Rosella.' He looked astonished and he said, 'Rosella! What! Do you make it out of *parrots*!' He had never heard of rosellas as a fruit. They must grow only in the north.

Rosella Jam

Prepare rosellas by cutting off tips and removing pods. Place tips and pods in a saucepan, cover with water and boil for one hour or until mixture is syrupy. Strain and add liquid to rosellas and boil for twenty to thirty minutes. Measure rosella mixture and add one cup of sugar to one cup of pulp and boil for another fifteen minutes, stirring continually. Bottle and seal while hot.

Melon and Lemon Jam

To five pounds of cut up melon allow five pounds of sugar and three sliced lemons. Put half of sugar on the melon overnight. In another dish place the sliced lemons and pour over three cups of boiling water. Let stand overnight. In the morning add to the melon, bring to boil, add remainder of sugar and boil till a clear amber colour.

About half an acre of garden was enclosed for vegetables down by the windmill; always a good supply of vegetables in rotation; some newly planted, some growing and some ready for use. Cauliflowers only grew in the cooler months of the year. Mother made marmalade, pickles and chutneys out of tomatoes and things from our garden, as most people did when they had to be self-sufficient. Most of what we needed we produced ourselves, meat, milk and butter, vegetables and fruit.

We used to milk about six or eight cows, quiet old things out of the herd. The cream was separated to make butter. Olive loved anything outdoors and it was her job to go and bring the cows up in the late afternoon and lock the calves up for the night. We would bring the young heifers up into the bails to get them used to it, and on one occasion Mother was pulling on the rope and the heifer reefed back and the rope slipped through her hand. There was blood everywhere and she said, 'Have any of you hurt your hand?' Then she looked and she said, 'Oh! I've cut off the end off my finger!" I was only a little chap and when I saw the blood pouring out of her hand I thought, 'Oh! That's the end of the world! Mother is going to die!' I said, 'Don't cry, Mother!' She told me, 'I'm not crying but I will have to have help.' Dad was away. He used to do a bit of droving to get money to keep the place going. Mother quietened us down and one of the boys rode to Robinson's, our neighbours, to come with his car and take her down the range to the doctor. The doctor removed the bone that was sticking out and pulled the skin back over the tip and she was all right. But, ah! That was a terrible moment when we thought our mother was going to die. Mother was everything to us!

The wash-house, with a big copper, was outside. Mother always made her own soap. All the bullock fat was kept and melted down and then strained. About four gallons was put into a big copper with caustic soda and borax, and boiled and boiled until it turned into an amber honey colour jelly in the bottom of the copper. You had to be careful not to let it boil over. Then Mother would tip it out into a big preserving pan, a big old enamel one about six inches deep. When it cooled down and set hard she cut it into bar soap. That was the only soap I ever knew for years. Mother was lucky in all this as she had a lady called Maddy – her name was really Mrs. Madden. She was the nurse that brought Dad into the world and she took Mother under her wing like a daughter and always lived with us. So she was always Maddy to us, like a grandma, and a wonderful help to Mother.

The shower house had water laid on by pipes from a windmill to a large tank on a twelve-foot stand. The floor was slatted and when we had water-melons they were put underneath to cool off. Toilets were another matter – quite a walk down past the mulberry trees; a two-seater, one for adults another for children; a pan system, treated with ashes from the fire after each use, and emptied every week. In later years, when we had septics, very good crops of bananas grew there.

Dad wouldn't have lawn around the house; just sand, kept raked. I suppose he thought it would show up any snake tracks! There were brooms made of sida retusa to keep it all swept nicely.

The girls had a cubby-house down on the bank of the creek where the roots of an old gum-tree had been scoured out, making a sort of cave. They played dressing-up and families, and, being the youngest I always had to be 'the baby'. Once, when Betty was going back to boarding-school, she said to Mother, 'Make sure you look after him while I am away! I want him to play with when I come back!' They might have been better off dressing up the dog!

OLIVE'S STORY

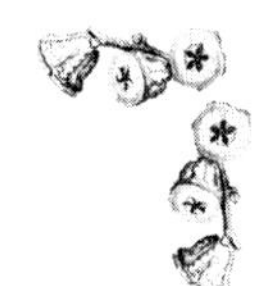

We killed all our own beef. Once they killed about eight miles from home and I at the age of eight years had to take the meat home leading a packhorse, and with a split bag over my saddle. The hot meat dripped blood and two dingoes followed me along the track all the way. I had to stop and get down to let down a set of slip-rails. I looked back and saw the dingoes standing watching me. I was off and through those rails as quick as never ever before. The dingoes stayed at the same distance the whole time. But while I was on horseback I was never frightened of anything.

Only once, I was riding up the bullock-wagon road and it had got much later than I thought. I heard someone, or something coming. I listened and I thought, 'Oh, Gosh! Is that the Ghost of Dead Man's Gully!' Two old tin-scratchers had a fight there once, and one shot the other and he had to be buried there. When the coffin came it was too short and they had to cut his knees and bend them up to fit him in. So I thought it was his ghost coming. In the half-dark I was terribly frightened but it was only Mr. Lafferty from the top of the range. He scolded me for being out so late on my own. He rode home with me; neighbours were so caring of one another in those days.

Not all the neighbours were so kind. There was a Mr. Moody who had a property, Myrtlebank, further out, about fifteen miles or so.Whenever they were going down to Townsville they would stay a couple of days with us, passing through. They had open buggies, a seat in the front and a seat in the back.They had a small pup and I just loved it and it would always come to me. And when they were going home Mr. Moody decided he was not having that pup in the buggy; that it had to run along behind. And it must have got tired and just sat in the grass. And Uncle Bill was coming home that way and it ran out and ran along with his dogs. A little puppy! And when I saw it coming back again, oh! wasn't I happy! So I had this little dog and I called him Specky because he was speckles all over. I trained him and he worked well with me. He was a good little dog; no doubt about it.

So when Mr. Moody came by next time, Mother said to him, 'Mr. Moody I would like to buy that dog off you. He works well for Olive, and I am telling you now, he won't work for anyone else!' But he said, 'Oh, No, no, no! When I get him home he will be a different dog! He will work for me alright!'

So a year went by and it was time for them to come again and I said to Ronnie, one of their boys, 'How's Specky?' And he said to me, 'Oh, we haven't got Specky any more. He wouldn't work for Dad so he shot him.' Oh! I nearly broke my heart! Those people! They always stayed with us and enjoyed our hospitality. If the dog wouldn't work for them they could easily have sent him back to me. Anyone passing by would have been glad to bring him. But that Mr. Moody was not a generous man!

My brother Fred was born at home because Mother woke up and realized it was her time. She put layers and layers of newspapers in the bed and she said to Father, 'Don't you go anywhere today! You might be needed here!' Not long after the baby was born I saw it with all the blood and the cord still attached. I had seen baby goats being born and I said to myself, 'That baby has come from Mother's tummy!' So after that I knew where babies came from although I never said so. They used to tell us that Dad brought them home in a sugar-bag hanging on his saddle. I was about six or seven at the time.

Once I lost my pony, Lovel, stolen by the brumbies. Sometimes I would see her with them but was never able to turn the mob and run them into a paddock. One day, I was out bringing in the cows and I thought 'I will just ride up to the Horse Camp and see if any brumbies are there'. I found Lovel, and she had just given birth to a foal, just able to stand up. I pulled that foal up over the pommel of my saddle and rode home with Lovel running close behind and sometimes kicking out at me. I won. And that was how we got Laurel, the black pony. A brumby sire. She grew to a good quiet pony, broken by Fred and myself.

We all had our own set jobs and were expected to do them. The garden had to be watered, the poultry fed and watered, eggs collected and the yard locked up.Corn from the corn patch had to be husked for their feed.The husks were dried and used to make mattresses for the smaller children.

There was also a herd of anything up to two hundred goats, which were kept for mutton. And of course, we would ride them as well. We all had our favourites, and we would race them. At night they had to be locked up because of the dingoes. When the cows were dry the goats were milked. Dad bought two big Angora billies, the ones with the curly hair. The next lot of kiddy-goats had the curls too. But the grass-seed got into it.

It was my job to bring the cows up by about 4.30 and to lock the calves up for the night. We separated the milk and churned the cream next day for butter. The butter-milk was always saved for drinking and for making scones and milk-loaf with fruit. Delicious!

Florence said that I always got the best jobs. She complained to mother, 'All Olive has to do is get on a pony and bring up a few cows!' So on one occasion Florence went for the cows and I did her jobs. Poor Florence! She returned very late, and no cows! Couldn't find them anywhere! Mother said, 'Olive! Get on to the pony and find the cows! I have to have milk for the baby!' I knew there were only a few places where the cows could be. I rode over to Spring Gully and there they were, mostly lying down. I soon got them home with the help of my little dog.

Every Monday was washing day, in three big tubs with a wash-board and wringer. It took all day. And then came the ironing with flat-irons heated on the top of the stove. We were a change daily lot of children so there was always plenty to be done. It was remarkable how well Mother turned us all out. We girls had frocks made of khaki drill trimmed with red rick-rack braid and another lot made of blue and white striped butchers' drill. We always looked well-dressed and clean. But once we got into real trouble! We were sliding down the banks of the creek on old bags. Oh! The colour of our clothes!

Mother and Dad had a couple of comical sayings. One was, 'Everyone to their own fancy, as the old woman said when she kissed the cow!' We would all laugh when she said it. And once, when Dad had to go to hospital to have a sun-spot removed, they shaved off his moustache. When Mother saw him she said, 'Oh, Father! You look like a motherless calf!' Oh! We laughed! And father, if he had been away for the day and met an old friend, would say, 'I met old so-and-so today and had a good *pitch* with him.' He never said 'yarn' or 'talk'; always 'pitch'.

Christmas was always kept as a very special time. The house was decorated with paper streamers and bells, brought out again year after year. Us kids thought it was great to hook the streamers up over the rafters and make the house ready for Christmas. If it was a dry, droughty year we would go down the creek and cut green bushes and stand them around the house. Ham today is just ordinary old tucker but in those days it was a specialty. Dad used to buy big hams, the biggest he could get, up from Townsville. They would come packed in a bag of oat-husks; each ham in its own cloth bag. We would gather round to help undo it and empty all the oat-husks to get this wonderful Christmas ham out!

The smelter chimney at The Argentine, the deserted gold and silver field "a couple of hours ride away" from Tabletop, where the children used to go gold-scratching with their father.

Santa Claus came every year. The girls always got a doll, a naked one. When they asked Mother why the cousins always got a doll with clothes on she told them that was because Santa Claus knew they had older sisters who understood how to make dolls' clothes. If it was raining on Christmas Eve we would all be down in the mouth and grizzling, 'It's raining and Santa Claus won't come!' One time Father said, 'Don't you worry! Santa won't let you down. But maybe you will have to look under your beds instead.' And in the morning we looked and there were presents and a red lolly-stocking each. One year when Olive was about nine she thought she hadn't got a present. Dad told her, 'Don't be sad, Little Girl. Perhaps if you go and look in the school room?' So she looked and she saw a beautiful new saddle. Olive was always the outdoors one of the girls.

For Christmas dinner we would always have a roast sucking-pig and there would be a big Christmas pudding made in a cloth with threepences and sixpences in. You would try to wade through two slices just to try to get a coin. At night there would be cold meats and salads and trifles and jellies. Christmas was when all the members of the family tried to get home. It was really important to Mother and Dad to have all the family home; from boarding school, or from wherever they happened to be away working.

Dad made the big long dining-room table himself, and for a seat along the side against the wall he carved out a log the full length of the table. It got a beautiful sheen from us sliding in and out to our places. Another special piece of furniture was Grandfather Fryer's desk that was brought out from England on the ship in 1865. He lost all his other furniture in the flood at Five Head Creek but the desk had been in his office at Carter and Fryer Pty Ltd in town.

Dad was very much a family man. He lived for his kids. Well, he had nine of us, so he must have! One day, Norma – the sister two years older than me – and I were having an argument about something, the way kids have, and I hauled off and hit her. And my father grabbed me and gave me a clip and he told me, 'Now, don't you ever hit your sister again! It's not right! Boys don't hit girls!' That's the only time I can remember my father going crook at me and giving me a whack. He made sure we knew what was right from wrong, but in all ways he was a very kind man.

We had an Aboriginal named Murray who lived with us as part of the family. He had a room on the end of the verandah. When he was a little baby he and his mother were part of a pygmy-sized tribe that lived somewhere up beyond the Wallaman Falls. One day, our Uncle Fred and his friend Freeman Lawrence were riding by – they had been up that way looking for land – and this young Aboriginal girl ran out with her baby in her arms screaming and begging them to save her. So they took her back to Townsville with them and she lived with the Lawrence family from then till the end of her life. They named the baby Murray and when he was a little bit older, he came to Tabletop and lived with us.

When Dad was a young fellow he used to be with the mounted police, up on Cape York Peninsula, breaking in horses for them. He used to tell us about the Chinese gold fossickers up around Cohen and Mein and those old gold-mining places. After he left the mounted police he went up the tip of the peninsula to the Jardines at Somerset, and helped them put up some of those old station buildings that used to be right at the water's edge. They are mainly all gone today. Dad could put his hand to any kind of building work. He was pretty handy.[3]

Dad was always keen on scratching a bit of gold. He used to take us out with him when the storm rains came and there was a bit of water around. We'd ride out to an old mining town about two or three hours from home, known as the Argentine.The name means 'silver' because silver was found there before gold. In its heyday in the 1880s the Argentine had several pubs and a butcher and baker and two or three stores. And of course there would have been Chinese gardeners. You always got them in any of those little mining places. But nothing was left only the brick chimney-stack of the smelter. Everything else had gone. We'd scratch around and Dad would say, 'No. That's not a good place! You've got to look for a likely part where the gold could catch up!' We never went home without a few colours of gold. And sometimes little bits of rough. And Dad would examine them and say, 'They haven't come far! You never know! We might find the lead some day.' Every wet season we went out and we looked forward to it. Mother had a gold-bar brooch made from a nugget Dad found at the Argentine.

In the days of the buckboard it was a day's journey to go down the range to Townsville. The day before, the wheels had to be greased and extra pads put on the brake blocks. A change of horses was sent on ahead. Umbrellas were stowed under the seats for the girls and women. The whole family stayed overnight with Grandma Evans at Lychette in Mundingburra and then a day's journey back up the range next day.

Then Dad bought a Model T Ford, a 'Tin Lizzie'. He built a shed at the foot of the range where they kept it. They used to drive out to the foot of the range. It would take them all day to get there, with all the sandy creeks. Then pack-horses would come down and pack the supplies up the range to home. The only other route to

Horseteams pulled wagons such as this on the road to Georgetown and the Gulf. The precipitous road came up the range at Thornton's Gap, not from Tabletop homestead.

bring in supplies was the old wagon-road across to Charters Towers. When a vehicle road was put in up Hervey's Range in the 1930s, Dad graduated to a Model A Ford. Going up the range the radiator would boil and we'd have to stop and put a stone in behind the wheel and wait till she cooled down. We always carried a couple of gallons of water, and when she was cool enough we'd top her up and off we'd go again. Sometimes we'd have to do that a couple of times to get up the range. We had that Model A right up until the War.

The bush pub at the top of the range from the old teamster days was called the Eureka. Originally Kidman owned all that Dotswood area and people by the name of Moody had a mining lease block in the middle of Dotswood. Kidman's didn't want anyone in the centre of their country so they made a deal to swap the block for the Eureka. The Moody's had the Eureka for twenty years and then they sold it to Dad. At one stage there was a family called McConachie running it. They had three little children, Joan, Jimmy and Betty. If Dad had been down to Townsville on business he always made a point of bringing them back some lollies. Once he came back late and was yarning away to their father about something important. In the end little Jimmy edged up beside him and whispered, 'Did you forget about the lollies this time, Mr. Fryer?' But of course, Dad hadn't. He pulled them out of his pocket. Dad would never disappoint a child.

In those days everybody was more or less scratching. It was only the love of the land that kept people in the bush. For work on the property Dad had a fairly heavy dray, with two horses – one in the shafts and one as an outrigger. That was for fencing or yard-building. There was also a spring-cart. And for mother there was the sulky. Not that she moved off the place very much. After I was born, in 1930, she never went down to Townsville for seven years.

Murray Laurence, who lived with the Fryer family at Tabletop from boyhood.

I didn't see the sea until I was about seven years old. Then Mother and Dad took me down to the coast at Townsville. I saw one of those shark-proof swimming enclosures, made out of tea-tree stakes. I said to Dad, 'Gee! What a silly place to put a cattle-yard, out in the water like that!' and they all laughed. They had been telling me how I'd be able to pick up shells when I was at the beach, but I was scared to walk along the edge of the water. I thought sharks'd get me. Then they said, 'Go on! Taste the water!' So I scooped up a handful and drank it. And I said, 'Ah! It's terrible! How do the cattle drink it!' Of course that was another great laugh!

We did most of our primary schooling by Correspondence, then we were all sent away to boarding school. Dad built a room on to the side of the dining-room and that was our school-room. We each had our own table and stool. The work came from the Correspondence School in Brisbane in weekly sets but as we had no weekly mail we would get a big batch at a time. We had governesses, who would have been on about ten shillings a week and their keep. Once we had a tutor, Mr. Price. He was sent away because he had a daughter with him who slapped Mabbs when she asked her why she didn't have a Mother. For a few years we had Miss Kent. She was out riding one day with Olive and me and her hairpins, tortoiseshell ones with gold rims, fell out of her hair. We had to go back and search and search until we found them. Later she went up to New Guinea and became a missionary. The one I remember most clearly is Miss Lapsley. She was very popular with all the family. But we had to show respect to her; always had to call her 'Miss Lapsley', never just her Christian name. Even Mother called her Miss Lapsley. Dad wouldn't have any disrespect from any of us towards adults. But sad to say she went down to Townsville to meet her sister off a train and got wet waiting on the platform and caught a chill and died. From time to time an itinerant teacher from the Education Department would arrive by buckboard to check how our work was getting on. [4]

From the school-room at home Olive and Florence went to St. Mary's in Herberton, and Betty, Mabs and Norma went to St. Anne's in Townsville. Edward went to Townsville Grammar School. Mother and Dad were very insistent that we all get a good education.

Us kids all had our own ponies. I don't remember learning to ride. I think it just came naturally to me. You would be put on a quiet old horse when you were a bit of a toddler and you'd learn to get your balance and hang on and that was that. We all helped with the stock-work. From the time I can remember I'd be there bum-trotting round the tail of a mob on dipping days. I could never get up enough speed to get up near the lead. As we got a bit older we worked our way up through the ranks and graduated to decent mustering horses.

Dad started out with Shorthorn/Hereford cross, which were the accepted herd in those days, and what he was used to at his parents' place on the Upper Ross. But with the tick problems we had at Tabletop, dipping constantly every three or four weeks, he would no sooner finish than it would be time to start again. So about 1940 he made the decision to get a couple of young Brahman bulls. He'd heard about them being more suitable to the tropics; tick resistant and better able to stand up to the heat. Also, at about that time buffalo fly were beginning to move down from the Gulf country.

He got his first two young bulls from Glen Prairie stud near Marlborough owned by William Angliss and Co. and a young quarter-cross bull from the Beake family at Christmas Creek out from Ingham. The Beakes originally introduced Brahmans to Australia in about 1914. They had them at the zoo in Melbourne as a bit of a curiosity. The progeny from these were crossed with shorthorns on Beakes' property at Rocky Ponds inland from Rockhampton. Christmas Creek had a quarter-cross bull for sale. Dad got hold of it, but of course, no roads or rail in those days, so the bull was walked down to Townsville meatworks with a mob of sale bullocks and then to get it up the range to Tabletop it was hitched to an old working-bullock and walked up.

Dad was the first in the Hervey's Range area to introduce the Brahman strain into his herd. It caused quite a bit of throwing off around the district. 'What do you want to go bringing in them yaks for?' people were saying. But the Aitkenson's up at Gunnawarra had also gone over to Brahman and gradually people saw the benefits of the breed and by the mid-fifties Brahmans began to be the accepted thing.

During the war years my sister, Norma found a plane that crashed on Tabletop. Two young American pilots were practising dog-fighting over the range and one of them got a bit too clever and dived too low. The wing just clipped the top of the timber and it went in.

The other plane came circling over the homestead. He dropped this long streamer, and written on it was 'Airplane – (that's how he spelt it) – crashed approximately one mile east of homestead. If the pilot is still living can you please wave. If he is dead please walk away from the site of the crash'.

So Norma and Dad rode out in different directions. Norma was the one who spotted the fire and cooeed out to Dad. The pilot – his name was Meadows – had somehow managed to drag himself clear of the wreckage before it burst into flames, but he was in a bad way. He had a broken pelvis and a broken leg. Norma was the first to get to him.

Edward Fryer, Ray's father, was the first grazier to introduce Brahmans to the Hervey's Range area.

The other plane was circling overhead to make sure they'd got the message. Dad and Norma waved their arms to show that the pilot was still alive. Then Norma stayed with him, while Dad rode back to the homestead to get water and blankets. They couldn't move him, he was in too much of a bad way, and terribly thirsty. He kept asking for water. Of course, I'm a curious kid, so I'm out there too, getting a good look at all that's going on.

This was all about four, maybe five o'clock in the afternoon, and the rescue team from the base-camp didn't get up through the range until about midnight. Eventually they got through and put him on a stretcher slung across the back of a weapons carrier. It must have been a hell of a trip down the range for him, with broken leg and arm and pelvis. They took him out to the big wartime hospital the Americans had out on the Black River. Norma used to visit him quite a lot, and even after the war was over they still kept in touch.

There were quite a few planes that came down on Tabletop country. One was a Wirraway, a trainer, made mostly of fabric on a wooden frame. The pilot must have done a pretty good job of bringing it in because both he and the instructor walked away. The authorities came up with old horse limbers and loaded the wreckage on and took it way. The chap who designed the Wirraway was "Winky" Wacket. His name still goes down pretty well in the north because he was a Townsville fellow.

Another crash was a Mitchell bomber coming from Charters Towers to Townsville. It clipped the top of a hill not far from home and exploded. There were about six or eight of them, all Yanks, on board and they were all killed. The authorities came up and took all the remains away, but even today you can still see bits of aluminium where that crash was.

The reason we got all these crashes was that Tabletop is on the Great Divide directly inland from where all the wartime air-strips were. Townsville was a major operations base once the Americans arrived and the Battle of the Coral Sea got underway. It is still a big training area and accidents still happen. In more recent years two Black Hawk helicopters collided not far away from almost the same spot where the Mitchell bomber crashed; hardly a stone's throw away. Seventeen men lost their lives. There is a beautiful memorial to them in the Palmetum in Townsville.

During the war it was nothing to see two or three hundred troops about our place. They'd be out on a training exercise and just come up out of the scrub. They'd set up this army cook-place, and I'd go and line up with them to get a feed of army stew! I thought it was great to get a feed with the army blokes like that!

Up on the mountain behind the homestead there was a trig point put in in 1942 by the Australian Army for mapping the area round Townsville and Charters Towers. There are trig points on all those mountains in the area. There was also a radio beacon which used to beep out a signal, as well as some sort of mirror arrangement called a helio which they could flick from one hill to another to send messages. The radio beacon was run off a six-volt battery. I got the job of changing the battery. I used to cart the battery up the range on a quiet old pack-horse, lug it up the last pinch myself and then hook it on. The job was worth about ten bob a week.[5] In those days any bob you could get was pretty welcome.

1 John Oliver Feetham, Bishop of North Queensland, 1913 to 1947, was known for his love of the Australian bush and its people, believing they epitomized the virtues of the Australian character. An early leader of the Brotherhood of the Good Shepherd, the 'Bush Brothers', the outstanding achievement of his episcopate was the foundation of the North Queensland schools; All Souls, St.Gabriels, St.Annes and St. Mary's. He was noted not only for his huge zest and enthusiasm when visiting the people of his far-flung diocese but for the personal eccentricity of preferring to sleep in a swag rather than a bed.

2 Gibson Wilde, Gateway to a Golden Land, page 215. Samuel Allen and Sons was an esteemed trading company, founded in 1872 and later acquiring a number of hotels. Edward Fryer's sister had married Christopher Allen.

3 Byerly, Frederick. (Ed.) The complete Jardine Expedition Journals, page 100. 'With the fresh horses (obtained by swimming them over to the mainland from Albany Island) they were enabled to take look about them and to select a site for the formation of a cattle station. A convenient spot was chosen at Vallack Point, about three miles from the settlement at Somerset.' The Settlement at Somerset had not long previously been established by the Queensland Government.

4 Miller, Lillian Ada. The Border and Beyond, p. 78; 'The Travelling Teachers Scheme began in 1901. Each teacher had his own district and was expected to visit each child in that district four times a year. He was supplied with a specially designed buggy, four horses and camping equipment.'

5 Ten shillings was the equivalent of a quarter of an average working man's weekly pay. When men joined the army at the outbreak of war they were said to be getting 'five bob a day' i.e. half of ten shillings. A 'bob' was the familiar term for one shilling.

two...

'A GOOD PADDOCK'

All Souls School

I went to boarding-school at All Souls, in Charters Towers. They used to say to me at home, before I left – you know how little kids leave food on their plates – 'You won't be doing that when you go to All Souls! You'll eat all of that!' My elder brother, Chris, he was at Souls, and he used to scare me with all these tales about how you would get a flogging for this or that or the other. The day came and he took me up on the train to the Towers. My heart was in my boots. I didn't know what to expect. Chris was an old hand by this time. He grabbed a taxi outside the station – Souls is a bit out of town – and we headed out. And when the taxi went through those big school gates, well, I could have been going into gaol, the way I felt. I was dead scared. I'd have been about nine.

The Head Master was Canon G.G. O'Keefe, an ex-army chaplain. Oh! He was a strict old bugger! He used to tell us 'Hard work and sound discipline never hurt anybody'! If he saw you sky-larking around or slacking he would say, 'Get your back into it, Boy! Hard work never hurt anybody!' The only time we were allowed out was to collect the scraps for the pigs from the big military camp nearby. We had pigs at the back of the school – not a pig-project – they were for the kids to eat. This was wartime! So it was a great thing to be told to get the old horse and dray out and take it over to the army camp to collect the scraps to feed the pigs. There was a lot of good-eating tucker in with them, too! Biscuits and so on. The cooks would give us a bit of a hand-out as well. You were on a good thing to get that job. And of course, when we got to the camp, well, they had a canteen, and the men gave us Club chocolate and everything!

Being wartime, we had to take our food-ration cards to school with us; for tea, sugar and butter. And one morning at breakfast they made an announcement; no more sugar! That was it! Nobody was to put sugar in their tea any more! Of course a moan went up, but after a couple of days we got used to it. I've never taken sugar in my tea from that day to this, and I'm probably healthier for it. As well, there was a big garden with a full time gardener. Us kids were allotted to do certain jobs on the weekends, weeding and watering and chipping and carting manure in the wheel-barrow. We were pretty well off for milk. The school had six or eight big old A.I.S cows; lovely old things; good milkers; gave a couple of gallons a day each. I used to like getting that job. I've always liked cows. The job I hated getting was cleaning out the pig pens. You had to scrub the troughs and turn them over and rake out the yards. Leave everything cleaned up. I'd dodge that if I could. Swap it for milking, any day! We got plenty of beef which the stations round about brought in. So that was the way the school faced up to the food shortages during the war-years.

Like all schools, we had air-raid drill. There were slit-trenches about four or five feet deep in the grounds, built in a zig-zag pattern to stop the bomb blast. At certain times of the day they would blow a siren and all us kids would pelt out and jump into the trenches until the all clear siren went. Which we thought was great.

Our uniform was khaki shorts and shirts from Aridas' in Charters Towers, and lace-up boots. For Sundays we had grey suits and a black and white tie and a boater hat known as a Donkey's Breakfast. The edges of those boaters were serrated and if you were mucking around and bumped into someone, it would almost take the hide off them.

We had chapel every day, and on Sunday a lot of people from the town used to come out and join in. The chapel had a classroom and dormitory underneath. We all had to take it in turns to be altar boy, robed-up in these long white gowns. We used to call them 'ghost coats'. Your shoes had to be just showing and that's all. You had a girth around your waist to hitch up your skirt and tie her up a bit. Then you had to learn how to kneel. You don't just plonk down like an old cow. You have to go down one knee at a time, and when you stand back up you stand with your legs straight. One of the senior boys, the Chapel Captain, was 'head stockman'. He'd eye us over to make sure we were right before we marched in. And when you were swinging the censor – the 'smoke machine' – well, there was a knack to it; on the forward swing you give it a bit of an extra heave and away she goes! You had to do so many laps of the chapel with it, then round the altar and bow. And when the old Bishop – actually he was my uncle – came up with his collar and hames on to run us through the crush for confirmation we'd have to cart his big chair out and put it in position at the front. Someone said to me recently, 'You! An Altar boy! You must have altered a bloody lot since then!'

There used to be a special dormitory for the little kids. An old lady, Mrs. Snowdon lived there and she was in charge of them. We used to call her Old Slipper because she would prowl round at night and if she caught you talking after lights out she would lay into you with this old slipper! You'd be squirming down in the blankets to try to dodge! And us bigger boys, we'd go down and look through the windows of the little kids' dormitory with our torches under our chins and go 'Wooo-oooo-ooo!', in spooky voices. They'd wake up and yell the place down. We'd take off and be in our beds, and, of course, we knew nothing about it! But one time the prefects got us and then weren't we up for a flogging!

Not that many floggings got handed out. The prefects would give you a bit of a clip under the ear if you hadn't made your bed properly. If someone was playing up they'd get called aside and the teacher would say to them, 'Look! I don't want to be caning you!' And they would talk about the problem and try to work it out. Or if

When All Souls was taken over by the Army for a hospital during the Battle of the Coral Sea, the boys moved into a "Tent School" at Dalrymple Crossing on the Burdekin.

Courtesy All Souls St Gabriels School Archive

one boy had a bit of a snout on another kid they were made to shake hands and forget it. Or you would get sent down to the oval to do some weeding as a punishment.

The teachers were a pretty decent mob. But once the war started they began leaving to join up. One chap named McKinnon, he got killed in action, only twenty-two years old. Another bloke, John Bartlett, was killed on his first operational flight over the North Sea. He was only twenty. He'd just been filling in time at Souls waiting to be old enough to join the RAAF. There was Mr. Evans. We used to call him 'Slimy'. And there was Miss Thornton in charge of the house-keeping side of things. She was six foot two! We used to call her 'Stork'!

Saturday mornings were free after you had cleaned your dormitory and tidied your locker and polished your boots and cleaned your sandshoes. If they weren't done properly then you missed out on sport and you pulled weeds! That oval at Souls! It was couch grass. They would line the two hundred and thirty-six of us up – not the prefects; they followed along behind – and we'd be down on our hands and knees crawling along and pulling up any bindi-eyes and weeds. We had to crawl across, and then when we got to the other side they would say, 'Now! Everyone come around here!' And they would line us all up again looking down the length of it, and say, 'Now! All down again!' And back we'd crawl down the length of it. After you had done that a couple of times you knew you had knees! We must have had the most prickle-free oval in the north!

There was a sick-bay with a trained sister and there was a special isolation ward down the flat. If you got sick they would park you down there and the sister would come down and have a look at you. We all seemed to end up with whatever was going around, whooping cough and chicken pox and measles. We all got through. None of us died.

Ray (holding book) and a mate, in a temporary wartime dormitory – 1941.

Courtesy All Souls St Gabriels School Archive

After prep of a night time they would give you half a slice of melon and lemon jam which was made by the school from pie-melons. We called it 'scrape' because we reckoned they scraped it on and then scraped it off again. When prep ended at night they would ring a bell and you'd line up at the 'scrape-post'. The prefects had trays of bread and melon and lemon jam and you lined up and got a slice. My best mate at Souls was always Bob Forster from out round Hughenden way. He and I always got into scrape-line together. We still laugh about it. That bloody old scrape-post is still at the school today sixty years on, but I don't know whether the kids line up for bread and melon and lemon jam after prep. Kids today are a bit more picky.

So I was there when the war started getting pretty rough in 1941. The Yanks were at Breddan Airstrip across the other side of the racecourse. We used to get up into the trees to see the bombers coming in; to count how many were coming back.

Then the schools were commandeered and turned into army hospitals; All Souls, Mount Carmel and St. Gabes. The Yanks took over Mount Carmel; the Australian Army had Souls. All us

Souls' boys were sent up to Dalrymple Crossing on the Burdekin. And we set up a tent school there. We were all in tents, supplied by the Department of Defence. There would have been about one hundred and eighty-six of us, all under canvas, out of the two hundred and fifty that had been at the school before the shift came. They brought the beds out from the school. Just dirt floors, but with corn-sacks for mats in between the beds. There would have been twelve kids in each tent. We thought it was great. All the classrooms and the dining-room were under canvas, the staff up one end of the camp, the boys down the other.

There were no showers. Our bath was straight over the bank and down into the creek. And the rules were; get changed: get your clothes off: put a towel round yourself and head for the creek. And you weren't allowed to pull your towel off until you were over the bank and could dive into the water. That was so as not to upset the ladies on the staff. No swimming togs. Just straight in. The water was shallow over the sand but anything up to eight feet further out.

The School Captain that year was a bloke named Reg Beck. Then we had the first Aboriginal School Captain for any school in Australia, Joe Croft. He wasn't picked just because he was an Aboriginal. He was picked because he was the best! He was a terrific fellow. He went on to become the engineer on the Mount Isa to Townsville railway and they say he walked every foot of the way during the building of it.

The classrooms were tents provided by the army, but the cook-house and dining room were corrugated-iron with concrete floors. There was a football field – the goal posts were gum-saplings cut down and stuck in the ground; and a cricket-pitch. There was a special tent for the chapel. We still had church six times a week and twice on Sunday! We were in that tent-school on Dalrymple Crossing for a year. But, that Christmas, during the Wet, while we were at home for the holidays, the whole thing was wiped out in a big flood that came down the Burdekin.

And of course, this was the war years, and petrol was rationed. So, after the holidays, when it was time to go back to school, we'd ride our horses down the range to catch the train. My big brother Gulliver would go with us with pack-horses to pack supplies back in. If it had been raining there were all those creeks at the foot of the range to be crossed and the road might be out, so we'd cut across the other way towards Mingela. That way we only had to cross the Fanning. We'd stop the night at Fanning River Downs and go on to Mingela to get the train next day.

Very often, the train would have been commandeered for the army for a troop-train. Wartime, and the troops had priority. And for us school kids they'd shunt a couple of cattle wagons on, and chuck a couple of bales of straw in on the floor, and rig a bit of a tarpaulin over the top for shade. We'd throw our ports up and sit on them. There'd be kids from all the schools – Thornburgh, Mount Carmel, All Souls. We thought it was great. It'd take us all day to get to the Towers, but we weren't in any hurry! The only stops were at Reid River, Macrossan and Selheim, which were all army camps. Selheim was a very big staging camp and there were a lot of troop movements backwards and forwards. We'd get into line with the troops and get a feed. It's only eighty miles up to the Towers but sometimes it would take all day and into the night to get there. You could be shunted on to a siding for a couple of hours waiting for a troop train to pass going down to Townsville. Sometimes we wouldn't get to the Towers till next day. That was all right by us! We'd be quite proud of being able to say we came back to school in a cattle wagon.

During the war years the boys were given tasks to help the school through the period of staff shortages and food rationing. Ray's favourite job was to drive the school cart to a nearby army camp for scraps for the school pigs.

Courtesy All Souls St Gabriels School Archive

After the tent-school on the Burdekin was washed out, the authorities allowed us to go back into the Towers and camp at the racecourse. Tents to sleep in. And the cooking and dining-room were under the grandstand. That would have been 1943. And after the Coral Sea Battle the war moved on to the north and we were allowed back to the school again. We'd been away two years. But they say that the results for Junior for the years that we were under canvas were the best the school ever had. That tough sort of life was suited to boys. It must have brought the best in us out. People complain about their boarding-schools but at Souls we did pretty well. It must have been a pretty good paddock.

I more or less ran away from school. I decided, bugger it! I'd had enough schooling. I didn't actually run away, but my sister Betty and her husband, Les Gilmore, were on Spring Valley up in the basalt country, and they lost their little girl Diane from some illness as a toddler. Losing her broke my sister up and she came down to spend a bit of time at home. I was sent up to Spring Valley to give Les a bit of a hand.

I decided I liked being away from school and wasn't going to have any more of it! I propped and told Mother and Dad I wouldn't go back. Dad said, 'Well, I'm very disappointed! I hoped you would have gone on and done your Senior!' That was what they called the last year of secondary schooling in those days. He had done his at Townsville Grammar School. But I wasn't having any of that! But Dad didn't believe in sons working for their fathers. He thought they should get out and knock round a bit – get a bit of experience of working under a boss. So I went out to the basalt country north of Hughenden – Chudleigh, Sturgeon, Tutley Park, those stations, and worked. Dad's idea was that you should learn to take orders before you start giving them yourself. And I did. I'd have been fifteen or so.

three...

'GETTING A BIT OF EXPERIENCE'

The Basalt Country; the Gulf; New Guinea; India

The basalt country is rough. Galloping around on those bloody rocks took a bit of getting used to. There weren't many fences but they had well-bred, handy horses. The basalt hillsides are impassable in places and you had to have cleared pads to get horses and stock through. But the basalt country, though it is rocky, grows good Mitchell grass and turns off very good cattle. It is classed as some of the best country in the north.

Millions of years ago there were volcanoes all through that area and the huge eruptions that came out of them sent flows[1] maybe sixty-five, seventy miles wide right across the area. What they call the Basalt Wall starts just south of Mount Garnet. It follows the valley of the Burdekin until it turns west out towards Richmond and continues towards Hughenden, about three hundred miles or so. You can see it on the horizon for miles, like a wave, one long, unbroken rock-flow.

The springs that come out of the basalt walls were the main source of water for properties in the area until artesian bores were put down. All across that part of Queensland they find dinosaur fossils. Down near Muttaburra, a chap named Des Pitman was putting in a dam on a property and found fossil bones that turned out to be the Muttaburrasaurus they have a replica of in Richmond.

Basalt rock is perforated, something like coral. Once I was out mustering and when we were setting up camp for the night I used a couple of basalt rocks to hold the corned-beef bucket on the fire. When we were in our swags asleep the bloody lot blew up! Sparks and coals and chunks of rock going everywhere! A bit of rock as big as your fist hit me in the ribs. Holy hell, didn't it hurt! I've still got the scar to this day. There must have been a pocket of air, or water, trapped inside the rock.

If your horse lost a shoe on that stony ground during the day when you were mustering you would have to pull up and tack another one on pretty quickly or he would go lame. So while I was there I learned to shoe pretty well. It was part of the game, carrying your shoeing gear with you in your saddle bag and keeping your own horses shod. But basalt cattlemen are good men! They know the job and most of them had worked in that basalt country all their lives.

Then, in 1948, my father passed away. I was eighteen. So I went back to Tabletop to give my mother and brother a hand. We bought a neighbouring property which doubled the size of Tabletop making it a reasonable sized place, carrying between three and four thousand head. From the old arsenic dips we switched over to Rucide, and Bercotox, Acattack and Tactick, new style dips which make a tick-prone property easier to run. It meant we only had to dip three or four times a year instead of every month.

Ray mustering on Tabletop aged about eighteen, not long after his father had died.

This was the early fifties and things were starting to come good after the war. A telephone line, the first in the area, was being put in from Townsville up over the range, and the local men were doing their fair share of the work, stringing the wire tree to tree. My brother Fred and I were doing our section with a couple of others, Geoff Yardley and Len Page. I was taking the tractor out to them and, crossing a bit of water in a gully I bogged it. We couldn't get it out that night so we left it where it was. Next morning I went back and managed to get it going, but, going up the embankment the wheels seemed to be locking so I gave her a few revs. What I didn't realize was that the water had made the brake linings swell. One wheel locked. The whole thing spun round and reared over. I could see it was going to roll so I tried to jump clear. But as it went over the side the tyre hit me in the middle of the back. I dragged myself back up to the road. The others came back with the truck and found me. They said, 'Christ! We'll have to get you down to hospital!'

Mother was quite calm about it. She had learned to take things in her life as they came. Dr. Gavin Douglas had some x-rays done and they found I had crushed five vertebrae in my spine. I was hospitalized for a fair while and after that I had to wear a brace, with two steel bands down either side of the spine with four heavy canvas girth-sort've things to strap around. It was hot gear to have to wear but if I didn't stick to it all my vertebrae would keep slipping apart. I'd only have to move a bit and the disks would slip and touch the spinal cord and I'd be

paralysed from the hips down. So I was out of action for eleven months, but I stuck with it and in the end it came good.

And so then I did a few droving trips, only four or five weeks at a time, from up in the Gulf to the meatworks in Townsville. I thought it was more or less a holiday to get up there and walk a few cattle through. In those days there used to be up to forty thousand head of cattle every year coming from the Gulf down over the range to the meatworks in Townsville. I've seen three mobs, six hundred a mob, pushing each other, a day apart. Most of that top country was owned by Kidman's under the name of Queensland Stations Limited. They had Bluff Downs, Vanrop, Eveleigh, Miranda – a mob of places.

On those trips the bullocks would get very sore-footed. That was when I learned to shoe a bullock. Lame bullocks always drop back to the tail of the mob, hobbling along. And one of us would always have a rope, not a lassoo like the Yanks have, just a coil of rope carried around one of the pack-horse's necks. We'd work up beside the lame bullock and drop it over his horns. Then when he passed a tree, we'd lap the rope round and pull him up to it. Then we'd leg rope him and pull him down and stretch his leg back so he couldn't kick and we'd tack slippers on him.

The correct word for a bullock shoe is a 'cue', but we always called them 'slippers'. The blacksmiths used to make cues for the working bullocks in the olden days, and they would flatten them on the end a bit.[2] But for shoeing lame bullocks in a droving mob you'd use your old worn-out horse-shoes that aren't worth using again. You cut them in half. A bullock's got a very thin shallow hoof, a cloven hoof. You tack the slipper one side at a time, with the thick side of the shoe to the outer edge and the thin, worn edge on the inner side. Most times you'd only get two nails in. Three is better. But you have to be a bit careful because a bullock has got a thinner hoof than a horse and if you get the nail too close in you will lame him. Of course, in that rocky country coming through the Upper Burdekin, the cues get pulled off, but at least the poor old fellow gets along for a bit. Otherwise they'd be always hobbling along on the tail there, holding you up. It's pretty rocky country once you get out from the river flats, but there's one thing about it, there was always plenty of water. There's the Walsh, the Douglas, the Keelbottom and the Star – good water all through, all year round.

We had to watch the cattle every night but towards the end, when they'd have settled down, we'd be able to get them in the corner of a paddock and hold them. There was no, 'They'll be right! Let's go!' about it. What Kidman's used to do was bring stores down to Bluff Downs and Dotswood and give them twelve to eighteen months fattening, and then push them down over the range to Townsville Meatworks.

That was the toughest part, bringing them down over the range. There was only the old wagon road where the old horse-teams used to go through to the Gulf. My parents used to tell us how those teams would get to the foot of the range and all they'd meet up. They'd hitch two teams to one wagon to get up the range through Thornton's Gap. At the top there was a bush pub, the Eureka Hotel. There'd be eight or ten wagons parked there before they all headed off. They'd mainly set off about April after the Wet. If they were going south to the Towers they'd cross the Burdekin at Dalrymple Crossing. If they were going north up around Lyndhurst, Vanrop, Eveleigh, or any of those places they'd follow the Burdekin up and cross somewhere near Blue Range. But once the railhead went through to Mungana and motor-vehicles came in, the days of the horse-team were over.

The stock route followed the old wagon track down the range. It was very narrow, with steep cuttings in places, and a decent sort of a drop over the edge. The horse-tailer and the cook would go on ahead and we'd start the cattle down, strung out, some men ahead to hold them back. Some at the back to push them along. You'd have to keep them moving but at the same time not let them get a rush on. In places you'd have to have men on the side to stop them going over the edge. And you couldn't let them get into a canter or they'd have got away at the bottom of the range and ended up God-knows where. It was all thick scrub country down at the foot of the range, big timber, lantana, and tea-tree swamp. You'd have had a hell of a job of it if they'd got away.

From the foot of the range it was about twenty miles to the outskirts of Townsville. We'd swim them across the Ross, camp on the other side and then follow the river down to where James Cook University and Lavarack Army Barracks are today.

The last night we'd camp back off the main road to Charters Towers and next morning, bring them to the bitumen. Well, those old bullocks, once they heard their feet going tap, tap, tap on that bitumen, they'd try to cut back. It could take a couple of hours just trying to get them on to the bitumen. It wasn't a cattleman's way, but you had to up them a bit to get them moving across. After that, we took them to either Ross River Meatworks or to Alligator Creek, owned by Swifts, another day's stage further down, six or eight mile.

After this I got a job on a live-stock boat, the Clausen Steamship Company's *Alondra*, taking horses to India. There was an Indian colonel in Townsville buying remounts for the Indian army to use up on the Nepalese border. The 'Alondra' had excellent standards of hygiene. When it came into Townsville it pulled in behind Magnetic Island and out went a Pest Control boat to spray it right through. Every surface had to be painted with lime; all the railings, the floors, the ramps. Going on board you had to stamp your boots in trays filled with disinfectant. Even in the early 'fifties they were aware of foot and mouth.

There were about four or five of us Aussies on board; something to do with insurance coverage. Most of the feeding and watering was done by Malays, about ten of them. We kept an eye on the horses and made sure none of them went down. There were about a hundred and sixty on board, standard stock-horses. My father had done much the same thing as a young man, though he was more involved in the buying and shipping side of things for J.S. Love. J.S. Love was the big name in shipping horses in the early days. He had a place outside Charters Towers, 'Egera' – it's cut up now – but it used to be his main depot. Once when he came back from India he brought a rickshaw plus an Indian fellow with him to pull him from the wharf, down Flinders Street and out to his place in Love's Lane, Mundingburra! The first and only rickshaw ever seen in Townsville.

Heading out for mustering camp, Tabletop about 1950. Swags on packhorse.

It was about a seventeen days' trip on the 'Alondra' to India. We pulled into Singapore to get another vet for a health clearance. I don't know why you would want a health clearance to go into India! It was the first time I had been away from Australia. When we were going up the the main channel of the Ganges, the Hoogli, to Calcutta, us Aussies were looking over the railing at all the shanty-towns and bullock-carts. Sudddenly one bloke yells, 'Hey! Look here!' and there's a body floating down the river! He goes racing up the steps, singing out to the captain. The captain goes, 'No worry! No worry!' We saw about four more bodies before we got into Calcutta! That was my first experience of India. Don't worry about anyone dead! There's plenty more! Once we docked we helped unload the horses which were haltered and led down one by one on to trucks. And then they flew us home from Delhi by Qantas.

After that trip I was offered a job by a woman vet who owned a property in New Guinea called Dumpu in the Markham Valley, right at the foot of Shaggy Ridge, a well-known battle-place of the Australian Army in World War Two. The World Bank was financing a lot of European people in New Guinea to try to get the cattle industry established. So the job was to load cattle in Townsville, or Rocky, or Princess Charlotte Bay, and then ship them to Lae where they were quarantined. We handled about three hundred a trip. We'd take them out to Nadzab, a big wartime strip about thirty or forty miles into the Markham

Valley, and from there we'd walk them in for about a week or ten days up through that kunai-grass country to Gusap and then on to Dumpu.

The cattle were shipped on a barge called the *Wewak*, so old and rusty you could've posted letters through the gaps in the paint-work. At Marina Plains, on Princess Charlotte Bay, a company called Marine Contractors had put in a set of yards with a very long race for loading cattle for the Queerah Meatworks in Cairns.

One time, the cattle were giving trouble. We couldn't get them yarded and then we couldn't get them down this long race on to the boat. So it was a couple of days before we eventually got them all on board. Afterwards the blokes had a bit of a celebration, knocking back a few too many rums. One of them was a character by the name of Tiger Davis. That country round Marina Plains is pretty flat, all salt pans and claypans. Driving back to the camp, we saw this dingo trotting across the track. He was that close I thought I had run over him. Tiger said, 'Go on! Get up on to him! I'll bull-dog the bastard!' So I took off across the flat after this dingo and next thing Tiger gives a yakkai, and he flies out, at about thirty mile an hour, grabs the dingo, wraps himself around it and rolls with it.

The dingo wonders what the hell is happening. He gives a yoik and the next thing he turns and fastens his teeth into the nearest bit of Tiger he can grab, which is Tiger's throat! Sinks his teeth right in! Bloody near tore Tiger's jugular out! So Tiger lets go and the dingo gallops off looking over his shoulder wondering what hit him. Tiger's lying there pumping blood from his throat. We did what we could; plugged his throat to stop the bleeding; got on to VKA Cairns Outpost Radio to the Aerial Ambulance. Took a bit of explaining! They came out, landing on one of the claypans, and flew him into Cairns Base Hospital. Tiger lived to tell the tale, but I don't think he bull-dogged too many dingoes after that !

Another time we were loading cattle at the town wharf in Rockhampton on to one of the Clausen boats, the 'Inga Clausen'; just a two-decker, with a ramp going down to the lower deck. There were some bulls from Lionel De Landel's place, Cherokee Stud, at Goovigen in the Callide Valley. They were using small trucks, and one had pulled away to make room for the next one to come in to the ramp. Suddenly this young bull decides to make a break for it. He comes flying down the ramp and jumps out. Now right along the riverbank just there was all grass and parkland, and you'd think this bull would have headed for the timber. But, no! He belts off up-town into the main street!

We all jump in to Lionel's Land Rover and after him! Right along where the Mall is today. The cops were out in force. They wanted to shoot him; a menace to public safety. But this was a valuable stud bull, and being Rocky, a cattle town, they stayed on the sidelines with their .303s at the ready. We managed to block him; got him cornered right there in front of the main shops. We threw him and loaded him on to the float and took him back down to the wharf. Rocky calls itself The Beef Capital of Australia, so for them this was all in a day's work.

Another time we were loading in Townsville. There was a race which hooked into the side of the boat to run the cattle down. As the tide went out the boat dropped below the level of the wharf and the ramp unhooked itself and dropped. Two of the bulls made a break for it. There was a very capable bloke named Len Carthew, in charge of livestock loading. He and I took off after the bulls in a Land Rover, down the road towards the Metropole Hotel. On the main road the cops held up the traffic for us. Eventually we blocked these two bulls and turned them back. Next thing they cantered into the bulk-loading sugar shed! We slammed the heavy gates shut, and here they are inside, climbing this mountain of raw sugar – up to their knees in it! Like climbing Mt. Vesuvius! And us up after them! Eventually we got round them, got them down and blocked them in a corner. They were stud bulls, used to being handled, so we hitched them on at the back of the Land Rover and walked them back, slowly, slowly, down to the loading wharf and got them back on board.

Those Clausen boats, they were that bloody hot to sleep in down in the crew's quarters that they would tell us, 'It's lovely and cool on deck. Here's a hammock. Sleep up on top.' I knew those old-time matelots in Nelson's day used to sleep in hammocks, but, hell, you get a bend in you like a banana! Getting into the bloody thing! That's the hardest part!

One trip, we got out from Cairns a day or so and struck bad weather. I began to wonder if the bloody old boat was a submarine, the way the waves were breaking over the bow. And I'm not the best sailor! I was that crook! The feed for the stock used to be stacked on the top deck, roped down, so that to feed them all we had to do was to chuck it down into the hold. But during this storm the waves were breaking right over the deck and half the feed was washed overboard. The rest was full of salt water. We made it round as far as Samarai, and into Milne Bay, into a bit of shelter.

The next thing we know the de-salinating plant is buggered. So there we are, down to our last feed for the stock and no bloody water as well! We called up Lae on the radio and told them we had an emergency and needed to get in urgently to unload. As we were coming in, we could see the big white passenger boat, the *Bulolo*, that used to do the islands and back down the coast to Brisbane, in at the wharf. In those days, stock had preference, so as this old cattle-boat is limping in, there's the *Bulolo* having to pull out. She'd been ordered to anchor out midstream to let us get in to the wharf to unload!

Once the stock were unloaded the owners would leave us to see them through the ten days quarantine and dipping. Then they had to be walked through the kunai-country and up into the Markham valley, usually about a ten days trip. The natives I had working for me, as far as cattle went, they didn't know a thing. If a cow walked towards them they would run away!

Along those roads in New Guinea you would see an old native fellow strolling along with a couple of spears and a bone through his nose, scratching himself, and coming along behind him would be his 'meri', his missus, and she would be loaded up with a bilum of kau kau, that's sweet potato, and a piccaninny sitting on top and a couple of banana suckers as well. You'd even see them with a piccaninny on one breast and a piglet on the other, or half a dozen piglets tied to her ankles;

Pack-horse with water drum, Tabletop, 1940s. The water was being 'packed' to a distant yard on the Fanning River boundary where no water was available to mix rucide for spraying against buffalo fly.

getting along with all this and the old fellow is strolling along up in front looking around. The first time I came across this I said to myself, 'Bloody hell! They've got these women trained pretty well up here!' They reckon they feed the women on pups to make them strong. No joking! They have certain dogs that are kept for eating. But they don't feed those dogs meat. They're fed on kau kau, so they are vegetarian dogs – and are supposed to be good eating.

The export company gave me a donga – a very nice, self-contained place. The first morning I was there, the screeching of the cockatoos in the trees outside! Big, hook-beaked things! I woke up wondering what the hell all the commotion was about! Two house-boys did the cooking and cleaning and washing, though most of the time I was away at the wharf or the research-station. But it was nice to have somewhere clean and comfortable to come back to and have a shower and lie down to cool off; the bed turned back, nice clean sheets, and a jug of fresh lime juice they called 'muli-water' in the fridge.

Somewhere along the line on one of these trips taking cattle into the Markham I ended up getting malaria. God! I was crook! I don't know how sick you've got to be before you die but, by God I was that sick I wished I could. I made it as far as Gusap and just slid off my horse and lay down beside the yards. I'd drag myself in and out of the river – the Umi – to try to cool off a bit. My head felt ready to burst. I thought to myself, 'I'm finished!' I really thought I'd had it. But Sid Staines, the manager, said,

'Come on! We'll get you up to the house. My wife will fix you. She's a trained sister.'

I was so dirty and filthy I felt ashamed of myself, but she said, 'Lie on the bed and we'll get those trousers off you.' I just didn't care. Then she said, 'This is going to hurt.' And she hit me just under the fleshy part with an injection of Nivaquin. The needle felt the size of a drinking-straw. Struth! Didn't it hurt! She said, 'In the morning you'll get another one.' I must have been delirious because everything seemed to be on fire. I felt I was being burned up. Every so often she would come in with fresh ice-packs. Jesus! I was crook! Shivering and shaking. One minute you're boiling hot and the next you are freezing.You don't know what the hell's going on around you and your head feels like one of those big kundu-drums they have up there – someone is banging on it and won't stop.

Unloading cattle at Lae.

After a night of this, she said, 'How are you doing?' and then she hit me with another injection. She kept this up for a couple of days. Then she started me on a course of tablets. After about the third or fourth day I started to come good. She and Sid told me that during the first night they thought I wasn't going to make it, I was that far over the 104 mark. But the cattle had to be got through to Dumpu so after a couple more days we left and moved on. But I was that sore from those bloody injections I was practically riding side-saddle!

Once we had some bulls for a very well-known man in the aviation game in New Guinea, Bobby Gibbs. Bobby had made a name for himself during the war as a fighter pilot. He had a property up at Bundi in the highlands. We had two stud bulls for him and he came down in his old Norseman to collect them. The bulls were about eighteen months old and, one big fella, we've got this halter on him but not roped down or anything. And Barbara Jeffcott, the local vet needled him and she said, 'He'll be right now! He won't come round for a good hour.' It was only going to take Bobby twenty minutes to fly him up to Dumpu. So we get this bull on board the Norseman, on the floor, lying down, head lolling, and Bobby climbs in and away he goes. The rest of us go back up to the house for a cup of tea. After a bit I could hear this plane circling round overhead, but no-one else is taking any notice of it, so I thought no more about it.

Next day, Bobby came back for the second bull. He told us what happened. He said, 'By Christ, I had an experience going home yesterday! My strip at Dumpu had clouded in and I couldn't see to land, so I was holding off till it cleared a bit, and suddenly that bloody bull gets up on his feet! And he's standing there behind me blowing down my bloody neck! ' The strip at Dumpu was very tight, at a hell of an angle on the side of the hill. So Bobby had turned back to Gusap. That was the plane I'd heard circling. And our Gusap strip had closed in too. So there he is, flying round and round in this old Norseman waiting for a break in the clouds and all the time this bloody old is bull right behind him, looking over his shoulder!

Next day when we were loading the second bull, we made sure he was needled and fully out to it. We had him roped down to the cargo ties in the floor, head and legs, the lot! And as luck would have it, the weather was as clear as a bell and Bobby had no trouble flying him back up into Bundi.

The clouds come in pretty quickly up in those valleys. Once I was flying with this pilot, and he's skimming along close in to the mountains on one side. I thought, 'Gees! This valley is wide enough! Why doesn't he get out a bit!' So I asked him. He told me, 'Well, you go up the middle of this valley, she'll maybe cloud in. If you're over on one side against the mountains you've got a bit of air space to turn round in without running into the offside hill.'

A lot of cattle that went up to New Guinea were for the Government Research Stations. They would ship them out from Lae in a Bristol Freighter; front-loading, up underneath the cock-pit. The truck would back in and the cattle were loaded and tethered head and tail across the fuselage, eleven or twelve at a time. One lot of females, good quality breeding stock, went up to Baiu River, in the Western Highlands.

One of these valuable cows died and word was sent down to Lae for the vet to go up to establish the cause of death. We tried for three days to get up there but the cloud cover was too low. So by the time we got there this cow had been lying out in the paddock three days, and was bloated to buggery, legs in the air, well and truly blown.

All the natives had serifs, long bush-knives, stuck through a bit of string around their waist. The vet said to one of them, 'OK. Open her up.' And he goes slash, with his bush-knife, across her belly. Well, holy hell! The smell! It was enough to make you throw your guts up. And the poor damned vet! He has to poke around amongst the entrails trying to establish the cause of death! I'm backing off, thinking, 'To hell with this!' I didn't see anything could be done as far as a post mortem went. She was too far gone. The poor bloody vet is going green around the gills. He looked across at me and said, 'What do you reckon? Do you think it could be snakebite?' I said, 'That's for certain!'

As we were walking back to the aircraft I looked over my shoulder and here's all these natives hacking and chopping into the carcass with their bush knives and they're running away towards their camp with big hunks of beef. I said, 'What are they going to do with it?' He told me, 'Oh, Don't you worry! They'll eat it! They've got cast-iron constitutions.' I thought, 'Hell! They'd need to!'

Cattle in a yard made from steel Marsden matting, used during the war in the construction of landing strips.

It used to amaze me in New Guinea the way that, if there was a wet night coming on when we were on the road with cattle, the boys would make a grass hut. A couple of them would go on ahead and they'd put up a *haus kunai* of grass laid like thatch. The first time I thought to myself, 'Now this is going to be lovely! We'll get a soaking for sure!' But to my surprise we had a good dry camp. No rain came through at all. New Guinea fellows seem to be a bit more energetic than Aboriginals. They slip into any job you give them, and they'll be laughing away and working in a team.

The timber they use in New Guinea for building stock-yards is the queelah. But a lot of yards were built out of Marsden matting, the steel mesh-matting that was laid down during the war for airstrips; each section about ten feet long and about eighteen inches wide. The sections lock into one another; a Yank invention. Using this steel matting their engineers could put in an airstrip in a matter of days – just grade her out and lay this Marsden matting down and she's ready for aircraft. There were hundreds of these landing strips all through New Guinea during the war. Afterwards this Marsden matting was lying around everywhere. The locals used it for everything; fences, sheds, chook-yards. To make a post they would bend one of these strips lengthwise into a u-shape. Then you bend a second length and lock the two together. It's a post! You get more of these lengths and lay them flat against your posts, Cobb and Co. them in place and you've got a post-and-rail yard!

The cattle we took up there were Brahman-cross. Whenever the cows calved you had to be careful not to let screw-worm flies get at them. It looks a bit like a blow-fly and it lays its eggs in any wet place on a beast; around the cord when the calf is born and around the cow's hind-quarters. There was an antiseptic grease that had to be rubbed on to the calf, around his ears and along his back to keep this screw-fly off him.

The native boys had been trained to grab the calf as soon as it was born to apply this grease. But when the old cow hears her calf bellowing and sees the boys have got hold of him, she'd be wanting to hook into them! Some of those old Brahman cows hadn't been dehorned and were toey old things! The boys had to be pretty light-footed shifting out of their road! I used to watch them handling these calves and think, thank Christ it's you fellows on the job and not me!

And that kunai grass, to look at it you would think it was rubbishing stuff ; it's that heavy and thick, like guinea grass. You wouldn't think cattle would touch it. But you burn it; you fire it up and if you get the wind behind it, wouldn't she go! It's the regrowth that cattle go for. So you keep burning it back all the year round. Kunai was the main fodder-grass in my time up there.

At first the beef that was produced in those places was for the local markets in the Highlands. They'd kill maybe three, some days maybe five a days a week. Towards the end of my time there abattoirs were built down in Lae, and once the roads were put through, they started moving cattle by truck. After that they were able to sell all round the local islands and even as far as the Philippines.

I was up there in Milne Bay doing this sort of thing for five years. I had two good mates, chaps by the name of Ray Currie and Jim Rice. And of course I was Fryer. So we were Currie and Rice and Fryer! We used to take out Golden Casket tickets and call our syndicate 'Fried Rice and Curry' but do you think we ever won a razoo! Not on your life! I saved every penny during my time in New Guinea because I had it in the back of my mind to eventually head for the Northern Territory and look around for a place of my own. It was something I had always wanted to do.

1 The Great Basalt Wall is the local name for the long basalt lava flows in the Nulla province, near Hughenden. Volcanoes in the area have been erupting sporadically for the past 5.2 million years.Toomba volcano is one of the youngest in the province. The Toomba flow extends from just beyond the crest of the Great Dividing Range inland from Townsville to about one hundred and fifty kilometres west, making it one of the longest known lava flows on earth.

2 Plowman, R.B; The Man from Oodnadatta, p.21, 'You hardly ever have to put a cue on a working bullock's front feet. A bullock does nearly all his work with his hind legs. Lays into his yoke with his neck and lifts while he shoves with his hind-quarters. Most of the weight's off his front feet when he is getting into it.'

four...

'REACHING UP TO TOUCH BOTTOM'

Starting Out at Urapunga

Once I had decided that Urapunga was the place I wanted, and put the deposit down, I was stony broke. I was reaching up to touch bottom; living on bugger all! I accepted I'd be living rough; under a couple of bits of paper-bark and a sheet of iron, you could say, for the first few years. The hut had a dirt floor with a bit of malthoid over it, and a few slabs of bush slate. The walls, just sheets of bark, didn't go up more than six or seven feet and were just tacked on to the cross-bars, any old how. A few sheets of iron for the roof, and that was about it. Spiders everywhere! Flies over everything. About a half a mile away, up over the ridge, was a big blacks' camp, with anything up to one hundred and fifty to two hundred people. And that was it.

But the rivers! The Wilton junctioned into the Roper not far below the homestead, both of them flowing strong with fresh clear water. The Wilton was just below the homestead, down over a steep bank. There were big old paperbarks and pandanus leaning out over the water and I jumped in for a bit of a clean-up. My old mate, Duncan, said to me, 'By Chrise, Boss! More better you look out long that saltie fella!' That was the first inkling I had that crocodiles were going to be a bit of a problem[1].

I started out by cleaning out the hut, getting rid of all the junk and burying it or burning it. I made myself a bed out of greenhide. A greenhide bed looks like something out of Saltbush Bill but they are comfortable enough. You cut out a hide and trim it to the right width, about an inch and a quarter, into one long strip. First you set put four posts in the ground with two rails along each side and with a spreader across each end. Some people prefer to have cross sticks for the supports. You drill a couple of holes with the brace and bit – a magic tool in the bush – and Cobb and Co. her up tight. Then you get the greenhide and work backwards and forwards across the framework – take a half-hitch, pull – backwards and forwards. The old gins showed me how to do it. I'd never seen a greenhide bed in my life. The gins at Urapunga were very capable people.

Another thing they showed me was to get the old carbide, after you've emptied the lamp, and mix it with water – it stinks like hell! – and pour it all around to keep the ants away from your food and eating utensils; keeps the cockroaches out as well. There was a bit of a galley at the front of the hut, three sheets of corrugated iron propped up for a wind break, and I did my own cooking in a camp oven in the ashes.

Come the wet season there were centipedes everywhere. The ground was swarming with them. They got into your swag, especially when you were camped out. I was bitten on the side of the face one night and it burnt for bloody hours! They leave some sort of chemical on your skin with their front nippers.There were also scorpions, which were a bloody sight worse! They could make you pretty crook. They were four inches long, or so. But even worse was the little greeny-blue bugger, not more than an inch and a half; but talk about sting! It could really knock you!

During the Wet the mossies could give you a towelling so I would go out and knock over a couple of anthills. It was an old bushman's trick my father had taught us. In the centre of an anthill there is a core that looks like honey-comb. It must have some chemical that ants secrete. When you burn it, it smoulders away and it is better than any mosquito coil or spray from a shop, and not at all unpleasant to smell, rather scented, though I suppose they would draw the line at it in Buckingham Palace. It might muck up the curtains! Sand-flies were a bit of a bugger; worse than mosquitoes. When they got really bad I would light a fallen tree out in the paddock for the horses and you would see them standing in the smoke, tail to head, head to tail, swishing their tails over one another to keep the sandflies away.

I kept my clothes in an old tin trunk; that was the only way to keep them out of the dirt and dust. So it was all pretty rough and ready but I just wanted to get on with the cattle work. I wanted to get the place up and running so I was prepared to rough it for as long as it took. I was always up and away by about four, five o'clock. And sometimes I'd be away in the mustering camp for three or four weeks at a time. But a swag under the stars suits me; the smell of the bush and the coolness of the night air after a hot day's work. Sometimes you almost feel the earth revolving in space, everything is so vast and beautiful.

The property was very badly run-down. There was no permanent set of yards. The cattle weren't controlled and the branded ones were just as wild as the cleanskins. I knew one of the first things I would have to do was to get a decent muster underway. I found the biggest percentage of the cattle were unbranded, and there were big mobs of scrub bulls. I asked some of the young blacks if they would like to work for me and they jumped at the chance. Those fellows turned out to be excellent stockmen. They loved the life. Most of them subsequently stayed with me for many years. They were a natural at cattle work and they respected Old Duncan and were used to taking orders from him. What he said went! Duncan was my right-hand man all through the years. He was an excellent horseman and he understood cattle. And as a tracker he was among the best. He could find his way anywhere, daytime or night

We got away to a late start for the first muster because it was already the middle of the year but it was essential to get a bit of money in to start running the place,

In the early years on Urapunga all supplies were shipped in by barge and unloaded on to the bank of the Roper, then transported up to the homestead by packhorse.

so we mustered everything that was saleable; any old scrubber bullocks, bulls, piker bullocks, old cracker cows, anything that could be sold. We got together a mob of about five hundred head to walk through to Elliot to be dipped and trucked to Alice Springs. That was my first income.

The next priority was to get a mob of decent horses. Dad used to say if you can't afford decent horses you shouldn't be in the game. The things that were there were a clapped-out bloody mob. So I went back over to Queensland and bought about eighty horses and trucked them to Mataranka and then walked them out, a week or ten day's walk. There were no horse-paddocks, no yards, or anything. There was only one old tumbled down bit of a paddock that I managed to get into a bit of shape, so all the horses had to be hobbled. The blackfellas and I used to hobble them at night and tail them during the day.

The country was so rough that horses had to be kept shod all the time. If a horse lost a shoe during the day you would have to pull up and tack a slipper on, or it wouldn't be long before he would go lame and that would mean he was off work. I bought horseshoes by the hundredweight bag round from Queensland Pastoral Supplies in Townsville; mainly size three and fours. Plus hobble-chains. Hobble-chains were always getting lost so we always took spares out with us; hobble-chains, shoes and buckles. We made our hobble-straps out of greenhide.

Then we started boundary musters with adjoining stations to sort out the cleanskins. During my early years none of the boundaries with Roper Valley, St. Vidgeon's, Mainoru or Arnhem Land were fenced and once or twice a year we joined forces with our neighbours and did a muster along the boundary. Our Urapunga brand was XTI. Each station's branded cattle were returned and the unbranded clean-skins were split evenly and then we went our own way.

The Barge *Fourcroy* landing supplies for Urapunga at Roper Mission landing.

So, no paddocks, no fences. Wire was something you didn't see. So as soon as I got some money in from the first sale of cattle I sent round to Queensland Pastoral Supplies for barbed wire and started putting in some decent paddocks. I built a small paddock of about twenty acres for the night horse. Then I built two bigger horse-paddocks further out; one about three hundred acres, and a six square mile one where I ran my work horses. Across the Wilton River I fenced off about twenty-five square mile for working-horses and it was also a holding-paddock for cattle that I was getting together to be walked through to Elliot. Then I fenced the Arnhem Land boundary right up into the hills. There was no timber out that way to cut posts so it was all steel pickets which I had got up from Queensland Pastoral Supplies. The government funded fifty percent because it was the boundary of the Aboriginal reserve. I got a contractor to help with that.

Each of the paddocks was named. There was Wilton River, Wallanji, named after a big waterhole there, which lasted all the year round, Elu, named after another waterhole, and the Eight Mile – I don't think it was actually eight mile from home but it was called that – Jalboi, after the river, Pumpkin Yard, and Roper River, which followed the Roper up. Then there was the Wilton Valley paddock where you could use the escarpment of the ranges for a lot of the boundary. Sandy Creek paddock had a big sandy-bottomed tributary of the Roper.

In all these paddocks we built holding-yards, a couple of hundred yards square, to hold cattle overnight while we were mustering. I built the yards in the lancewood scrub using as many standing trees as possible for posts, cutting out the trees in the centre for railings. Lancewood scrub was pretty thick all through that country and we'd cut a big mob of rails and Cobb and Co them into place with wire. We had no chain-saws, just a couple of axes. At each holding paddock we built a race so we could run the old bullocks up it to knock their horns off all the quicker. We built sets of yards like that every eight to ten mile.

Once I was building a yard with a very well-respected old Aboriginal Chinese man, Tex Camfu; a good horseman and a very good cattleman, and we'd run out of wire. He said, 'We'll blow one of those old scrub bulls out and use the greenhide.' So we shot this bull and made greenhide rope, stranding it out as well as we could, tying it and stretching it. We finished building the yards like that, by tying them up with greenhide.

Another big paddock, right up the top of the place, about twenty-five mile out, was on a waterhole that never went dry known as Ah Cup's. It was out on a big plain off the bank of the Wilton, on the boundary between Mainoru and Urapunga. A Chinese named Ah Cup is buried there. His grave is marked by a big mound of stones and a plate with his name punched into it. They say Ah Cup was one of a mob of Chinese prospectors going through to Pine Creek in the gold rush days. The old blackfellas told me this Ah Cup got in tow with the young gins there at the lagoon, and settled in to stay. It must have been a bit like heaven to him! Then he died. I don't know what the cause of death was but I could use my imagination!

Ah Cup's waterhole was never known to go dry. One year when we had very little feed left in the big horse-paddock I moved all my horses out there, and put Old Duncan in charge of them with a couple of young fellows to off-side for him, until the Wet came.

The biggest paddock I had was Wilton Valley. I built two holding-yards in it about six miles apart, to save driving the cattle the distance. I got form-boards and cement and rails and put in grids on the road in accordance with specifications that the Main Roads gave me.

One day the blackfellas were all singing out as I rode up. I said, 'What's wrong?' They told me, 'Big cheeky-fella snake in there!' I said, 'Where?' They said, 'There! Him run that long-grass.' I said, 'Well, he's way out here in this back country. He's not doing us any harm. Just get out of his road!' But they reckoned 'Him cheeky-fella. Proper bad one. Killim finis!" So we chucked a match and set fire to the grass and out he came! Oh! He was a big fellow! A king brown. Must have been close on six foot! You don't get any second chances where they are concerned.[2]

Something that took a bit of getting used to, when I first went to that Top End country, was the way some of the things that the blacks and I said to one another could have totally different meanings. For instance, the word, 'Yes', or 'Yo-i'. 'Yes' could mean 'No'. One day we lost a couple of pack mules, and I sent a young fellow called Eddie back to have a look for them. Later on, I saw him riding back along the road. I said to him, 'You didn't get those mules, eh, Eddie?' He said, 'Yo-i.' I said to him, 'Oh, Good on you, Mate! Thanks very much.' And he rode on home.

And next day I went back to the camp and there are no mules there. I said to the fellows, 'What happened to those mules Eddies said he got? They said to me, 'Him bin look'im. Him no pine 'em.' I said to them, 'The bastard! He told me he had!' We had to go looking for them and later on I said to Eddie, 'Hey! What's this rot you told me about getting those mules!' He said to me, 'No-got! Maluka! Me talk tru.' I said, 'I asked you when I saw you coming, 'You didn't get those mules, eh?' And you said 'Yo-i'. It suddenly dawned on me that what he meant was, Yes, he hadn't got them! I knew I would have to put things to them so that there could be no misunderstandings.

But sometimes you had to laugh. I sent one young blackfella on ahead of us one day, and I said to him, 'If you get to the gate before we do, put a bush on it.'And he said, 'Yo-i! Righto, Maluka. Me savvy. S'posim me get there first me put bush long gate. S'posim you get there first you take him off!'

They never said 'morning' or 'evening'. It was 'sun come up' and 'sun go down'. And midday they would call 'sun on top'. East was 'sun-up' and west was 'sun-go-down'. But they knew a lot more English than I did blackfella talk. They seem to handle other languages better than we do, maybe from hearing different tribal dialects from when they are little kids in the camp or when they go away to big ceremonies.They get a bit of an ear for it. There is also a sign language which they use to signal to one another when they are out hunting. And the kids pick these language skills up from early childhood round the camp. I made a bit of an effort to pick up some of their words.

The first school at Urapunga was what they called a pastoral school, a galvanised building with push-out shutters, and back and front verandah, with a room on one end for the teacher. The government supplied the money – I think it might have been about five hundred pounds – to buy the iron and cement. I bought the timber from Roper River Mission where there was a sawmill. Everything else was brought up by barge and unloaded on the bank and from there we carted it up by pack-mule.There were about twenty-five or thirty kids in the school.

Every morning they would come galloping down from the camp and they were run through the shower and cleaned their teeth. I made the bell out of a piece of inch steel bent into a triangle, hanging up on a bit of chain. There was another piece of steel to bang it with. Then they would change into their clean clothes and be ready for school. A couple of the old gins were in charge of the clothes. They took the dirty camp clothes away and washed them down the river, banging them against a tree stump to get the dirt out of them; a 'coolibah' wash! Then they would spread them out on the bushes or along the fence to dry. They brought them back nice and clean for the kids to change back into when school was finished.

There used to be quite a bit in the way of supplementary food brought in to boost the kids' diet; tinned orange juice, and other fruit juices, in those big five pound tins. And powdered Sunshine milk. The teacher organized one of the big kids to mix in a bucket. At morning smoko-time all the kids lined up with their pannikins. Sometimes there'd be Milo added in, a couple of mugsful to the bucket. This was all to improve their general health, to get a bit of extra feed into them. It was all shipped from the east coast on the barge and we packed it up from the landing on mules.

Until he could build a proper homestead on Urapunga, Ray built "a decent sort of a shed, accommodation up one and stores down the other; nothing flash but it kept the rain out."

The schoolteacher, a nice-enough young fellow from down Victoria way, not long out of Training College, said to me, 'How do you get on about washing here?' I said, 'Oh, well. There're tubs and things. But those old gins, they're good on the washing. They'll do it for you. You give them a few bob, whatever you think it's worth to you.' So he did this. The old ladies used to get his clothes and take them down the river to wash them

But after a bit this young chap comes to me and he says, 'Do those women do your washing?' And I said, 'Yeah. When I'm home I get them to do it. I do it myself when I'm out in the stock-camp.' He said, 'I don't know what's happening to my clothes. I've got no buttons left on my shirts. And the hems are coming down. And they've got rips all over them. I never tore my clothes like that! I don't understand what's happening to them!"

I said to him, 'Oh, Hell! You want to go down the river one day when the old women are doing the washing! They're probably doing a coolibah on them. That's why they are losing all those buttons and getting a bit frayed!' He said, 'What's a coolibah?' I told him, 'Oh, well. They wet the clothes in the river and then they get the soap powder and they sprinkle it on and then they flog them up against that old coolibah tree down there. You'll see the soap all white around the base of it. And they hang them over the barbed wire fence to dry. If the breeze gets up a bit they pull them off. That's how your things are getting a few rips.'

He said, 'Oh, Dear! I'll have to start doing my own!' I said, 'Well, it's either a coolibah or a Do It Yourself one!' That young chap only stayed one or two years there, but he was a different man towards the end. And later on when I got a bit of money behind me I got some thirty two volt washing machines for the old ladies to make life a bit easier for them.

The next priority I had was to start work on a decent set of main yards. I began putting them in about a quarter of a mile from where I planned the future homestead would be, far enough away from the dust. In later years I moved them even further. They were five-rail lancewood, mortised into timber posts of ironwood. Ironwood is a rough-barked timber, very hard. You know where it gets its name when you start to cut it with an axe. We cut all the posts by hand and carted them in. I treated the bases with creosote and arsenic pentoxide against white-ants before I put them into the ground; never above the ground because stock will lick it and it can knock them.

I like to set my gates high. The gate is always the weakest part of any fence and if a beast is going to try to jump out of the yard it will always try at the lowest part. So if you set your gates high the beast is less likely to crash them. I can't stand a gate that has to be picked up and dragged. There should be a foot's clearance under a gate. They're not meant to block lizards.

The main yards were six foot to the top rail and the receiving yards were four foot six; just one rail, with four cables which I got from the mines at Mount Isa. You could buy the cables after they were taken out of the shaft. They were still good enough for fencing. The drafting yards were six foot. The crush was ten panels, each nine-foot, with one section a speying-bail and one an ordinary bail.The round yard was a six-way draft. Later on, when I could afford it, I put in a race to run the calves down, with a steel branding and castrating cradle, made by Morriseys in Jandowie.

Outside the yards were four receiving paddocks where you could bring in as many cattle as you mustered for the day. We used to bring in three or four hundred cattle a day because by the time you got them in and drafted and took them back to paddocks, well, that was ample for a day's work. I was a great believer in trying to get your work done before sundown. My father always told us it was a bad boss who worked cattle after dark. He used to say that if the head stockman didn't have his cattle yarded before sun-down he wasn't a good man at the job. He said you should have your cattle yarded-up in the daylight where everyone can see what they are doing.

All the main yards had watering-points. I started off by pumping from the river through old galvanized piping into a tank but then as time went by I got black poly-piping and pumped directly into troughs in the yards from a tank set on a pushed-up mound.

Cattle that were held overnight we turned out next morning and returned to different paddocks, putting our breeders in good paddocks. At certain times of the year when we had pulled weaners off they were locked up in the yards and fed on hay or whatever feed we could get. I bought an old mowing-machine that I could pull behind a Toyota to cut a bit of hay. No such thing as baling. I would just scratch it together and take it up and tip it into them

In that Top End country you have to wait for the country to dry out before you can move around and begin your mustering. I began making preparations well before the end of the Wet. Horses had to be got in out of the horse-paddocks and drafted and shod. The stock-boys weren't much good at shoeing; they just couldn't seem to get the hang. If they tacked on a set of shoes they would be off again the very first day. But Old Duncan was very handy, so he and I did most of the shoeing.

For a muster I would take four horses per man, with a pack-horse or pack-mule shared between two men for their swags and gear, and a few spares. So with eight to ten men we took about forty-five head of horses with us. Each horse had its own hobbles on a raw greenhide strap around its neck. One pack-mule was generally for the shoeing gear. You had to have a few sets of spare shoes, and your hammers and rasps and pritchel – which is what you use if the nail won't fit through the shoe; you drive a pritchel in to widen the holes. As well you had to take a shovel and an axe and maybe a roll of wire and pliers in case a fence was down, and a .303.

Another mule carried the canteens of water and the tarpaulins and D-billies. They are flat on one side to fit against the pack-saddle and fit one inside the other in a set of six. I also used a couple of old flour drums – they have a well-turned edge – for cooking the corned-beef. Other packs had spuds and onions, flour, rice, dehydrated vegetables, syrup, jam, salt-beef. And plenty of sugar! Those blacks ate more sugar than anything else. You could stand a spoon up in their tea! All the things you would need for eight or ten men for four weeks out.

I never built any mustering-huts. We always put up two big tarpaulins, about sixteen by twenty feet; the tent sticks were left in position so all that had to be done was to throw the tarps over. One was for the boys and the other one was where I kept the tucker and rolled my own swag out.

I have my own way of rolling a swag. I reckon a six by eight is no good for a swag-cover. You've got no side flaps. I get mine made with a flap of Birkmyre – that stuff they make horse-rugs for race horses out of; it's waterproof – on either side and at each end. That gives you a good long swag that you can carry over a pack-horse, a U-shaped one. They reckon in the olden days if your mate died when you were out bush you put him over a log overnight so that he would be the right shape to sling over a pack-horse to bring him back!

Before we set up camp I'd get the men to clean up around the area, especially if there was any grass that might have grown since you used the camp last. I'd tell the boys to bring plenty of wood and I'd get a good fire going and unpack the packs. I had a couple of cook-packs with all the gear necessary for getting a meal together; Stan Norgren, my saddler, made leather pouches for the knives and forks, the butchering knife and the steel, and one that you could put three tins of syrup into so that they couldn't pop their lids. There's nothing worse than getting golden syrup through everything! I'd always put a rail up between the trees where the packs were hung, and another for the saddles.

I would detail off two blokes as horse-tailers, whose job it would be to look after the horses. At the end of the day they would take the horses out a bit from the camp and hobble them. I did the cooking in the camp but when those fellows with the horses went back to camp after dinner-camp when we were mustering I would tell them to put the corned-beef on to get it started. Then when I got back to camp I would chuck in some spuds and onions and boil it up and we had a decent feed. A rule was everybody had to have a sluice-up before they ate. I like a bit of cleanliness around a camp.

"In the original bark hut there was no kitchen. There was a bit of a galley, three sheets of iron propped up for a wind-break. I did my own cooking in a camp-oven in the ashes."

I would have a tarp spread out on the ground where I would have everything set out and I would have the stew, or curry, or corned beef or whatever it was, in camp ovens beside the fire. Everybody could help themselves to what they wanted then when they'd finished they would scrape their plates and I'd have put out a big dish of hot water with some soap in and everybody washed up their own plate and knife and fork. And at night before I turned in I would knock up dampers for the next day in big bedourie ovens. I would generally take the first watch and then I would shake up the next fellow, usually the horse-tailer, because he and I were the ones that had to make the earliest start next day. Or if, for some reason, the cattle were really toey I might have the whole camp up until they settled down. If you had cattle in the holding yards and there was a storm brewing, a clap of thunder would make them jump up. Anything could make cattle toey – a possom running up a tree or a limb falling and they could take off.

It's a funny thing, but about midnight, cattle will get up, stand up, and mill around a bit and then lie down again on their other side. You hear all these stories about cattle being more likely to rush if they are tired; they are half asleep and something startles them and they hit their feet and go. I think it is right that tired cattle are more inclined to jump at night. That's why you keep riding around them singing or whistling to keep them a bit alert that you are there.You don't like to see them all lying down asleep at the same time. It's better to see some standing up.

When that morning star rose, about four o'clock I would sing out to the horse-boys to get up and bring the horses up. A couple of the horses would have a bell on them so they would know which direction to go looking for them. When they brought the horses in to the camp you'd catch your horse for the day and saddle him and tell the horse-tailers what other horses you would need that afternoon. I would tell them the direction we were heading, so they would know which direction to bring the change-horses along to the dinner-camp. They would get on to our tracks and follow us out with the fresh horses. We would let our morning horse go and catch the fresh ones; they were called the dinner-horses. Dinner was a cut lunch of damper and beef which you cut yourself in the morning and took out in your saddle bag. If there was no water where we were going to have dinner-camp we would take one pack-horse with canteens of water; the flat-sided ones.

I'd always have the camp laid out so that the fire was between the tents and the cattle. If you have a good fire and the cattle rush, the mob would split and not come over the top of you. When I was a young bloke I was taking a mob of six hundred Fanning River bullocks for old Harry Clarke down to Ross River Meatworks. I had a young fellow with me by the name of Craig Vincent. And late one night a bloody bloke and his sheila were driving round in a jeep and they didn't know we had cattle there and they came up out of the creek and their headlights hit them. Well! Didn't the mob jump! The fire was down and the cattle came through the camp right over the top of us! We had the ridge-pole of the tent on to a tree and Craig went to swing up. He was on the ridge-pole and I was right behind him! Somehow I jammed into him and drove his shoulder into the branch above him. Afterwards he caught his horse but he couldn't get on, his arm was so sore. So next day I got him into Townsville hospital and they x-rayed his shoulder and found it was broken! So that is why I always have a decent sort of fire between the cattle and the camp. It will split the cattle if they rush.

I usually took a mob of coachers out with me, quiet, strong cattle used to being handled. Any unbranded scrub cattle we came across we would get round and push in among the coachers. It helped to settle them down and they would be much easier to handle. Any bulls were thrown and had their horns knocked off. Then they'd be pushed into the coachers as well. The coaching mob had to be in good condition because you would be walking them for the best part of a month. And when we had a big enough mob we headed back and put them into the new paddocks I was putting in.Then we would repeat the whole process. When we headed out again we took a different mob of coachers. I didn't use the same ones over. I would give them a spell. Those old coachers would get that quiet they would come up and camp around your fire at night.

We used to get hot, dry winds and some terrible hot days. If there was timber with a bit of shade for the cattle we would pull up and hold them until the real heat of the day was past. Then later, we would poke them along to the holding yard or the camp. At the end of each day we would take the horses down to the waterhole and get a quart-pot and wash their backs to get the dirt and sweat off to stop them from scalding.

When we ran short of meat in camp we would knock over a killer. We'd slit its jugular to bleed it, then lay the hide back on to a good pile of clean branches and bone it out there and then. We'd cut out what fresh meat we could use that night and salt the rest. We always carried a half a bag of coarse salt for this purpose. I'd butcher the meat and stack it on the hide and salt it down; throw a few branches over it to keep the flies off. After a day or two you'd pack it in the pack-bags and you'd use that until it was all gone. Then you'd knock another killer. If we came across young buffaloes we would blow one of them out for a killer. They weren't bad eating, though I'd sooner red-beef, any day. But if we started to cut out of tucker I'd send one boy back with a pack-horse to the hut to pick up a bit more.

We used a lot of salt, not just for salting down beef. The stock like it for a lick in the Wet. The horses relished it. So we used to go down in the old blitz to the mouth of the Roper; a pretty rough road down through St. Vidgeon's. Urapunga was eighty-four miles upstream by river but by road through the ridges and scrub it must have been close on a hundred. At the mouth of the river there was a tidal creek on the southern side where a salt flat used to flood at king tide. During neap tides the water would evaporate and leave a good, thick deposit of salt.[3]

We would go down for a couple of days at a time and camp there and shovel the salt into bags. The clean stuff we kept separately to take home and it was used for cooking and to salt beef. It was surprising how clean you could get some of it. It was easy enough to shovel up. You just had to be careful that you didn't dig your shovel too deep. Any that wasn't perfectly clean was kept for the stock. The horses really went for it during the Wet and it was cheaper to get lick for them in this way than having it shipped round from Townsville or Cairns on the barge.

A bit of a problem at Urapunga could be quicksand. Sometimes when you were crossing creeks you would hit a patch and your horse would flounder right down to his belly and fall on his side, whinnying and squealing. He would strike out and try to get up and flounder again and squeal. And you're bogging in the quicksand yourself and can't do much to help him. You couldn't always tell where a patch of it would be. Sometimes it would look smooth and glassy. It is generally not in the water but just off the stream. The blackfellas might say, 'Hey! Maluka! You don't want go there! You bog there!' You would look at it and think, 'Yes, by God! I might too!' You got that way you would know by the look of it.

Once the monsoonal rains set in, Urapunga averaged about thirty or thirty-five inches a year. We didn't get cyclones because once a cyclone crosses the coast it loses a lot of its intensity but we would get high winds off them – maybe lose some sheets of iron off the roof – but we'd get a hell of a lot of rain. One year we got an earlier Wet; it started in October and the river came down. Rain pelted and pelted and never let up. And once the river gets to a certain height there's no way a beast can swim it. No way I'd be in there, either! I had all these cattle ready and a sale lined up for them but I just couldn't deliver them. I didn't get those cattle away to be sold until August, September the following year, ten months later.

Pack-horses carrying in supplies from Roper River Mission landing to Urapunga. "Everything had to be packed up from the landing on mules or pack-horses."

And a wet night's camp! If you're lucky enough to get your tent up before the storm comes, you end up, eight or ten blacks and yourself, huddling under it, and if you're on flat country you've got to dig a drain around it, otherwise three or four inches of water will come straight through; dirt and mud, all through your swag! Next morning you're hanging your blankets out hoping to Christ they dry out a bit before you get back that night so you can get a bit of sleep. The blow-flies get into them and once they're fly-blown they stink like hell. Once the eggs get right in, there's only one way to get rid of them and that's to throw them over a decent sort of an ant-hill. The ants get in and do a good job of cleaning the maggots and eggs up.

Once we were camped at Sturt Plain, out from Dunmara, in an old Nissen hut. And bloody big storms! The next day there were little fish about half an inch to an inch long – clear little fellows, you could almost see right through them – in the puddle holes! The blackfellas told me they had seen the same thing down in Alice! But how the hell do they stay alive when they must hit the ground so hard coming down out of the sky like that![4]

An on-going problem at Urapunga was the fitness of the horses. Horses don't have a long life in the Top End. There is a disease they are prone to called walkabout disease. They say it is caused by them eating a bluey-green bush with a yellow flower, pollopodium pea. Horses fall away and go blind, and can't stop walking; or they fall arse-over head down gullies and creeks.

The occasional one would get over it but they were never much good afterwards. They would walk into your tent. Anything! You would see them lying on their side throwing their head back over their ribs, groaning. I would shoot any that I saw down like that. It was all you could do for them. There didn't seem to be any cure for it. I cut open a few of them after they had died, and the livers seemed to be shrivelled up like an old dried-up bit of leather. Walkabout even hit the brumbies, running wild. It seems to be very bad in the Kimberley and the Territory. For this reason a lot of people used mules. Mules don't seem to be affected by it.

I had about a hundred and twenty to a hundred and thirty horses on the place. About three times a year I would muster the big horse paddock, pull out the ones I wanted, and turn out those that had been working. They wouldn't be worked again until the following year. I would muster the colts at about eighteen months old and bring them into the paddock near the homestead. I built a set of horse yards with a round yard and every morning we would run the colts up and give them a bit of feed, oats or anything cheap I had been able to get up from down south. They were castrated and branded and recorded. The blacks liked naming them after themselves, or names like 'Trumby' after the Slim Dusty song, or 'Migaloo', which would be for a whitey fellow – 'Migaloo' means 'white man'; so does 'Balanda', another name they liked for a grey. Then the details would be entered in the Record Book; the name, date, and identification; 'star and blaze' or 'three white feet' or 'one white hind'.

During the Wet, to fill in time and make a bit of fun for the boys, we would get a couple of colts each and break them in. We would throw a rope on them and then collar-rope them with a rope from their neck down to their hind foot, and pull that up so they couldn't go down. Then you use a bit of bag and rub them all over and keep moving around them until they get to understand that you are not going to harm them. Then you put mouthing-gear on them, which is a means of tying their head down with a bridle to a back-band. That gets them so that their their head arches in a nice way and then you get them going round and round the yard like that.You get them in long driving reins and drive them round, so that they begin to understand what's expected of them and how to respond to a bridle.

The main thing is to handle them as much as possible; get a halter on them and get them quiet and get them to face you. For the first few times out of the yard they would be pretty useless but once you get them going and they have got used to blocking up cattle, they get used to the work like the other horses. Some would be a lot smarter than others. For a couple of years after a colt has been broken in he's still learning on the job. Everything you teach him has to be done in the right way, and done consistently, a bit like getting the best out of a kid. And just like a kid he learns by repetition. A horse that is badly taught and doesn't understand what is required of him is likely to end up with a bad temperament, and turn into a bolter or wanting to get his head down and pelt you off. Some would turn out useless. Any that showed a bad temperament, any viciousness, I would put a bullet through their head. I don't mind a horse with a bit of spirit but a horse that has an ugly streak, that will turn and lash out at you with his hoofs for no reason, well, you are better off without him in a stock-camp. I had one hanging on to my shoulder one time! I was trying to get some front shoes on him, and he just swung around and sank his teeth into me. I kicked him in the guts a couple of times until he let go of me! I have still got a scar on my arm! He never tried it again. But it is no use risking the life of a man for the sake of an ugly-tempered horse. Or if he was just a moody mongrel I'd shove a pack on him and use him as a pack-horse. Sometimes that will bring them to their senses.

I have always loved horses and I would have liked to have started a breeding programme on Urapunga but the walkabout disease beat me. Early on in the piece I brought up a beautiful stallion from Charters Towers but he only lasted three years before it hit him. The same thing happened to the breeding mares. So then I got a horse-dealer by the name of Tom Cannon in the Towers to bring me up a semi-load, about twenty head, every twelve to eighteen months. I was paying about $75 to $100 a head.

When we were broncoing on a muster I used mules a lot. I'd pack with mules, too. Horses, if you didn't have them shod, or if you lost a shoe during the day, well, you'd have to pull up – you'd always carry spare shoes – and tack another one on. But mules, they just job along, carry a pack all the time, and never seem to go lame on you. Mules have got hard feet.

Breaking in a mule is much the same principle as breaking in a horse. You throw a rope on him and pull him up, and bag him down and get him quiet. Some mules are sour buggers; touch them on the forehead and they'll kick you in the belly, sort of thing. I've had mules that when you'd go to pack them, you would tie them to a tree with a halter on, then throw a rope on his hind leg and stretch him right out, otherwise he'd kick you when you were putting the girth and pack on him. Once I had the pack on I'd let him go. He would kick the rope off his foot and run along with the horses. But the most important thing when working with mules is to remember to put your swag on a civil-tempered one. Put it on a nasty bugger and he takes off with it! Well, you've got to have your swag of a night time, eh!

But some quiet old jenny-mules you could use for broncoing. Mules can be male or female. They are the first cross of the horse with the donkey. The jenny mule, she will breed, but the male can't breed. Maybe that's what he's cranky about!

Mules can get a long way at night in hobbles; jumping feet together. I had one old Aboriginal ringer, Hinkler Daiwanna – he was a good old man at tracking. Daiwanna was his tribal name but he was just a piccanniny in the year that Bert Hinkler flew over so he was always known as Hinkler. He lived into his nineties. But old Hinkler could be tracking these bloody mules for two or three miles every morning, so I thought, to hell with that! So to save him, we'd sideline them; a hind leg to a foreleg, with a chain a bit longer than an ordinary hobble-chain and using ordinary hobble-straps. It's sometimes called Scotch hobbling; when you run the chain from the near-side to the off-side hind. But I have seen horses get the other foot over the chain and trip themselves over. In the morning they'd be lying on the ground and I don't like seeing horses or mules down like that, so I would side-line mine from front leg to back. But mostly mules. That puts a stop to their little gallop!

There was one old jenny, a friendly old thing; at night she would always come up close by wherever I was and camp. One night it was pouring rain. The roof of the hut had no guttering and the rain's pouring down off the edge. After I had finished my washing-up in an old tin dish, I ducked outside to throw the water away. Well, this poor old jenny-mule, she was standing out there under the edge of the lean-to to get out of the rain and when I ran out to chuck the dish of water I ran straight into her backside. I got a hell of a fright. But so did she! She lashed out with both heels and knocked me arse over tip! Flat on my back in the mud! It wasn't her fault! But, gee, was I sore for a few days afterwards! There's nothing like a kick in the guts from a mule to let you know you've got them!

There are mobs of donkeys all through the Top End, especially in the rougher areas in the ranges, brought in originally for the Maranboy gold diggings, between Urapunga and Katherine. That country was ideal for donkeys and they bred up. Apart from eating a bit of grass they weren't a big problem to us though we would shoot a few out from time to time to keep their numbers down.

Robin-John Scuthorpe breaking-in a pack-mule at Urapunga.

One night when I was driving over to Mainoru I came across a big mob of donkeys straggling across the road. They scattered in all directions, but one little fellow – he can't have been much more than a few days old – he just propped in the head-lights not knowing which way to run. I opened the door, jumped out and grabbed him, and shoved him down under the seat in front of me. When I got to Mainoru I carried him in my arms – they are all dangly legs, you know – and shoved him inside the cook's bedroom and closed the door. Well, after about five minutes didn't all hell break loose! Donkey, he's hee-hawing; Cook, she's screaming! She promised she'd kill me when she got hold of me! But talk about laugh! They had that donkey there as a pet around the place for a good many years.

So the first ten years on Urapunga were pretty rough. I lived off a bank-draft and a mortgage. I was paying interest only and not letting my debt increase, and putting any money I could scrape together into improvements. I lived hard, and had a few dry gullies, but I got by. And eventually cattle numbers bred up until after ten years I started to get my head above water. My idea of happy was marking out a fence-line. I couldn't afford bull-dozers so I used to clear a chain width with a chain-saw and drag the trees out of the way and burn them and then start running the new fence. I put in decent yards and bought portable panels. In the end I had about seven and a half thousand head of cattle and was turning off about six or seven hundred head of steers. At the beginning I was getting about fifty dollars a head but in those days you did a lot more with your dollar than you do today. For example, wire, when I started out was twenty dollars a coil. Now it's a hundred and ten!

When I had been on the place about twelve or eighteen months, I ordered some iron and cement round from Queensland Pastoral Supplies, and built myself a decent sort of a shed to live in; stores up one end, accommodation at the other, with a temporary shower. I put in a ten horsepower centrifugal pump to bring water up from the Wilton. The shed wasn't anything flash but at least it could be kept clean and the roof kept the rain out. I put a match to the original bark hut and stood back and watched it go up! Didn't I enjoy giving those bloody spiders and cockroaches their cremation! I still got those big bush cockroaches when the storms came in the Wet. You would see them flying in. I used to spray all the time.They just seem to be part of things up there in that country.

1 Leichhardt, Ludwig, *Journal of an Overland Expedition in Australia*; pp.442, 3; 'Oct. 19th. ... I observed a green belt of trees to the northward, and on riding towards it, I found myself on the banks of a freshwater river from 500 to 800 yards broad, with not very high banks....The water was slightly muddy as if a fresh had come down it; the tide rose a full three feet. It was the river Mr. Roper had seen two days before and I named it after him.'...'Oct. 20th...We travelled about ten miles N.60deg. W up the river...Oct.24th...a ledge of rocks crossed the bed, over which a considerable stream formed a small fall and rapids; above this a fine sheet of water overhung with shady tea-tree, casuarinas and pandanus, which made this crossing place extremely lovely.'

2 Pseudechis australis; active at night, the king brown is the heaviest-built snake in Australia, growing to a length of 3 metres. It has the largest output of venom of any Australian snake, producing up to 180mg and can be very aggressive.

3 ibid, page 346. 'I found the broad bed of a creek one mass of the purest, whitest salt...in ten minutes we collecteded sufficient for our needs for the rest of the journey. Ship loads of pure salt could have been collected here in a very short time. Its appearance was quite wonderful to me.'

4 Durack, Mary. *Kings in Grass Castles*; page 127. 'There was a time when a deluge of tiny fish and frogs fell from the heavens with the rains.'

five...

'KANGAROO DREAMING'

The Rittarangu and Njandi People

The tribes at Urapunga were the Rittarangus and the Njandi. They used to call themselves 'salt waters'. The salt water black is taller and darker than the inland fellow. They told me that Urapunga means 'The Land of the Dreaming Kangaroo'. The Rittarangu and the Njandi spoke the same language and got on well together. They used to call me Maluka[1]; which is their way of saying Boss. A lot of them had been born on the place. There were also a few Nalakan people, from Elsey way, whose language was very similar, according to Old Duncan.

The men from those tribes were very good stockmen. Bruce Simpson, a well known drover, told me that he always tried to get men from the Roper River area because they were superior when it came to stockwork.The Alawa men, from south of the river, towards Nutwood Downs and Nathan River, didn't go in for stockwork very much. Alawas were alright in their own country, but if they got into Mataranka or Katherine, they'd fight and brawl with the tribes from the Kimberleys. So I stuck to the Rittarangus, Njandis and Nalakans because being the same language group there'd be less fighting. Duncan told me that in the old times the Njandis were a very peaceful people. They avoided tribal fighting and would hide out in caves in the hills if there was trouble brewing.

At times there would be groups of Warramungas and Wailbri from down around Banka Banka that would work their way up to Urapunga on foot and then there could be fights in the camp. Or else they would come on 'blackfella business', initiation ceremonies or 'payback'. Or sometimes a stranger would lob in from down south, a 'visita', which usually meant something was getting too hot for him where he came from, and he suddenly remembered he had an 'Auntie bilong 'im' at Urapunga.

I got on very well with the Aborigines. They tried to teach me how to make fire their way. I'd be rubbing away on the stick, rub, rub, rub and I'd get the smoke coming and I'm blowing and blowing, puff, puff, puff, but, ah! I could never get it to light. They'd fall around laughing! They were a happy people; always ready to see the funny side of things. Once, I got this directive from Aboriginal Affairs in Darwin; all the pastoralists across the Top End were told that from then on we were not to call them 'blackfellas' any more. They made it official; we had to call them 'Aboriginals'. I told old Duncan Yappanala, my head man. Oh, he laughed. He said, 'Bull-shit! We call you 'whitefella'. You call us 'blackfella'. That's all right!' As far as he was concerned 'blackfella' was OK by him.[2]

And in any case, they use the word 'blackfella' for themselves. When they were arranging important ceremonies or if there was a dispute going on between tribes or skin-groups, they would tell you straight out to your face, 'That blackfella business.' It meant it was nothing to do with you and not to ask too many questions. I had no problem with that. Blackfella business was blackfella business. I kept out of it.

When I first went into that country I was bloody raw as anything. I was used to the type of blackfellas that I'd met up in the Gulf who'd been living on stations for a couple of generations and were used to wearing clothes and speaking English. But in Arnhem Land they were still getting around dressed in ngagas, or loin cloths, and the old gins in the raw! The men would have a bit of twisted string around their waist with a tomahawk stuck through, and the gins without a stitch on! They would come in out of the bush for a handout. What they wanted was 'tea and chuga'. And, of course, 'bacca'.

The first six months that I was there they were all a bit wary of me, looking to see how I would shape up. Once they realized that I was fair dinkum with them they more or less accepted me. There were certain places on Urapunga where there were rock-paintings and gradually they began to show me these places and tell me about them, their stories and the meanings. They would tell me, 'You can't take pictures that one.' or 'Women can't look long that one,' and so on. I got to know several places where there were cave paintings that I never let on about to any outsiders because they had been shown to me in good faith.

They told me that 'Urapunga' meant 'place of the dreaming kangaroo' and how the creeks came to be where they were and how the dreamtime kangaroo hopped into the mountains and knocked the valley between this range of hills and that. I would pull their leg, and say 'Gammon!' but they would say, 'Yeah! That one all right! Old man he bin tell me all 'bout him!' I used to think, 'Oh, well! As long as they are happy with it.' They would say 'Whitefella, he don't savvee same like blackfella.'

They were always having corroborees up in the camp. It used to go on all the time. At night you could hear them, singing away and having a great old time. Sometimes the old fellows would come down to me during the day and they would say, 'You come tonight. We-fella makim' big sing!' I'd go up for an hour or so. They would be sitting around a fire in a big circle; one fella playing the 'bumboo' – their word for didgeridoo – leg out in front, holding it with big toe, another one on the click-sticks, singing away. They would not be painted-up for these dances; usually they made do by grabbing a handful of wet ash and smearing it over their chest and back. I've even seen them use flour and water. They'd still have their work trousers on, or a pair of shorts. Emu dance, Buffalo dance.

In the Kangaroo Hunt one fellow is the kangaroo and he stretches up and looks around and gives himself a bit of a scratch, and the others all come in line with sticks for hunting spears, lifting their feet and placing them down carefully, rolling their foot inwards – a hunting way of walking. The 'roo' sniffs the air and senses danger. He goes to hop away. But they spear him and down he goes. The 'roo' grips the spear under his arm as though it's in his guts, and rolls on the ground and kicks his legs and then he 'dies'. Then all the hunters spin round and kick a bit of gravel and give a final stamp and a yell, 'Ai!' and stroll off. And that's it. After a bit of a break they start up again. Maybe this time it is How Jacob got Pelted Off His Horse in the Horse-yards! That's always good for a laugh! Or How Duncan got Kicked in the Behind By the Mule. They kill themselves over that!

The women, they're stripped down to the waist with paint on their faces. Women didn't dance in the circle, just off to one side doing a sort of shuffle-dance in a semi-circle of their own. And this goes on for half the night; kids running around; dogs scratching themselves or starting up fights. Everybody happy as Larry.

Even out in the mustering camp after tea was over at night the young fellows would have a little fire going and start up a bit of a sing-song clicking away on the clap-sticks. I'd listen to them from my swag. And when we were boundary-mustering, they would have a get-together with blacks from other stations. Each stock camp had about eight or ten blackfellas and when two or three camps got together, they would be singing away in their camp half the night.

And when we had been out mustering three or four weeks and were only a day or two from home, they would ride up on to a hill and light up the spinifex and send up black smoke. The old gins would see it and they would say, 'Oh! Stock-camp bin comin'!' and they would be jumping around with joy. They could judge how long it would be till the boys were back. And the big excitement when we got in and yarded up! All the little piccaninny fellows full of excitement on the top rail at the yards. It was a big thing to see their brothers and fathers come back, and all the unsaddling and unloading of the packs and swags and gear. But the first night home there wouldn't be much in the way of corroboreeing. They had other things on their minds!

The Urapunga people still maintained a lot of their tribal ways. At the week-end they would head off in family groups, trailing a mob of dogs like a bloody fox-hunting turn-out, off after wallabies or freshies – freshwater crocodiles – the small, fish-eating variety. They also went after the long-necked turtles in the creeks and lagoons, and emus and bush turkeys. Those valleys on Urapunga were like a supermarket to them.

The women loved to go digging sand-goannas.There were long sand-ridges that must have been formed a long time ago when the river had a different course. After a decent storm these sand-ridges would be full of goanna holes and the women would sit round them with their digging sticks, sand flying everywhere. When they got down maybe three or four feet they'd see his tail and grab him and haul him out. The poor bastard is walking up the air trying to escape, but they break his legs and chuck him under a tree until its time to cook him; that's the blackfella equivalent of sticking him in the Esky! If he is lucky they might crack his head against a tree trunk before chucking him on the ashes to cook. They say the tail is good eating, like fish, but I could never come at it myself. I've seen too many of the buggers gorging on the carcass of dead beasts.

The little girls have dilly-bags and digging-sticks and they tag along with the women, copying what they do, and all the time they are picking up bush knowledge, learning what foods can be eaten and which are 'cheeky-fellow'. The boys aren't taken on kangaroo hunts with the men. They'd be too noisy or not be able to keep up. But they have little spears and shanghais and go off hunting lizards or budgerigars or finches. When they catch enough they make a little fire and chuck them on the coals and eat them. Crunch up the bones and beaks half raw! But they grin and tell you 'Em 'i numba one good tucker!'

The rivers were full of fish but the funny thing was it was the old women who did most of the fishing. You'd see them coming back to camp late afternoon with their fingers hooked through the gills of a bloody big barra'. Once the rivers start to run with a bit of fresh at the beginning of the Wet, the barramundi come up from the salt water. The Fisheries people told me that barra' go out to sea to breed but they like to come up into the fresh water, especially the nice quiet side creeks and gullies. A barra' can swim upstream when there is fresh in the river, but if he turns to go down stream he gets mud into his gills then he goes belly-up. You can tell a salt water barra' because he is bright and silvery, but one that has been up in the fresh for a while or maybe got himself trapped in a lagoon at the end of the Wet has a dark gray or black look about him.

Another thing the women go after is a very big freshwater snake called a file-snake, a big harmless old thing that lives in the waterholes and lagoons among the lily roots. You see the gins among the lily pads feeling round with their feet for them and the next thing they duck down and grab one of these file snakes behind the neck. They come up with bits of water-lily all over them, and one of these snakes, up to five or six foot in length, thick as a man's arm; harmless old things but to the blacks, 'Good tucker!'

In the rivers of Arnhem Land, and right across to the Kimberleys, wherever you get fresh running water you will find big yabbies called tjerapin. They are almost transparent and up to eight or ten inches long. The blacks feel around under the rocks for them. Roper Bar was a great place for them. And when we were mustering, at the end of the day's work, if we happened to be camped on a creek or one of the rivers, the boys would get into the water and lift up the rocks feeling for tjerapin to chuck on the coals to cook. But one old fellow told me that you can put a trap in – an old flour drum on its side will do – and use a piece of old washing soap for a bait, and you'll get two or three every time.

Sometimes when we were mustering we'd be riding along and we'd startle up a little mob of what are known as flock pigeons – maybe six or eight of them at a time. They'd suddenly fly up ahead of us out of the grass. The boys were that damned good with their whips, they could flick one of these things on the wing! Out of mid-air! Then they would wring its neck and hang it on their saddle. When we got back to camp they would get some mud and cover it in mud and chuck it in the hot ashes and cover it up. Later on, they'd rake it out. The mud sets hard and when they crack it open all the feathers and skin come away. The intestines roll up into a hard little ball and they hook that out with their fingers and chuck it away. And that's a meal!

I picked up quite a bit of their language just by listening to them talking away to one another in the stockcamp. The freshwater croc, he was a *nanguru*; the goanna was a *burngurunga*; emus, they were *warapun*; the long-necked turtle fellow, he was a *bakaras*, and a barra', he was an *amarigee*. After a few years there I'd lived so close to them and spent so much time with them that a friend from down south said to me once, 'Listen, Mate! You've been up in this country too long! It's getting that way that you're starting to sound like an old blackfella yourself!'

Knuckey's Bluff, across the airstrip at Urapunga, where the Aboriginal people liked to burn-off the grass to hunt for blue-tongue lizards.

Round certain springs and waterholes you would come across big mounds of freshwater mussel shells. 'That ceremony place long time ago' the boys told me. They didn't use the word 'corroboree', always 'ceremony'. Some of these middens were waist high. They must have represented hundreds of years of get-togethers that took place there.

The old pensioner blackfellas, what they liked to do was just sit under a tree talking. You'd see them sitting there in the morning when you were riding out, all sitting there looking in one direction. And when you came back late afternoon they would still be sitting in the same place and all still looking in that same direction! They wouldn't have moved. It was just their way.

Sometimes you'd come across family groups, way out somewhere, sitting under a bit of shade and the women would be making animal tracks in the sand with their fingers for the kids to guess at. It was a game but all the time the kids are learning. Another thing the women and girls did was tell circle-stories. You'd see them with a bit of a twig and they'd be brushing the sand in front of them smoothing it out and making patterns in the dust. I thought it was just a way of passing the time, but what they were doing was telling the tribal stories and making the sand-pictures of the story as they went along. Then it would be someone else's turn and the next one takes over and does the same thing. This is how the women pass on knowledge to the girls.

Once I came across an Aboriginal burial ground in the Wilton valley. I rode out looking for some horses that had strayed and I came upon a natural rock stack. I thought I'd take a look around to see if there were any cave-shelters. I got a hell of a shock when I saw all these bones and wrapped-up bundles shoved in on the ledges and in the crevices in the rocks. I told Roy Kulukundu, one of the older men.

He scowled and said, 'What-for you bin lookim long that place!' I said, 'I didn't know it was there. I was just looking for horses and I just came across it by chance.' He said, 'That one bad place! You not go there!' I could see that he wasn't very happy. I told him, 'Look, I wasn't sticking my nose into blackfella business. I just happened to come across it.' He said, 'That one someting bilong blackfella! More better you not go long that place! Proppa bad one!'

I think he was telling me that there were bad spirits there that could harm me. I didn't want to offend the poor old bugger so I told him I would steer clear of it and he seemed satisfied. Nothing more was ever said about it.

In the camp, if anyone was dying they carried them somewhere out bush. They wanted to get them out of the huts because if someone died in a hut no-one could live in it again. The spirit of the dead person would be hanging round. They burn all the dead person's clothes in case the spirit comes back for them. Everything had to be burned. Even if a person died some other place, like Katherine, they would still smoke their hut to be on the safe side. They got a fire going with green branches so that the smoke blew through the door. Then they ran in and out jabbing this way and that with their spears, yak-ai-ing and yelling to scare the debil-debils out.

One of the Church Missionary Society chaps told me that over at Anuragu on Groote Eylandt somebody died in hospital up in Darwin and the body was sent back by plane to Groote for burial. The relatives were burning the hut and the clothes, and the next thing they started trying to burn the plane! One fellow had a tin of petrol and he was trying to throw it over the plane to get it going! The mission staff came racing down to stop them. The old fellows said, 'We gotta burn the plane! We got to do it proppa!'. The pilot's revving the motor and motoring round the airstrip to keep one step ahead of them! In the end the missionary got them calmed down. He told them, 'Look! You can't go burning the plane! Just smoke it! Get some green branches going and let the smoke go blow through! That'll do!' But the old fellows were grumbling and saying, 'It gotta be done proper! In the Dreamtime we always burn the aeroplane!'

When someone died in the camp they had a burial service, a religious one, at the cemetery up the back of the ridge. The old women would make 'sorry-cuts' on their foreheads with a couple of rocks, one in each hand, and belt their heads until the blood was pouring down their faces. Then they would hang over the grave-side and let the blood drip down on to the coffin, and start wailing. About a year later they dug the body up again and collected the leg bones and the skull. They wrapped them in paper-bark and tied the bundle with string made out of women's hair. You would see the women rolling the string on their thighs. Old Sam told me that when he was a kid the bones were placed inside a hollow branch, specially decorated. Now they are just wrapped in paperbark. Relatives came for these big ceremonies from all over the Top End. They would fly in by Connellan Air and there would be a very big corroboree. I used to give Old Duncan the Toyota and tell him to go out and shoot a couple of scrub bulls to feed them all. Duncan was straight. I knew he wouldn't touch the station stock.

They invited me to these ceremonies, big affairs with up to a couple of hundred extra people. These big ceremonies were called *met*, with a very important songman. The singing and clicking would go on all night for about a week. The boss-man of it all was the *janguyya*. He would be an old bloke with cicatrice-cuts all over his arms and his chest – they make the cuts when they are young and pack them with ash to make them stand out. And he would have a hole through his nose where they would have put a bone in the old days. These old men still had a lot of influence. Then, at sunrise on the final night, as soon as the sun hit the horizon, that was it. It was all over and done with. Everyone got their gear and climbed into Connellan's plane, or on to their trucks and off they went. None of this foot-walking the bones back to their Dreaming! These days they put them in an overnight bag and hop on Connair! No more walk-about. Nowadays it's all fly-about!

There were times when the old men from the camp would come and tell me that the *kadaitcha* man was in the Roper area. 'Old Feather Foot' they used to call him; 'Old Featherfoot 'im bin come!'. The *kadaitcha* man was supposed to get around with feathers on his feet so as not to leave tracks. This ability to leave no tracks gave the *kadaitcha* man powerful magic. No-one ever knew where he was. Or where he would be. He had a hell of a hold over them. He would come on some secret blackfella business, usually something to do with a wrong-skin marriage or a broken tribal law. The old fellows only told me as much as they wanted to tell me. I didn't get the whole story. The *kadaitcha* man who came into the Roper area would have walked across from Borroloola or the Northern Tablelands. The camp got edgy when he was around; the women scared and not wanting to be away from their own campfire come night-time and huddling together and looking over their shoulder into the dark. The stock-boys acted tough but they had the wind up as much as the rest.

'Bush Fairies' were another thing that scared hell out of them. These bush fairies were supposed to be little men that came round the camp when there was trouble brewing. Some sort of a warning. They were supposed to be about the size of pixies; 'Him little fella, that's all.' These bush-fairies meant trouble and people had to keep on the good side of them. I've seen their tracks myself, and, hell, didn't

The Ruined City: a spectacular rock-formation about twenty-five miles north-east of Urapunga on the Arnhem Land boundary. Dissected sandstone plateaux have eroded to create unusual stone out-croppings in a maze of stunning complexity. The Ruined City was Sam Thompson's 'Dreaming'. He took Ray through it. Ray said "It had the same feeling as being in a cathedral. You had to keep your voice down a bit."

the blacks get the wind up when they knew these bush fairies were poking about. Myself, I thought it was the old fellows trying to scare a bit of respect into the young people. I worked out how they made the tracks.You close your fist and press the side of it into the sand. Then you use your little finger and go dab, dab, dab five times around the top edge for toes. It makes a little foot-track. You would see these bush fairy tracks in the soft sand down near the river. Even the stockmen would tell you, 'Bush fairy, him been lookim!' and they would be a bit subdued. If I pulled their leg about it they would tell me, 'That blackfella business! Whitefella no savvee 'im!'

In traditional Aboriginal marriage a young girl is 'promised' to a tribal elder almost from birth. It was a sort of old-age pension. The system meant that when the old fellows were past being able to hunt for themselves they would have a young girl to look after them. There was one old chap ancient as the hills, with one of these young girls – he was that clapped-out he must have needed a bloody winch to do the job! A young fellow sneaked into the camp and took her and they cleared off together up the Wilton River valley. Well! Holy hell! There was uproar! And this old fellow, and a few more with him, went after them! The young bloke took her right up the valley then doubled back and across on to the salt water coast. But those old fellows were right on their trail. They caught up with them when they were asleep.

In tribal law, the punishment was that they formed a circle. They had their hunting spears. And they forced him into the centre of the circle and took turns at throwing these bloody great hunting spears at him. They had to aim below the knee, and if he was to duck out of that ring and make a run for it then the next spear is through his back. They gave him the works! I couldn't go interfering. That was blackfella law; their way of dealing with it. The young fellow had about eight or ten spears hanging out of him. As for the girl, the old fellow took her away somewhere. I never ever saw her come back our way again.

Over time, Duncan Yappanala taught me a lot about the blackfella way of handling things. One was that it is the 'Uncle' that takes charge of a young person's relationships in the tribe. It doesn't mean 'Uncle' the way we mean it. It is more something like 'god-father' or 'authority figure'. The 'uncle' is the one who dishes out any discipline to the young boy or girl. He is also the one that does the marriage arrangements. And – not in the missions or where the missionaries have had any influence – the 'Uncle' is the one who has first sex with the girl when she starts being a woman. That's his right. And according to what Duncan told me, the 'Uncle' has the right to come back to her at any time.

For the important ceremonies they would go away up-river somewhere. They would say to me, 'We got big blackfella business going on, makim-man ceremony', and invite me. There was a 'doctor man', a real old skinny fellow called Willie Munumua. He lived by blackfella law and he would foot-walk from station to station, living off the land. You might not see him for months on end and then they'd tell me, 'That Willie, 'im bin come back.' Then they would get the young boys and start the circumcision ceremonies.

They would take them away up-river and teach them blackfella law and then they would bring them back. For the circumcision the boy was laid across his uncle. The uncle lies flat on his back and he wraps his arms around the boy while the doctor-man does the operation.The kid's not to squeal or carry on. The 'doctor-man' would use a razor blade, but, even so, there were times when I had to race the ones that had gone wrong over to the mission hospital for a patch-up job.

I said to Old Duncan one time, 'By Chrise! That bloody man-makin's a rough one, eh!' 'Arrh!' he reckoned, 'In my day they use that sharp stone! That proper cruel-one, that time!' I thought to myself, 'Thank God I'm white!'

The women had their own ceremonies but they were never held anywhere near the homestead. They would go up-river and meet women from other stations for their own turn-outs. There were times when you would know there was some sort of trouble in the camp. You would feel the atmosphere, but nobody would say what was going on. I would know it was 'blackfella business' and keep out of it. But at times the house-girls wouldn't turn up, and I would know there was something brewing. I said to one of the old fellows, 'What's going on? None of those women came down, clean house, the last couple of days?' 'Aw,' he said, 'They got women's-business. They got problem.' And after a while I found out. One of the young girls had got pregnant to some wrong-skin fellow. I said, 'What they do now?' He said, 'They get rid of that piccaninny.' Apparently, what happens is that the women take the girl out bush and they stretch her out flat and hold her down. Then they pile big rocks on her stomach to get rid of the baby. Apparently it worked. I don't know how they didn't end up killing her.

A directive came from Welfare that we were to stamp down on the practice. The police did what they could, but there wasn't much any of us could do. The trackers didn't want to have anything to do with it. As far as they were concerned it was 'somethin' bilong womens' and they were keeping out of it. It was the blackfella way of handling things and whitefellas shouldn't interfere.

The most important thing in tribal law was the 'skin-group'[3] or *moity*. Kinship lines meant everything to them. It was a system they had worked out themselves over thousands of years to prevent in-breeding. There will be a line of people in one moity who can only marry the people of a certain line in another moity. There were certain relationships within the tribe where a young man, or a girl, couldn't 'look.' They were 'wrong-skin'. And if you happened to be talking to them about that person, they would half-look away over their shoulder. They couldn't even 'hear' the name, let alone say it. Not being able to 'look' at someone meant they were banned from any relationship. A young fellow might be told that a certain little girl was his mother-in-law and that when he went hunting he would have to give her part of his kill and that if she had a daughter in the future that would be his wife. Everything they did was based on this skin-group idea. They had obligations to certain people and they could expect pay-back from them. It was complicated by our way of thinking but you had to respect it.

Tradition was everything to those old blokes. It made them cranky that the young fellows weren't following the old ways. You never saw a stricter man than old Duncan. If those young teenage fellows were playing up he would pick up a stick and flog them! He was only a little fellow himself, 'eight stone, wringing wet', but he would double a length of stirrup leather around his waist like a belt. I said to him once, 'What you got there, Duncan? You going out bull-throwing?' He told me, 'No. I'm just looking that young fellow over there. Him too-much cheeky-fella.' And all of a sudden he up-him! He chased this young fellow round the camp and he's yelling at him! He couldn't block him with pace but he could block him with his tongue! He got him on the ground and he put foot on this kid's neck. The kid's yelling and roaring. But Duncan's telling him, 'I give you plenty more! You cheeky-fellow!' This is just not his own kids. Anybody's kids! He would straighten them all up.

There were some marvellous things to see up in that country. If you cross the Hodgson and drive up along the bank a bit there's a rock bar right across the river. Up a bit further there is a perfect set of dinosaur tracks. The blacks showed them to me. They reckon ' big bird bin walkabout there!'

If you follow the old road into Mainoru and cross the Mainoru River, there's a flat sandstone area where there are more dinosaur tracks. The old people from Mainoru showed them to me. When the water clears after the Wet, there are lovely sandy banks, and a waterfall you can sit under. Beautiful water! Crystal clear! It is a lovely spot and wouldn't be a bad place to camp, but by gee! The flying foxes! Millions of them! The smell of them!

Another beautiful place is the Ruined City. It is a rock formation about twenty-five miles north-east of Urapunga on the Arnhem Land border. It must be twenty miles square with columns of rock about sixty to a hundred feet high, packed together like The Destruction of Pompei. Someone said the columns look like giant chess pieces because they are squarish at the base but taper to spires and columns at the top, like cathedrals or castle-turrets, and all the colours of sandstone from pale blondy-coloured to purple and orange. There are passageways like streets and places where springs come out of the rocks and make soaks and pools. It is a spectacular place and has a feeling something like being in a cathedral, a special place, where you have to keep your voice down a bit out of respect.

Rock formations in Urapunga's Eight Mile paddock. It was in these rock shelters that the three young men who accompanied Ray on his epic walk from Mainoru before his mother's death, decided they would 'sit little bit' to look for bush tucker.

Some of the Urapunga Aborigines were scared to go there, but, strangely, some didn't worry about it at all. Old Sam Thompson took me through it. He told me it was his Dreaming and that he was boss-man there. Every so often Sam would come down to the house and we would have a cuppa-tea and some spotted dog – that's damper with a handful of currants and sultanas thrown in – I used to make a lot of them. Another chap, Silas Roberts – he had an Aboriginal tribal name but he preferred being known as Silas – he was the Aboriginal Magistrate for the area; his job was to sit next to the judge at trials of Aboriginals in Katherine or Darwin, and advise them on what the tribal law of the case was. He and Sam and I would sit and yarn for hours. I learned a lot from them.

Sam was an important man in the tribe. He had warrior markings across his chest and his arms. His father had been a tribal leader in the Roper River area and Sam could remember when he was a kid seeing his father kill a crocodile that had taken an old woman. She was swimming back across the river after a lily-diving expedition at the Four Mile, which is what they used to call the barge landing. This croc had been taking the station nanny-goats when they came down to drink, but this time he took the woman instead. Sam's father killed it and when he opened it up with an axe he found the head of the old woman inside. Sam lived by the old tribal law, but he also took his duties in the Anglican church – taking the plate around and swinging the smoke-machine on Sundays – very seriously. I had a lot of time for Old Sam. He was as fine a man as you would meet.

One day I got a letter from the Aboriginal Welfare Department offering me £5 a head if I would issue rations to the two tribes. They put it to me that I should keep a record of who I fed, and the skin-group they belonged to, their estimated age, their family, their language group, their health, and when they scratched their backsides! It would have been a full-time job! And too much of a tie. I had to be out mustering for weeks at a time. At that stage I was practically living out in the stock-camp. I told them I couldn't take the job on. I didn't have the time and I was trying to get a cattle station up and running. Also that I had to get all my supplies round from Queensland by barge and then everything had to be unloaded off the river-bank and packed up by mule to the homestead. I bailed up on it!

Old Harry Gee, he was head of Aboriginal Affairs in Darwin, came down and he said, 'But it's your responsibility! These people are your work-force!' I said, 'What! Two hundred of them! No bloody way! Ten, or maybe fifteen! And their families! I'm feeding them and paying the award. But not the bloody rest! I'm not responsible for them! Look, I'm flat out feeding my bloody self at this stage! I can't look after all of them!' Oh, didn't he get nasty with me!

So I said, 'Right! There is one thing I will do. I'll kill so many beasts a week for them. What do you want? One a week? Two a week?' I thought to myself, 'This is going to be a bit of money coming in!'

He said, 'What are you going to charge?' I said, 'The same as I would get for them in Alice Springs. Fifty pounds!' 'Oh, but.' he said, 'You'd have no expense! They would go out and get the killers themselves!'

I said, 'Like bloody hell they will! Start them off going out and spearing cattle whenever they feel like a feed! No bloody way!' I used to do all my killing. We always had a mob with a few decent killers up in a handy paddock and I'd run one into the yard and shoot him myself and bleed him. I made sure I handled it all.

He said, 'No. We won't be paying you that. We'll be paying you less costs! Less five pound a head.' I used to walk my cattle into Elliot, about a two week walk. And he's going to dock me five pound a head! I said to him, 'How much do you get paid? Look! You're the brother-in-law of Paul Bloody Prime-Minister's-Mate down in Canberra! You get jack-knifed into your job by him and you come up here and start telling me how to run a cattle station, and what I can and can't do!'

Oh! Didn't he get nasty with me! But my father used to say 'If you think something and you know it's right then bloody-well say it! Even if people do get offended. At least they know how they stand with you. And you know where you stand.' So I said to him, 'How would I get paid for this?' He said, 'Oh, you'd have to put a requisition form into the Welfare Office.'

So, OK, I did this. I started killing for the blacks in the camp. And I put in these forms. And waited. And I waited six months. And twelve months went by and I'm still not getting paid! And, meantime, of course, I'm having to pay interest to the bank! I was getting jack of it! So I got on to Gee's office in Darwin but he still wouldn't see me. So I went up to his office; big bloody name across the door, 'Harry Gee'. I thought, 'That's the one! I'm going to get him!' So I opened the door and here's old Harry sitting at his desk. He said, 'What are you doing in my office!' I said, 'I've come here to get my payment. I've been decent enough to kill for those blacks as you wanted and now I want to be paid! I've got mortgage repayments to meet.'

He said, 'I don't talk to the likes of you! Get out of my office! Or I'll get the police to remove you!' If anyone ever wanted a good clip under the ear old Harry did!

I was very friendly with a solicitor-fellow named Ian Barker. He's a Q.C. now down in Sydney. He did the signing-up of the place for me originally and he used to bring his kids down home and go fishing quite often. He laughed when I told him what had happened. He said, 'You having problems with your old mate!' I said, 'He's no bloody mate of mine!'

So he says, 'We'll have to straighten this old fellow out! We'll write him a couple of letters.' He wrote a letter about how I had supplied beef for over twelve months to the Department of Aboriginal Affairs and never received any payment. He made three copies; one for me, one for Harry Gee and one for the Northern Territory News. On the bottom of old Harry's copy he wrote, 'Immediate action on this matter is required or the third copy of this letter will be dispatched forthwith to the press.' He sent the letter around and we waited. And the phone rings and it's Harry Gee. He says, 'I have your letter about your client Ray Fryer.....' Ian says, 'Yes, Ray is an old mate of mine. I know him quite well!' He's grinning across the desk at me. And Harry says, 'I will have a cheque delivered down to you right away.'

So, anyhow, I got the cheque! And Ian says to me, 'Look, Mate! If I was you I'd get down to the bank and slip that cheque in quick before bloody old Harry reneges on it!' And I'm telling you! It's a wonder my boots didn't scorch a hole in the footpath I was that quick getting to the bank to put that bloody cheque in!'

1 A term made familiar to Australian readers of the early 1900s by its use in Mrs. Aeneas Gunn's *We of the Never Never*. The term is common for 'Boss' among northern tribes of the Territory, where pronunciation places the accent on the first syllable, similar to 'mulga'.

2 Reynolds, Henry; *Race Relations in North Queensland*, James Cook University, 1993. "The term whitefella was in use by tribes who had no previous contact with Europeans as early as the 1830s. Explorers and settlers came across Aborigines who used the term white-fellow when speaking of the Europeans. This happened to Mitchell, Macpherson and Leichhardt in different parts of Queensland in the 1840s and to Carnegie in the Western Desert in 1896. Mitchell commented, 'We heard calls in various directions and 'whitefellow' pronounced very loudly and distinctly. *Whitefellow* appears to be their name for our race...'

3 The skin-group or moity is the way in which kinship relationships decide the intricate patterns of reciprocal duties and obligations owed by members of the tribe to one another, especially in relation to determining marriage. Reynolds (*The Other Side of the Frontier*, p. 69 records, 'reciprocity was so fundamental to Aboriginal society that they had no word meaning 'thank you'. Food was distributed among those present, not as a gift, but as a right.'

six...

'GETTING MY HEAD ABOVE WATER'

Bull Catching, Broncoing and Buffaloes

At the end of each muster we went after any bulls that had slipped out of the mob and got back into the timber. I rigged a couple of old Toyotas with heavy bull-bars and side rails, and wired old tyres on the front to go after them. Once you got a bull out into the open you could get up on him, lap him round the flat. I handled the driving and had a strapper beside me. Once the bull started to lose pace he would start coming round trying to hook you. Then you could get up on him and push him until you got him over. The strapper jumped out and tied his legs. You could leave him and come back later with a truck, pull him up on a skid and take him back to the yard.

It's a game that's tough on tyres and vehicles. I had a young fellow named Scottie Burke working for me for quite a few years, a happy-go-lucky young fellow, always laughing. He and I were out once up the Wilton valley looking for bulls. We had three spare tyres with us and we blew two. I said to Scottie, 'Hey! We've only got one spare left and we're thirty miles from home. We had better head back.'

On the way back across the top of the valley we saw two beautiful big bulls. Scottie said, 'Go on! Get up the bastards!' We got the first one and I was giving the second fellow a lap, and wham! I hit a rock; did the front tyre. So that was the end of that! Then, Righto! It's coming on dark and we've got to get home. We had about a seven mile foot-walk! And bloody Scottie kept laughing! He wouldn't let up! Couldn't get over the fact that we could blow so many tyres and get no-where! I said, 'Shut up! And just walk!' There's not a lot of point in going out after $1800 worth of bulls if you are going to do in $800 worth of tyres! I have found when you are driving in bad stony country, or crossing rocky creek beds, that it is better to go over the sharp pointy ones than to risk ripping the walls out of your tyres by running beside them. And when you are thinking of driving into that sort of country it is better to have your tyres up to 60lbs pressure.

I always carried a horn-saw in a scabbard on my saddle for de-horning the bulls. Or, if it happened that I didn't have a saw with me, I'd use my pocket knife. I'd cut the hide around the base of the horn on the head. Then I'd get a good solid stick about three feet long and give the horn a good knock down the side of the cheek.

You had to be careful to strike downwards. If you swung at it sideways you'd risk smashing part of the skull away and you'd lose your beast. After a day of this kind of work you'd need a decent sort of a waterhole for a clean up.

When we were de-horning like this I always cut a wad of hair off the beast's tail which I rolled up into a ball and wedged into the wound to stop the bleeding, if we didn't have any sulphanilamide with us, which is what we usually treateded wounds with. A funny thing, once. We had a late camp, no lights, and everyone's as hungry as hell. I'm making a big stew in this big old camp-oven. And I'm poking round in the packs for the salt to give it a bit of flavour. I come on this tin. No lights or anything and it feels like crystals so it must be salt. So I throw half a handful of this stuff in. Everyone ate the stew. A couple even backed up for more. Afterwards one of them said to me, 'Stew was OK but it seemed to have a sort of a bite to it. Seemed to get around your tongue.' And I agreed. It did have a sort of a bite to it. So in the morning I look at this flaming tin and I see it is the sulphanilamide! But it didn't seem to kill any of us!

When I first went to Urapunga all the cattle were mongrel scrub short-horn, run-out type of things. I could see that the only thing I could do would be to bring in bulls from Queensland to try to upgrade the breeding. So as soon as I started to get a bit of money together I began trucking in bulls from Tabletop, and later, when I could afford it, I started buying Brahman-cross bulls from around the area to put the Brahman breed into them. It was a slow process but after about ten years you could see the difference in the standard of the cattle.

There's this story about these two bulls; a young fellow, rearing-to-go and this real old-timer. They're up on the ridge

1. The quarry is sighted. In the years when Ray was strugging to pay off his mortgage "anything that could be sold was sold" including scrub bulls which had to be hunted down one at a time.
The vehicle pursues the bull until it tires sufficiently to turn on its pursuer. It is then 'bumped' using the heavy tyres strapped to the bumper, until it falls.

Courtesy Professor Gordon Grigg

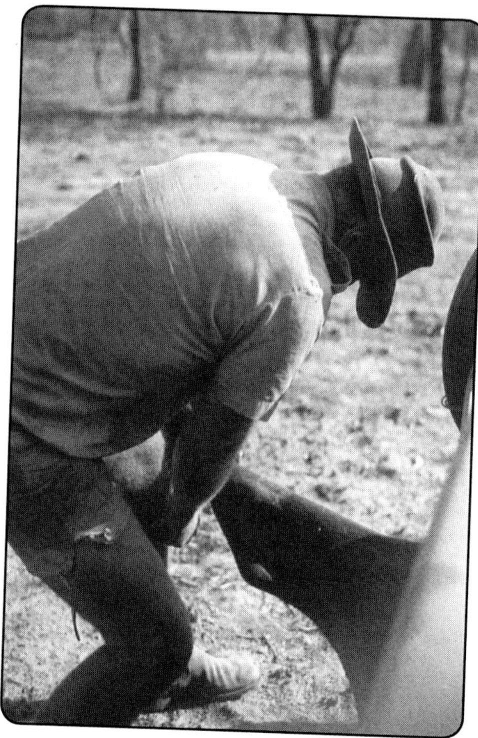

and they look down and see all these young cows and heifers out on the flat. And the young bull says to the old bull, 'Come on! Quick! Let's race down and do a few!' And the old bull says, 'No we won't! We'll walk down nice and slow and do the lot!'

I kept my bulls for about four or five years, no more. By then he's starting to get a bit clapped out. Another thing is that you don't want him breeding with his own progeny. When it got to that point he would be sent to the meatworks.

2. Once the bull is down, the 'strapper', in this case Ray himself, leaps out to secure its legs.

Courtesy Professor Gordon Grigg

I like to see a beast with a good square shoulder, with no bow in his back or any sagging. When you come to his hip-bones you don't want him to cut away. You want him to come back to the butt of his tail and down at a right-angle. You want the top-side to go right down to the back of his knee, and, say you are standing above him in a crush, you don't want to see any suck-in behind the shoulders. You want him well filled-out behind the shoulders, with a good round rib-cage. You want a big heavy bone in the leg; and the leg short to the ground. Thick-set. Not long, skinny lanky bloody things. A wide forehead. When you see a beast with a long, skinny nose, it shows a sign of in-breeding. In Brahman cattle I like the big grey whitey fellows. In Santa Gertrudas the reds are beautiful. The Braford, or Hereford-Brahman cross, they're nice, too, but they are not hardy enough for the North. For the North you can't beat the whitey Brahmans.

After you have castrated a beast, the purse, or the bag, that the testicles were in, builds fat and instead of hanging down it holds up firmly. It is called the cod. When beasts are putting on weight they cod up and it is a very good sign of their condition. You will hear the auctioneer say, 'Now these beasts are well codded-up. Have a look for yourself.'

We used to brand the calves out bush. We would brand them first in case they got away and went bush. There were no yards, just a bronco-panel which we would drag them up to. Broncoing was the method used for branding all over the north at one time. They say it was introduced into Australia in the late 1800s by a fellow from one of those Central American countries. A bronco-panel is two sets of good solid rails, end on to each other, with a twelve inch slot between them. As the calf is pulled up the rope slides along the top rail and drops into the slot. You use a bronco-panel when you don't have a branding cradle, but now that there are portable yards and branding cradles and crushes, broncoing is not used as much as it was in the early days and it has become more of a competitive sport.

But on Urapunga it was the only means we had of branding. I just couldn't afford to build the yards and crushes you need for cradles, so in the outer paddocks I put in bronco yards, each about a hundred yards in length and fifty yards wide. The cattle bunch together down one end and you can ride into them, select a calf and throw your rope on him. Then you snig him up to the bronco panel using a good reliable old horse, or mule. We mainly used jenny-mules.They were calmer and more reliable to work with and easier to handle. Some of them get that knowing they can almost do the job without being told.

If you are using a bronco-horse or mule it can be rigged two ways; either with a breast-plate, a wide band around the horse's chest with a girth over the saddle, with a big ring on either side which you buckled your bronco rope to for catching, or, on some places they prefer a horse-collar with a set of hames to pull with. I've used both methods but out in the stock-camp it was easier not to have to cart a horse-collar around.

Once the calf has been pulled up to the panel you have two fellows to catch the front and hind leg, slip the rope around the panel, throw him and stretch him out. Then he is branded, castrated, ear-marked and dehorned. With a big big mob of cattle you have two fellows cutting out and snigging-up so it is one continuous run up to the panel all the time. Once you have finished with the calf and he is turned loose he runs back bellowing to his mother. We found calves heal quicker if they get some mother's milk into them straight afterwards. Then the cows and calves would be let go.

The ropes we used for broncoing were greenhide. After we killed the hides weren't wasted. We'd use them to make greenhide ropes. We would strip the hide out, cut it round and round in circles, in one long continuous strip about an inch wide, until you've cut the whole hide out. Then you twist it up while it's fresh, in about thirty or forty foot lengths. They have to be stretched out – they are a bit stiff at the start – but you pull them around a post or a rail to get them a bit more flexible. After you use them for a while they start to become a bit more pliable.

Some people, when they cut the strip for a new rope, before they twist it, put water in an old carbide drum and shove the strip in and boil it up. That strips off all the hair. But I have found that when rope is boiled up with carbide like that, once it starts to get a bit of use there is not enough stretch in it and it can snap. But if you drag them they become more pliable. One way to drag a rope is to hitch it on behind a truck with a bit of wire, and hook an old hobble chain on to the

3. The bull is secured to trees to be dehorned and castrated. Pictured: Ray keeping tension on while Moses Silver removes the tips with a horn-saw.

Courtesy Professor Gordon Grigg

other end and drag it round the paddock for a bit. That gets rid of the hair and makes it just like a piece of kid. It also puts the twist into it that is the sign of a good rope. My mate Wayne McCulloch, a well-known horse-tailer down at Stonehenge, uses this method.

Another old mate of mine, George Booth, who does beautiful whip-plaiting, taught me another trick. It is to save the liver from the kill and when you've cut the hide into your strip, use it, not the fat, to run up and down the length of it. If you put grease on it won't twist, but if you use liver it will twist beautifully, and it is this twist, the lay of the rope, which gives it its expansion, and it will stay pliable and soft. A well-made greenhide rope is excellent and has a lot of uses on any cattle property.

Once I had got the new set of main yards at the homestead built I put in a crush and a cradle there and we'd take the mob back in and draft-out there. But in the further-out paddocks I continued to use the bronco yards in the old way. You'd always had to have it in mind that the sale mob had to be ready for the walk into Elliot before the Wet set in because once those rivers came down you had no hope of getting across.

It was about a two to three week walk through to Elliot. The next property to us was Hodgson Downs and from there we went on through to Nutwood, a Vestey's place. Some of these places had yards that they would allow us to use, so we would put the cattle in, or hold them in the corner of a paddock at night. Eight to ten miles was considered a good day's stage. You had to work your days out to where you could next get water. At times the stock would have to go two days without. A lot of the country was high lancewood, which was not the best to get through. Then on through to Dunmara and from there we followed Bucket Creek through to Sturt Plain and on down to Newcastle Waters where there was good water. From Newcastle Waters we would cross the Stuart Highway to Number Seven bore at Elliot. At Elliot the cattle were dipped and trucked down to Alice Springs for sale.

There were quite a few old piker bullocks hiding out in the scrub. Ten, twenty years old, some of them; big old fellows, often in very good condition. A piker bullock is generally a warrigal, a wild old bastard that has been branded young and dodged being mustered. Cunning old buggers, they'd lie low in those lancewood scrubs during the day. But early in the morning they'd come out for a feed and then you could pick them up.

4. The bull is snigged on a skid to a waiting truck and then loaded aboard for transport to the abattoir.

Courtesy Professor Gordon Grigg

A lot of them had never had their horns knocked. They are big old spikey-horn fellows, troublesome things to handle. If you got an old piker bullock and gave him a bit of a bumping around, he would sulk! He would lie down and that would be that. You couldn't tie him up to a tree like you could a bull. An old scrub bull, you can throw him and knock his horns off and tie him up to a tree, and a day or two later he is still there. But if you did that to a piker bullock nine times out of ten he would die in the night. They seem to lose the will to live.

Once when we were mustering we threw this old scrubber bull, and knocked his horns off but he wouldn't go into the mob. He swung out wide and beat us down over the river bank, into thick scrubby stuff. We couldn't see where he'd got to. Generally you see a bit of movement, and you know he's gone that way or this. I said to the Jacob, 'Here. Hold my horse and I'll go in and see where he is.' So I'm crawling in and around, looking for him, and, next thing! Bang! I'm hitting the ground! I didn't hear a thing until suddenly there was this big rush of leaves. Next second he's hooking into me. He had no horns but he gave me a good going over with his big bony forehead. I was pretty bruised and bashed about. I crawled on to my horse and rode back to the homestead – took me a couple of days, just poking along steady and feeling pretty crook.

The policeman's wife at Roper Bar was a trained sister. So I got myself into the Toyota and drove over to see her. I told her 'I don't feel too good. I've been spitting a bit of blood.' She took one look at me and got straight on the police radio – they worked off a police sched – and the next thing she came back and said, 'Air Med are coming out to pick you up.' They flew me into Katherine hospital; a broken shoulder; broken ribs, and a punctured lung. They doped me up pretty solidly and I came right again. After a couple of weeks, the copper, Peter Wotten, came and collected me and drove me back out home.

Another time I had a young fellow by the name of Ben Hall working for me. No relation to the bush-ranger! He was a good man! He came from outside Broken Hill. One time we had been out bull-catching all day and it was just coming on dark and we were heading for home with a load of about eight bulls on the back of the truck; red-beef scrubbers.When Ben was driving he was a bit inclined to put his foot down, and I said to him, 'Hey! You want to steady up a bit!' We came to a bit of a jump-up and the truck lurched, and of course, the weight of the bulls slewed over to one side. And, next thing, the bloody crate tipped off the truck. Well! There were bulls heading in all directions! Round us! Past us! Kicking their heels and galloping! Anyway! Ben just laughed and said, 'Looks like we've got to go and get some more, eh!' We went back home and got a couple of Toyotas and some ropes and pulled the crate out of the gully. We stood it on its end and finally got it loaded back up. Went home, made some straps and some anchor bolts and welded it back on. Made sure it didn't fall off again next time!

You get a lot of old scrub bulls out in that rough country and often, when you run a mob of cattle in, those gnarly old bulls would go rank and start hooking into everything. I've seen them, as soon as they get jammed up in a yard and they know they can't get out, they will start ripping the guts out of whatever's nearest them. They'd open a cow up and her guts would be hanging out. I always kept a rifle in the truck and as soon as a mob was yarded I'd jump up on the top rail and watch, and if there was an old bull starting any trouble I'd blow him out quick smart before he started ripping into the others.

There were buffalo all through that country and they would come down from Arnhem Land at times in fair mobs.[1] One time we were mustering up the top end of Urapunga, at Ah Cup's waterhole, on the big open plains out there. The blackfellas were all camped under the trees, not far from the waterhole, and I was a bit further back. During the night, I woke up with this hell of a yak-ai-ing and yelling going on. I jumped up, and through the camp comes this bloody old buffalo! He swung right at my swag! Blowing and making those bloody pig-squealing noises they make when they are stirred. Didn't I shift myself behind a tree! In the morning the blackfellas said to me, 'By Chrise, Maluka! That buffalo, him close-up bin hook you!' And there were his tracks. Almost on top of me! Luckily for me the boys had all sung out or he'd have had me. He put the shift on me alright!

Another time we were bull-catching on the southern side towards St.Vidgeon's, and we were camped beside a big spring there with a couple of Toyota bull-catchers and the pick-up truck. In the middle of the night this old buffalo turns up, snorting and grunting and squealing and ripping into door of the truck. Almost on top of my swag! Jesus! Didn't I shift! I out of my swag and underneath the truck pretty damned smart! All the other fellows flew up over the side and into it. There wasn't much we could do until he snorted off back the way he'd come. But, actually, we were camped a bit too close to a pad where the buffs came in to water. We were on his territory and it was his way of seeing us off!

When I first started off I sold whatever could be sold to pay off the bank, and so, although there wasn't that much money in catching buffaloes it all helped. So we'd muster them and truck them to the abattoir in Darwin. I'd get a chopper in and set up portable yards with big long hessian wings, and the chopper would poke them into the yards. Those old buffalo, it's surprising how well they would answer to the chopper. Once you got them moving you could poke them along towards the waterhole. They'd wait there while you'd go out and get a few more. Once you'd got a reasonable mob you'd poke them along and try to get them inside the hessian wings. We would run those wings back a quarter of a mile on either side.

But after that things got tough. They didn't like to be loaded. Now, cattle, you can get them running up the race, one behind the other, and you can keep them following along. But not those bloody buffalo! They just wouldn't go! They'd bail up! When a buff bails up on you he stays bailed up! He's not going to shift. So you had to make the race very wide, the width of a Toyota and push them up, one by one. We'd tie a panel of hide on the front of the bull-bar. If you didn't do that they'd be inclined to climb back over the top of the bonnet and you could have ended up with one sitting on your lap. So we would get them one at a time in front of the Toyota and jam them up the race into the loading gates of the truck. It was a slow process but the only way to get the job done.

One time, we had a set of portable yards with big hessian wings, a couple of hundred yards long, running out on either side. The chopper pilot was bringing in a mob of about a hundred to a hundred and fifty. It was a boundary muster and my mate – Tommy Castelli, from Mainoru – he and I were waiting out wide of the wings with a couple of Toyota bull-catchers to push them in. The mob were heading towards the wings, steady, steady, and Tommy and I were trying to keep just the right pressure on them so they would go in straight down the wings and into the yard. Well, the hessian for the wings was new, and new hessian has a strong smell about it, like wet bag. And I could see this old bull in the lead had got a whiff of it and had veered away. And I thought, if he goes, the whole mob will follow him! We'll lose the bloody lot! When the bull was about a hundred feet off the hessian

I put my foot down and went like hell to block him. I thought, 'I'll cut the bastard off even if I have to ram him!'

The truck had two big tyres wired on to the bull-bar. I thought, 'If I can just get up on him! I'll give him a thump in the ribs that'll turn him!' He saw me coming and started galloping. As I came up on to him he jumped. Next thing he is straddling the bonnet! His hind quarters right through the wind-screen! I thought, 'Hell! I'll be wearing him on my lap!' And I'm trying to get out! And his hoof is through the steering wheel! He's kicking! Kicking me in the ribs and kicking at my head! The next thing there's a bloody great lurch and the steering wheel comes off and goes flying across the flat! Then, thank Christ! He slides off the bonnet, hits his feet and goes off galloping!

Meanwhile the chopper dropped down to about ten feet and followed the mob in and got all the rest of them yarded. Tommy Castelli came over and he said, 'Are you right?' I said, 'Oh, yeah! If I can find the bloody steering-wheel I'll be right!' We found it out on the flat and jammed it back on, enough that we could steer it going steady, until we got home and got another wheel. I had a couple of old buggered-up Toyotas in a stack up the back. So I got another steering-wheel off one of them, put it on, put the nut on, no hassles at all; away we went again next day, no worries.

When you were trucking them, buffalo didn't travel well in the heat. In the real hot weather I used to go ahead of the transport truck with a pump, and wherever I could get a bit of water on the side of the road I would set the pump up and as soon as the truck arrived I would give them a good quenching. I'd spray as much water over them as I could and then the truck would head off again. We'd do this all the way north to Darwin. Otherwise they go down with the heat. He's an unusual beast, the old buff. He seems more like a pig. He's got bristles on him like a pig and not hair like cattle. And he's got to be able to wallow, like a pig. He loves mud and can't stand the heat unless he's wet.

We never made that much money out of them, but when you're trying to get on your feet you will give anything a go to get your interest at the bank paid. For ten years I was just paying the interest and that's all. But apart from that it was worthwhile to muster the buffalo whenever they came down from Arnhem Land in those big mobs because being a wallowing animal they mess up your waterholes and there is always the chance of them spreading disease. But later on, when the BTEC Scheme came in to eradicate brucellosis, they blew most of the buff away, and everyone thought that would be the end of them. But a few survived that cull in odd pockets here and there because once the BTEC Scheme finished their numbers bred up again.

I've got the horns of a buffalo that I shot on the other side of Roper Bar police station on the Borroloola road which are rated fifth in the world. I was going over to Roper Bar that day and I just happened to spot this big old fellow swimming the river. I thought to myself, 'Hell! That's a great set of horns! I'll have them!' I went to the police station and I said to my mate, Graham Chung, 'Hey! Can you lend me the police Toyota and a .303?' And I tracked this old buff along. A buff's track is more rounded than a red-beef; a red-beef is pointed – until I could see muddy water in his tracks and I knew he wasn't that far ahead of me. Then I came over this ridge and saw where his tracks went off into a billabong. He was out in the water a bit, just standing there with his head lifted up, sniffing. I put one into his shoulder – a heart shot – and dropped him. Then of course there was no way in the world I could get him out. He was right out in the water. So there was nothing I could do but wait until the carcass rotted. A couple of months later I went back with an axe and chopped the horns out. I brought them home and put them on an ant's nest for a few months to let the ants clean them out thoroughly. There was a young chap working at Urapunga at the time who was good at working leather and he mounted them for me and put the Urapunga brand, XTI, on them.

Scottie Burke, who "laughed all the bloody way back" when Ray and he had staked three tyres on the Toyota and had to walk home.

To be rated, buffalo horns are measured around the base of the skull, up to the tip and back down the length. Then they double that to get the rating. A chap by the name of Billy Fordham, up at Oenpelli, has the biggest set of buffalo horns in the world, not just in Australia. There's a chap by the name of Max Davidson, in Darwin, who is the official registrar. He measured mine and gave them the rating of number five on the world scale. They are sixty three inches from tip to tip.The number of grooves indicates the age of the bull. The older the bull the more grooves they have. My fellow would have been between eighteen to twenty years old.

We would also get those banteng cattle moving down from Arnhem Land. The banteng were brought in originally from Java for the settlement on the Coburg Peninsula in the early 1800s. When it folded they ran wild and their numbers bred up. The Territory's got more banteng than anywhere else in the world now. In Indonesia they've almost wiped them out to the point of extinction. Banteng are right through the Top End. They are small beasts which look more like jersey cattle but with longish horns that sweep back over their skull. The bull is a bit heavier than the cows and a bit darker. The cows tend

to yellow. Big game hunters from all over the world come to the Top End to shoot them for trophies, so I suppose there might be a bob or two in it for the traditional land owners. Myself, I don't think it is much of an achievement to sneak up and blow an old banteng out.

One of the main pasture-grasses on Urapunga was buffel. It is an introduced species that has spread pretty much across the north. They reckon it came into Australia originally in the lining of Afghans' packs. When you pull gidgee you generally seed with buffel. It does well in that dry pebbly country, all through Cloncurry, Mt. Isa, and through those inland hills. I don't think the environmentalists are too happy about it because it takes over from the natural pasture but as far as I'm concerned they are not as good. Buffel is a high protein feed and the cattle go for it. It survives in the driest of times and comes good after heavy cropping. If you get a fall of rain it responds quickly and it is a heavy seed producer. If you look under any tuft of buffel you will see the ground littered with seeds. The worst of it is that it is a devil to get into your radiator. I used to tie a piece of heavy shade-cloth over mine and when it got full I'd just chuck it away and get another piece. Some people use fly-wire, but shade-cloth is just as good. Some say buffel causes a condition called 'big-head' in horses; it seems to make them stiff in the joints if there's no other fodder available. But as far as I'm concerned she's a useful grass for cattle and that's the main thing. A funny thing is that you will notice that kangaroos don't go for it much if they can get other feed.

The Aborigines used to burn off the grass along the creeks and around the waterholes to get new growth coming through as soon as the Wet set in. It was their way of managing their hunting grounds. They knew the wallabies would come looking for green pickings. A couple of the old men would come and tell me that they were going to start burning off. I knew it was part of their way of life so I never interfered. They would say, 'Maluka, we like burnim grass long that Knuckey's Bluff. More betta catchim that blue-tongue fella.' And I would tell them OK. Those poor old blueies, they can't more very fast; once fire goes through they've had it, so they were easy tucker for the blacks.[2] You'd see the kite-hawks circling round too, looking for lizards and snakes. Leichhardt saw the smoke from Aboriginal burning-off fires when he came through in the 1840s.

The working dogs I had were a bull-terrier cattle-dog cross. If an old bull tried to break away those dogs would get round them and grab them by the nose. That would slow them down a bit. There were people round the Top End that bred these dogs especially. Old Duncan Yappanala looked after ours and I drenched them myself regularly to make sure they didn't get wormy like the camp dogs. But in that climate if dogs got overheated they would fit; foam at the mouth and go mad. All you could do was to try to wet them and cool them down, but in those fits they were that savage that you had to watch out for your hand or they would fasten on to you! [3]

One of my mates, Laurie Pointing, – he started off as a ringer out round Dirranbandi way, but later he joined the police force and ended up Inspector in the Rockhampton district – he had a dog he was very fond of, a red heeler, a very smart dog. Laurie reckons one time there, he was helping muster on a neighbouring property and it just happened to be Good Friday. Now, Laurie, he's a Catholic, a good bloke. So he says to this neighbour at dinner-camp when they are all slipping into the corned beef sandwiches, 'Look, No thanks. I'm a Catholic, see, and I can't eat meat today. It's Good Friday.' And the dog is there and he's picking up on all this. And that night, when Laurie goes to give him a feed, he opens a tin of Pal and puts it down for him and he goes back inside. After a while he hears the dog whingeing and complaining out in the dark. So he goes out. And there's this dog, he hasn't touched the Pal and he's got his nose stuck in a sardine tin!

And another time, Laurie's in town in his old truck. And this dog used to sit up on the passenger seat beside him. And this dog was that smart, he knew the cops were pretty strict about seat belts, so he used to pull the seat-belt across himself with his paw. He couldn't do it up, of course, but he used to just hold it down with his paw on the seat beside him. And one time, they're driving through town, and this dog suddenly sticks his left paw out the window. And Laurie's thinking, 'What's the bloody old fool think he's doing!' And then he looks down and he sees that his left-hand indicator isn't working!

Yes! A good dog is an asset in a stock-camp. A smart dog, that knows his job, and can get around the mob and get after a breakaway without being told, and turn him back into the mob, well, he's as good as an extra man on a camp. I've had some good dogs in my day but one thing I won't have and that's another man feeding my dog or calling him over to him. Most ringers are the same with their dog. A man's dog is his dog. You don't go fondling it or chucking it a bit of your tucker. Most cattle dogs are one-man dogs. I like that about a dog.

One of the problems with the blacks' camps on stations, and in the communities too, is the number of dogs they have. They never seem to get rid of any. No matter how many pups the old bitches have they always keep the lot of them. It gets that way that there are dogs everywhere, half of them starving to death, mangy and ticky and covered with sores. You'd see the flies on the dogs and the next thing they're swarming in the kids' eyes. And full of worms, a real health hazard. A lot of them were so far gone they wouldn't have any hair left on them, they'd be just skin stretched over bones, gone in the back quarters. They got that way they were a real menace. If they came down hanging round the homestead I'd get the rifle and blow'em out. It was the only thing to do. It used to upset them a bit up in the camp; they'd set up a yakkai and bit of a wail, but it was something that had to be done. The numbers of dogs would get out of hand. The police from Roper Bar used to come over from time to time and blow a few of 'em out to try to keep the numbers down. But no matter what you did there were always a hell of a lot of these mangy, diseased old camp dogs around.

There was a lot of hepatitis right across the Top End during the seventies. It was up in the camp and we evacuated a few people to Darwin. I was always going on at the blacks to keep the camp clean and burn their rubbish or bury it but if I didn't they would get slack. The piccaninnies would just squat down and do their business anywhere. I told the women to clean up after them but it didn't seem to worry them much. So I ended up getting hepatitis myself. It was the Wet and I got that way I could hardly get around. When you'd go to pass water it looked like coco cola! I thought, 'Hell! Something's not too bloody good here!'

"After a day like that you need a good clean up." Ray at the end of a day's bull-chasing.

So I went over to Roper Bar and saw the policeman's wife, and she said, 'I'm getting straight on to Air Med!' They came down and flew me up to Darwin and I had three weeks in hospital. I came home, and they had told me what to eat and what to avoid and I wasn't going too bad. But I hate just sitting around twiddling my thumbs and scratching myself so after a couple of weeks of this, I started mucking about with the horses. And, bang! Another bloody attack of hepatitis! I ended up in hospital in Darwin again! Even longer the second time! God! It makes you crook. And afterwards you are as weak as a kitten. No strength in you at all. But eventually I got over it. After that I put my foot down about the numbers of camp dogs. They could only have so many per family and that was it!

During that outbreak of hepatitis they slapped a quarantine order on Urapunga. No-one could move off the place and no-one could come in. And it just so happened that there was a mob of outsiders there for some big blackfella ceremony. I ended up feeding the whole bloody lot of them for the duration. I couldn't let the poor buggers starve! However about twelve months later, a cheque for nineteen hundred quid turns up in the mail! 'In recognition of my services'! Old Harry Gee must have thought he would get in one jump ahead of me!

And as the years went by and I started to get on my feet I built cement-floored steel huts, with steel shutters to replace the gunyahs in the camp. I used to make sure that they hosed out the new huts to keep the place clean. And I put in three septic systems, and an ablution block. Keeping the flies down, that was the main thing, or you would see the kids' eyes crusty with flies. I wasn't having that. So I used to keep on to them all the time about cleanliness. The Welfare Department and the Education Department reckoned our camp was one of the best around the Top End for health and hygiene. We always got very good reports.

I had a tractor and trailer and every Saturday morning when I was home we would go through the camp and pick up any tins or paper or bones and rubbish lying around. Everything had to be either burned or thrown into a pit and buried. Doing that kept the place pretty well cleaned up. I laid on the water so that there was a bit of grass growing around the camp to keep the dust down and give the kids somewhere to play. If there was no-one telling them to clean up it was just not done. Everything was just left lying around breeding flies and mosquitos. In their nomadic days if their camp got dirty and people started getting sick they just shifted camp. They would be camped on the river and every so often they would just pull out and move up or down the river a bit, or out to a billabong. And in those days they didn't have all the tins and bottles that are left lying around now.

We used to do aerial baiting for the dingoes with a poison called Ten-Eighty. We would shoot a couple of bulls and chop them up into hand-sized pieces and the bloke from the government department – they wouldn't allow us to use Ten-Eighty ourselves, and they still won't, either – he used to inject the meat. Then we would load a couple of big garbo bins full of baits into the back of the plane and fly up over the rough hill country, but mainly along the water-courses, because the dingo, he won't go far from water. I'd sit beside the pilot and we'd follow the main cattle-pads where dingoes were likely to be. And you just keep dropping the baits down a funnel. Once those dingoes took a Ten-Eighty bait they must have been affected by the sun. They would always get in under a log or in the shade before they died. But Ten-Eighty is a very good dingo control.

I'd always keep a few of the baits back, and when we were coming back to land – the pilot would always make a left-hand circuit; they fly over the strip then turn and come back in for landing I'd get him to go out wide, well clear of the camp, and I'd drop a string of these Ten-Eighty baits. They would wipe out a few of the sick old dogs and reduce the numbers round the camp for a while. But it wouldn't be long before the numbers would start to build up again.

The Department issues you with red plastic signs that you had to tack on to your gates posts; 'Ten Eighty baits laid here'. One time, a tourist fellow from down south called in and he said to me, really seriously, 'Why do you always lay exactly one thousand and eighty baits? Is there a reason?' Gees, I laughed.

We mustered a lot with helicopters, using them to push the cattle out of the rough country. I had to do it on a bank loan, though most of those helicopter companies would give you a month to pay. Helicopters are here to stay, and most places use choppers for mustering but I've always been keen on horses, so though

I used helicopters a fair bit I've always maintained a mob of good working horses as well. When we were mustering we'd let the choppers bring the cattle in out of the rough country and from there on we worked them with horses. As time went on and we could afford it I bought an old grader and put tracks through the ridges so we could get cattle trucks right into even the furtherest out yards.

The Bell helicopter following the crash at Montala yards on the Mainoru boundary.

Only once did we have any real trouble with the helicopter, when we had a crash. We were mustering on the boundary of Mainoru and Urapunga at the time, and yarding cattle at a place called Montala. The pilot got down a bit low. I said to him, 'Hey! Watch out! There's a tree behind us!' It was a dry tree; no leaves. He said, 'Shut us! Who's flying this thing!' Next thing, he backed into the tree and hit it with the tail rotor. Of course, that threw the whole thing all off balance. We started spinning and the main rotor smacked into another tree. We spun some more and knocked the tail off on another tree. It all happened so quick, you didn't have time to think. The chopper spun in circles and then it came down, luckily, the right way up.

We jumped out but the pilot was still inside and the bloody thing was on fire. I grabbed a shovel out of the truck and scraped up dirt to throw over it. Then we dragged the pilot clear. He had serious back injuries but we moved him as best we could, otherwise, he would have been a goner. That night, Air Med flew a plane down from Darwin and took us all back up. Three days of check-ups at the hospital and we were back down at Mainoru again, though walking round a bit stiff-legged.

The pilot wasn't so lucky. He was flown down south, crippled for a fair while. He was a Pommy fellow; an ex-Grenadier Guard, Arthur Blundell. A good man. But, bloody hell! Every bone in my body was aching for weeks afterwards!

Every year there was a get-together at Mataranka for a big rodeo and camp draft week-end and everyone from round the area turned up for it. It lasted from the Friday to Saturday and on the Sunday they held the finals. We all took our swags and camped at the hot springs. It is a beautiful place, big clumps of pandanus all around, and the water bubbling up clear blue and warm. It made you feel good just to be there.

It just so happened, one time that we were there, that NTEC, the Northern Territory Electricity Commission, had just connected the power through to the area, and off-cuts of the power poles were lying all round the place. Those poles were always treated against white-ants by putting them into steam tanks to pump a solution of copper chronium arsenate into them. But we didn't know this.

We gathered them all up and made up a big cooking fire. Before the rodeo I always killed a bullock so that I could take in enough steak to have a big cook-up on the coals on the Saturday night for every one to get a decent feed.

So we came back from a swim down in the springs and the coals are just right for cooking. We're all starving and everybody gets themselves set with bread and throws their steak on these nice red coals. The billies are boiling and we all get a good feed into us.

But somewhere in the early hours of the morning, Oh, Christ! Everyone was crook. Blokes were heading off into the bushes and throwing their guts up. And the pain! Like giving birth to a coil of barbed wire!

Next day in at Mataranka I was talking to one of the NTEC fellows about what had happened. He said, 'Oh, Hell! You don't go burning that bloody wood with that copper arsenate in it! It'll make you crook!' So that was how we found out that we'd been poisoned by the fumes that came off the coals. But, oh, well! None of us died!

1 Leichhardt, Ludwig. Journal, page 524. On the introduction of buffalo to the Top End, Leichhardt records, 11th December, 1845, 'we found a well-beaten path and several places where these animals were accustomed to camp. Brown and Mr. Roper pursued one on horseback and after a long run succeeded in killing it. It was a young bull, about three years old, and in most excellent condition. This was a most excellent event for us for our meat-bags were almost empty...We could now share freely with our black friends. They called the buffalo 'annoborro', and stated that the country ahead of us was full of them. These animals are the off-spring of the stock which had either strayed from Raffles Bay or had been left behind when that establishment was abandoned. They were originallly introduced from the Malay Islands.'

2 ibid, p. 355; 'The natives seemed to have burned the grass systematically along every watercourse and round every waterhole in order to have them surrounded with long grass as soon as the rain set in. It is no doubt associated with the management of their runs.'

3 ibid, p.438; Leichhardt, in 1845, was deeply grieved by the loss from heat stroke, of the expedition's dog which had accompanied the party from Moreton Bay 'They found him almost dead, stretched out in the deep cattle track which he had not quitted even to find a shady place. They bought him back to camp. I put his whole body with the exception of the head, under water, and bled him. He lived six hours longer, when he began to bark as if raving, and to move his legs slightly as dogs do when dreaming. It seems he died of inflamation of the brain.'

seven...

'SUGAR-BAG COUNTRY'

In the Stock Camp; A Long Walk

It was twenty miles down-river from Roper Bar to Roper River Mission and for another thirty miles below that you'll see paper-barks and pandanus all along the banks. To me there is something special about a pandanus; they have a lovely look about them. But fifty miles down-stream mangrove starts to take over. It is flood-plain country and at times the river loops around so that you have the sun on one shoulder one minute and next it's on the other. One long section is called Catalina Strait where there was a flying-boat base after the Japs bombed Darwin. The Roper is one of the major river systems of the north and fair sized boats can get the eighty miles up to Roper Bar. But right the way down to the mouth you've got to watch what you are doing; there are little islands and sandbars and rock outcrops, and the bottom is changing all the time; sometimes she's sandy, then you'll get mud and next she's bottoming out over stone or sand-bars. The bar at the mouth changes from one wet season to another so the channel is not marked. When the tide rises in the Gulf it pushes the fresh in the river back and puts a four foot rise and fall at Roper Bar. There'd be up to twenty-five feet of water there. And even above the bar, you can put a boat into the water and go upstream another twenty or thirty miles. A beautiful river.

The Wilton junctions into the Roper just below Urapunga homestead.The Wilton is also beautiful river, never known to go dry, but rocky compared to the Roper; rock-bars and ledges right along. Hard work taking a boat up.

Once those rivers come down at the beginning of the Wet you would be cut off for three or four months at a time. So, before the Wet set in, we would have to stock up on stores. We used to get them round by barge from Cairns, two or three times a year. It was no use running out of things you needed to see you through.

The barge, a John Burke Steamship Company vessel, came through Torres Strait, round the tip of Cape York and down into the Gulf to service Mornington Island Mission, Groote Eylandt, and the rivers in the Gulf. On its way north, it'd do Rose River and the Roper. It came up-river and brought in supplies and fuel and building materials to Urapunga, St.Vidgeon's station and Roper River Mission.

We'd get two or three tons of flour in twenty-five pound bags. But after a few years it came in drums, and then there was less worry about storing it, because it was all sealed. The sugar came in bags, so I always sprayed around the walls and floor to keep cockroaches away, because once the rains came, cockroaches, big fellows, up to an inch and a half to two inches long, came flying around. Sugar was a basic; it was no good running out of sugar; the blacks loved it; they would walk away from you if you couldn't keep the sugar supply up to them. Then there had to be tea, powdered milk, dehydrated vegetables, jams and syrup, and tinned fruit, custard powder, rice, and plenty of tobacco! Log Cabin they liked best. All the things you would need to see you through the Wet; all had to be got round on the barge.

The barge crew weren't fussy how they handled your cargo. They used to pull up close to the bank where there was a good depth; fifteen to twenty feet of water. They had long planks that they would drop across and they would cart all your loading over and dump it on the bank. I used pack-horses or pack-mules to pack everything back up to the homestead but later on I got an old blitz that could go anywhere and I would take it down to the river; some young fellas from the camp in the back; and we would load her up and make as many trips backwards and forwards as it took to get it all under cover.

The barge had a big loading door at the front and once I had several ton of barbed wire I'd ordered. And the bloody door hadn't been shut properly and the wire had been getting washed with salt water. I wouldn't take delivery of it. I was that disgusted with it. The old skipper said, 'Well, I'll chuck it up on the bank there, and it's up to you.' I said, 'Chuck it where you like. I won't be using it.' That rusty wire was there for years. I got on to Queensland Pastoral Supplies in Brisbane, and they sent another loading next trip. This time they made bloody sure it was packed properly in the hold.

I always kept plenty of clothes in the station store. A mob down in Adelaide, Trims, was our supplier. I'd send down to them and get so many pairs of R.M. Williams boots, just the two sizes, large and small; Akubras, and all the coloured checked shirts you could get. The blacks loved those flash shirts. And cotton dresses for the women. They could get any extras that they wanted, like biscuits – 'bizzacits' or 'chuga' – always sugar, they could never get enough, tobacco and matches, or tinned fish, 'tinna pish' – or tinned fruit, apricots especially, condensed milk, Johnson's Baby Powder, or Lux toilet soap and California Poppy hair-oil – they loved that! I opened the store two or three nights a week. When I was out in the stock-camp the school-teacher ran it.

As soon as the Wet season started coming to an end I would say to Old Duncan, 'Well, we'd better make a start on shoeing up, eh!' We'd get a plant of horses shod and we'd start picking the stock-boys we would take. I'd say, 'You pick who you want; but I've got my eye on a couple of really top fellows. I definitely want those two, but you can pick out the others.' And he'd come back and tell me who he wanted. I'd sit down with him and discuss what we were going to be doing, and when we would be heading out.

He'd say, 'I gotta coupla them school-kids we gotta take. I gotta learn them.' I'd say, 'OK, Take two young fellas along. Time we started training them up.'

Loading cattle out of portable yards. A 4WD bull-catcher is being used to push them up the race.

Once we got going his hardest job would be to keep those young fellas quiet; they were like pups with two tails – out of school! and working with the men! They couldn't shut up! Mustering in that country you had to poke along, steady, steady, and be quiet about it. Once the cattle got wind that you were around they were likely to take off. And these young fellas would be yakking away. Duncan would drop back and go for them. 'You gotta keep quiet! Bullock, him hear you coming, we don't see him, y'know!' Or at night, in the camp, you'd hear them with one of those little transistor radios in their swag. They used to love to try to get the Country and Western session from 4LG Longreach. In the end you would have to shut them up or they'd have been listening all night. As long as that bloody hillbilly session was going you couldn't get any sleep. It would be eleven or twelve at night and they would still be going. I'd yell out, 'Hey! You fellas! Give it a break! We've got work to do tomorrow!'

But one night this storm was coming up. I could hear the static crackling in their radio. And one of them says, 'Hey! Must be something broke in that wireless, eh!' He gives it a bit of a shake and then he gets his knife and he takes the back off and he gets the speaker out. And I'm thinking to myself, 'Well, good-o! That's it! There'll be no more wireless now! A man might get a decent night's sleep!'

Next morning I gave him a call at four o'clock and, bugger me! The next moment he turns this thing on and it's belting out Slim Dusty at me! He'd put it back together and got it all going!

If we ran short of tucker when we were mustering I would send one of the boys back in to the homestead with a pack-horse to get what we needed. So, one time there, I had sent Arnold, one of Duncan's boys back in and it just happened to be a night when the Salvation Army padre was showing some films to the camp. One was about the Americans landing on the moon.

And next night, when young Arnold gets back to the stock camp, there was a big full moon, and I hear the young fellas talking. Arnold is telling them that a man had landed on the moon and had been walking round up there. And one of the others is saying, 'Ah! Gammon! You can't go that moon! It all same aeroplane! You go up there no air. What you can breathe!'

And Arnold says, 'Not gammon! True! He bin go up orright! He been walkabout up there.' And the other fella says, 'OK! How he bin breathe?' And Arnold tells him, 'Aw! I bin lookim! Him bin take two bag wind along him.' He meant the oxygen tanks that he had seen the astronauts wearing in the documentary. As far as he was concerned they were bags of wind.

Jacob used to be a great one for a bit of talk when we were sitting around the fire, and one night we were talking about different countries and different animals, and he said, 'That panda fellow. Him not real one, eh! Him all-same toy.'

I said, 'Well, now. That panda, he's a bear sort of fellow. He comes from up round China and Mongolia way. He eat them bamboo shoots, like you see up in Pine Creek.' He said, 'True? No gammon now! Him not toy-fella? Me bin lookim' long Katherine Store and me reckon him one toy-fella! Thas-all!' And he is sitting there looking serious for a while then suddenly he looks at me and he says, 'Orright! That fella, Mickey Mouse. Wannem country bilong him?

Well, I couldn't help laughing. I said, 'Well, I'm buggered if I know, Jacob! I don't know much about that Mickey Mouse! All I know for sure is that those panda-fellas come from China and eat bamboo. But that Mickey Mouse-fella, he's got me tossed.'

The Urapunga Aboriginals were excellent stockmen, excellent horsemen. Smart with wild cattle! And when it came to throwing bulls, well, they couldn't be beaten! Bull-throwing is a knack they seem to have naturally. Oh! They were good! When you are throwing a bull, it's not strength that counts but skill. Some of those fellows were only slight in build, but you'd see them, they'd get a bull moving, and once he was in a bit of a high canter, they'd slip off their horse, give him a slap to get him out of harm's way, grab the bull by the tail and down him. Perfect timing!

Arnold Duncan, only a slightly built little fellow, used to amaze me. He would lap an old bull and then he would fly off, and grab the tail of the bull and hit the ground galloping. The bull would be taking him anywhere he wanted to. But once he steadied up and is coming around to hook him, Arnold would give the tail a quick twist and down the bull goes! It was amazing to watch.

And if a bull got one of them bailed up, well, the first thing they would do was chuck their hat on the ground in front of him. And as he went to hook the hat they would fly in and grab him by the tail. If they missed him that time the next thing they would do was to pull off their shirt and chuck the shirt at him. And if the bull kept charging these things they would end up throwing their boots at him! And when the bull gets to the stage where he is shaking his head and wondering what the hell is coming next, they'd fly in and grab him by the tail. They'd give it a twist, and, by God! The next thing he's down! Tail-throwing is a bloody art-form to those fellas on the Roper! They are world-class at it. I've thrown a few bulls in my time, but, by God! Nothing like the skill those young fellas on Urapunga had! Once the bull is down you tie him. Then he is de-horned, castrated and earmarked. After a day of that you needed a good clean-up. Your clothes are stiff with blood.

There are no better trackers than those blacks up there. When you were out looking for cattle you would come on to a river and get on to the tracks of the cattle heading out from water and they would be able to tell you how many there were, what age they were, what size. They could follow them, cantering along, looking down and reading the ground like we would a book. They would say 'Not far now, Maluka. Not far.' And if the cattle had got a fright and had taken off galloping they could tell you how fast they had been moving and what had startled them, until eventually we would see their dust up ahead and get on to them.

They love sugar. If you ran out they would belly-ache, 'Hey! Maluka! You bin perishin' us long chuga!' On a three or four week mustering camp, you'd have to pack a mule with two seventies of sugar. One Wet we got held up for a while and the sugar cut out. One old boy came up to me and he said, 'Hey! Maluka! What you gunna do 'bout that chuga? 'Well,' I said, 'She's run out, has she?' He said, 'Yoi. S'pose I ride back in. You give me one pack-horse. I bring one bag chuga.' 'All right,' I said.

Well, he rode back home and next day I see him coming back with, not one, but two bags of sugar.Two seventies! I laughed to myself. But I thought, 'Oh, All right! No sweat! Let them have it!' Sugar meant everything to them; they drink it by the pannikinful.

They love anything sweet. That's "sugar-bag" country all through that Top End; native-bee nests all through. If the boys came across a tree with a nest they'd chop it out. Beautiful honey, very strong, made by little black bees; no sting to them. They'd scoop it out and eat it by the handful. Sometimes there'd be a nest in the crack of the rocks but that would have them tossed. They wouldn't be able to get at it then.[1]

Most of our mustering camps were near water. The branches of the Roper were pretty good fishing places and there was one hole on the Jalboi River, north of the Roper, where there was a big paperbark leaning out over the water. In the middle of the day when the sun was just in the right position, you could balance out along that trunk and see big barramundi just hanging in the shadow. I'd take a .303 and shoot to stun. Then quick as a flash, one of the boys would dive in and grab him before he sank or swam away. There are crocs in those waterholes but the boys didn't care. They'd just jump in and grab them.

Sometimes we'd pull up and rest for a day and then another thing they liked to do was get in the water in the small creeks and go after freshwater crocodiles. They'd be in the mud, or in holes in the bank, and the boys would pull them out and cook them them. 'Good tucker!'

Micky Hall on Trumby in Eight Mile paddock.

When the mustering was finished we had to walk the cattle through to Elliot. We'd start out a month before we were due to load them to get them cleared. They had to dipped, spelled for four days and then dipped again. This was to get clearance to cross the tick line, about eighty miles south of Elliot. Once you got clearance they could go to Alice or wherever you wanted to send them in the south.

The solution used for the dip was arsenic and caustic soda. She was a wild old dip! They put a high charge in at times and then don't the cattle baulk and give you hell! Clarrie Pankhurst[2] was telling me that at Anthony's Lagoon, one time, the local policeman was in charge and he over-strengthened the solution and over three hundred head of cattle died.

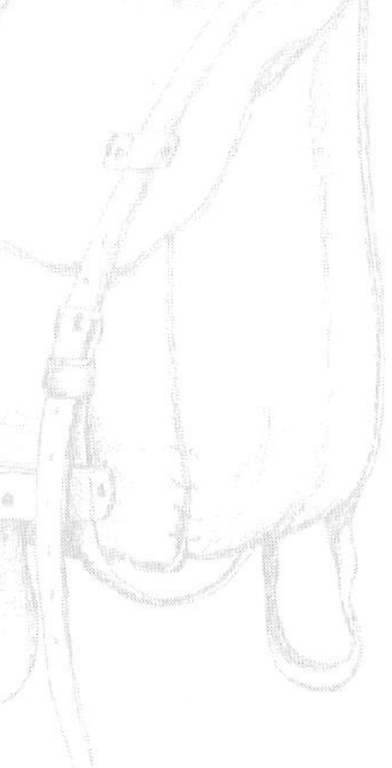

We were supposed to dip the horses as well but it knocks them around. They hit their shoulders and belt themselves against the sides. I'm against dipping horses. It's a terrible thing to do to them. If a horse has got ticks I'd sooner just hold him and get a good spray and spray him properly. For horses, spraying is bad enough but dipping is out.

One year early in the seventies when we were there, there was the biggest plague of rats that you could ever see. The rats were that thick that you would have to suspend your packs and saddles by a wire or the rats would have chewed them to pieces. And at night, when you tried to get some sleep, bloody rats would be running over you all night long. Running over your face! Chewing your boots! What we ended up doing was getting grass and sticks and building a circle of fire right round the camp and light it up before we went to bed. The hot ash stopped them. When you see a rat plague, it's not in hundreds, it's in thousands!

They were that bloody thick that in the morning hundreds and hundreds of them had fallen into the dip. The stock inspector at Elliot at the time was a bloke by the name of Frank Blakey. When Frank came down in the morning I said, 'I'm buggered if I know, Frank, if we're going to dip, what are we supposed to do about all those bloody rats!'

He went over and he had a look in the dip and he said, 'Bloody hell! We'll have to get rid of the bastards!' He went back into Elliot and came back with a roll of wire netting. And him and I on each end of it, we dragged that dip over and over. We'd drag the mesh along and we'd get hundreds and hundreds of the bloody things. They were floating about eighteen inches deep. And we'd haul them up on to the walk-out of the dip. And Arnold and Jacob were on the shovel and threw them into big piles for burning. We kept this up until we got most of them out and then we could start jumping the cattle through.

I have never seen anything like that in my life. I have spoken to other bush fellows and they say, yeah, they have seen the same thing. And your horses with greenhide hobble-straps, when they pull up for a bit of a camp at night, the rats would chew the bloody hobble-straps off while sleeping! Bloody rats around his fetlocks chewing the hobble-straps off him!

The rats lasted in that area for a couple of weeks and then they all disappeared. And everywhere you would go you would see a mob of dead cats. They said they ate so many of these rats that it killed them.

Those rats went right through from beyond Newcastle Waters up into the Gulf and then they just seemed to disappear.[3] I've told people about it and I could see they didn't really believe it; seemed to think I was bunging it on a bit. I was glad when an old mate of mine, Charlie Rayment, a well-known drover down in Winton, backed me up. He said he had seen the same thing, with horses getting around in the morning with their hobble-straps chewed off. And Edna Zigenbine, a well-respected lady-drover who used to bring cattle across the Murranji, remembers a rat plague in the Territory in about '42 or '43 when the rats were so bad that they destroyed turkey-nest dams by borrowing through the walls.

It's a funny thing about those cats you see out there in the Territory, especially when you are driving across the Barkly at night. You see hundreds of cats' eyes glowing in the headlights. But some of those areas are completely waterless. I have asked some of the locals about it and they say the same thing; where do the buggers drink? Some places there would be twenty-five or thirty miles to the nearest water, but you see cats right through there. Big fellas, they are, too. Much bigger than a domestic cat. If you shine a spotlight along a gully at night you will see all these eyes! How do they survive?

Aboriginals are excellent stockmen; you could say there are none better. But they are buggers when it comes to gambling. One time, we were down at Sturt Plain, just north of Newcastle Waters, and I went down to the camp one night and

I said to this bloke, 'You get them horses pretty early, eh! When that first star come up you make sure you get them.' And then I looked and I saw him sitting on top of his swag and hardly any clothes on! I said, 'Where's your bloody clothes?' And this other fella, he's sitting there on top of the biggest swag you've ever seen! And he's scowling.

My bloke said, 'That fella bin win'em las' night at card.' I went over to the other fella and I said to him – he was one of those blokes from around Newcastle Waters way – I said, 'Look! You'd better give him some of his clothes back, eh?' He just ignored me. Looked the other way. I said, 'Crikey! Well, lend them back to him, or something. We've got to get going!'

So he gave him one boot. I said, 'One boot's no bloody good! Give him two boot!' So he chucks over another boot, and a pair of strides. But that's all! No way was he going to hand over anything else! He'd won it all on the card game and he was going to stick with it.

So when we got down to Elliot I bought our fella some clothes to see him through the trip. But, yeah, they're awful fellas for gambling. And in all my years in the Territory, I never could make out the game. They'd all be sitting there; chuck a boot in, or a hat, or a bit of money. Anything. It wasn't poker. They'd just deal out the cards all round and one fella would chuck his hand into the ring and he'd scoop up all the winnings. There was never any disputing about whether he had won it or didn't win it. They didn't seem to worry much. It was their way.

But they were very good stockmen. There were times when I have had one or two white ringers working for me but for the most part I'd prefer Aboriginal stockmen. They know the country and they enjoy the work. You get white fellas; a few weeks out in the camp and they want to push off into town. But Aborginal stockman are good men; good horsemen; good bushmen. Very loyal.

One time there, we were coming on to camp and there was a big storm coming up. I said to the bloke bringing the horses along, 'You'd better slip along ahead and unpack those horses and hobble them out and put the tent up.' We got the cattle to the yard just as it was starting to rain. Lighting ripping down; and thunder! So we all get in under this big tarp that's strung on a rope between two trees. Next thing the bloody lighting struck the tree at one end of the rope. Flattened the lot of us! The tree flew to bits. The tent collapsed, and us all under it. I don't know how none of us were killed. We crawled out from underneath it; branches and bits of wood everywhere. The tree just a wreck of a stump. No-one dead. My ears were ringing for days!

One year it was very wet, an exceptionally wet year, and everything was flooded. All the airstrips were out and it was impossible to get any vehicles in and out of Mainoru. The country was that bloody saturated that horses were bogging belly deep. And I got word over Outpost Radio that my mother was very sick and not expected to last.

I thought to myself, 'Well, I'm going to do my best to get there!' And the blackfellas there with me said, 'Mumma bilong you close up finish, eh, Maluka? What you gunna do?' I said, 'I'm going to walk out of here!' They reckoned, 'You no more can walk! You get bushed! I said, 'Bushed be buggered! I've been in this country long enough to find my way round!' Anyway, three of them, Timothy Silver, Micky Hall and Jacob Carew, decided they would go with me. They wanted to get home. They hadn't been back to their women and kids for three or four weeks.

I said to the manager of Mainoru, a bloke by the name of Kevin Analsark, 'It's too bloody boggy to ride. If the horse bogged I wouldn't be able to leave it. It'd take days and I mightn't make it. Walking out is the only way. I'm going to foot-walk.' He said, 'It's a bloody long way! How long do you reckon it'll take you?' I said, 'Oh, I'll probably do it in about three days.'

So I went to the store and I got four tins of bully beef and four packets of Sayo biscuits. I thought to myself, 'Now, that'll do me.' And I said to the blackfellas, 'Now, if you fellas are coming you'd better get some tucker to take. Get some beef and biscuits or whatever you want from the store. I'll settle for it'.

Aboriginal stockmen of Urapunga. Mickey Hall with brindle, Moses Silver against tree. Ray believed the men of the Rittarangu and Njandi tribes to be superb stockmen. Most of them had been born on Urapunga.

But they reckoned, 'Aw! We-fella, we don't carry tucker! Plenty good bush tucker long that country!'

I said, 'Well, I'm buggered if I know about that. But I think you should get a bit of tucker to see you on the way.' But, no! They didn't need store-tucker. There'd be plenty of bush tucker.

So we headed off. The first day we must have gone about fifteen mile and we pulled up that night. I said to these fellows, 'Where's all this bloody bush tucker you were talking about!' They said, 'Aw, We don't know, Mate. We prob'ly get him tomorrow!' So I give them a couple of tins of beef and some of the biscuits and they had a bit of a feed. And I thought to myself, 'Jesus! This is getting bad! I'm down to one tin of beef and one packet of biscuits!'

So we put in a wet bloody night; raining all night; trying to get a bit of a camp at the foot of a tree. Next morning, soon as daylight came, we headed off, and the blackfellas are getting a bit slow. I said, 'Look, if you fellas can't keep up, I got to get going! I got to get there!' So they managed to keep up with me eventually, looking for bush tucker and God only knows what.' They couldn't find a goanna or any bloody thing. So that night I gave them the last of the biscuits and I ate the last tin of beef. We got a bit of a fire going but it was another wet night, and then headed off again as soon as daylight broke.

We got to a stock-yard about twelve miles from home, and they reckoned, 'We-fella sit round here, Old Man. We get plenty bush tucker round here!' So I kept walking. I was that buggered and hungry! And I was getting a bit sore in my boots. I thought to myself, 'Jesus! If these boots fall off my feet I'll be finished!' But anyway, I made it. I got to Urapunga that night.

Luckily there was a break in the weather and I got a charter plane in from Groote Eylandt. They came and picked me up and we got to Normanton. Half the strip was under water. There was just enough room for a light aircraft so we landed there and connected with a Bush Pilot flight to Cairns. I managed to get a flight out of Cairns to Townsville. I made it to the hospital just before my mother passed away.

But, by God, I'll never forget that walk! Bloody wet nights and out of tucker. If it was dry weather and a man could poke along nice and steady, well, it wouldn't have been much, but she was a pretty rough old stage coming through! But I made it, and that was the main thing. I would never have forgiven myself if I hadn't got to see my mother before she passed away.

1 Sugar-bag, the honey of the native bee, a non-stinging variety, smaller than the European bee, which deposits its aromatic honey without any wax comb, in trees and logs and rock crevices. Ludwig Leichhardt noted in his journal of 10th November, 1845, 'little bees came like flies on our hands, on my paper, and on our soup plates, and indicated an abundance of honey.'

2 Famous for the laconic comment, having lost his eye-sight, 'That's what a man gets for spending all his life looking up the arses of a thousand head of bullocks on the Murranji track.'

3 Buchanan, Bobbie; *Keep the Branding Iron Hot*, p.99. 'Inverway suffered a rat plague which lasted nine months.' Durack, Mary; *Kings in Grass Castles*; p.127 '...the rats came surging in a low-moving grey wave, tumbling, struggling and squeaking... No-one knew where they came from or where they disappeared'

eight...

'ROPER BAR'

The O.T.; The Duracks' Camp; The Police Station

The Roper is a magnificent river. When the Overland Telegraph – the O.T. as it is always called – was being built back in the 1870s, the Roper was the main means of transport in the area. The chief depot for the northern section of the line was Roper Bar, eighty-four miles upstream from the Gulf. All the bullock teams came in just below the Bar to pick up supplies for the construction teams working on the Line. There were two teams, one working north from Beltana in South Australia and the northern team working southwards from Palmerston. There is a memorial cairn along the Stuart Highway where the two teams eventually met up, with a Latin motto, 'Finis Corunus Opus : Success crowns the work'. There were four hundred men working on the northern section so Roper Bar would have been a busy place.

All the supplies were brought round from Adelaide by ship. A hell of a trip! They could have got things much quicker from Brisbane or Sydney but in those days the states were at one another's throats. Australia wasn't Australia then; just a lot of separate states. There was a lot of rivalry between them, and the Northern Territory was regarded as part of South Australia. You'll see it marked like that in old school atlases. That's why all the supplies were brought round from Adelaide. The boats they had were the Omeo, the Tararua and a little old paddle steamer, the *Young Australia*. One trip they brought five hundred bullocks! Roper Bar was known as Rocky Bar in those days, or sometimes Leichhardt's Bar.

And one time, when they needed fresh horses at the settlement – maybe the horses they had were knocked about by walkabout disease – they were shipped round on the *Young Australia*; right round the eastern coast and through the Torres Straits, into the Gulf and then up the Roper! You would think twice about doing it today! A fair sort of a trip for the horses! They unloaded them at Roper Bar and the *Young Australia* pushed off for the return journey. She hit an unchartered rock in the river and sank. The wreck is there to this day, or what is left of it.[1] It's about an hour's drive down the river, just inside the Arnhem Land boundary.You can see the steel water-tank on the rocks about a hundred yards out from the bank, sticking out of the water. One of the paddle-wheels is still there under water. They reckon that all the passengers were hitting the rum the night before so she was late

Roper Bar Crossing, 84 miles (145 kilometres) upstream from the mouth of the Roper River. It has become a popular tourist camping spot but crocodiles are often sighted in the vicinity and it is not a safe place to swim.

Courtesy Professor Harry Messel, University of Sydney Research Team, 1971.

getting underway and that the captain had gone below to have breakfast. Which doesn't seem a very skipperly thing to be doing when your're taking a paddle-steamer down an uncharted river! More likely he had a decent sort of a hang-over!

The early settlement was built at the foot of a hill called Depot Hill so that there would be somewhere to escape to if the river came down in a big flood. They'd have been able to tell how high she runs in the Wet because of the flood-debris in the trees, thirty or forty feet up. One year, during the Dry, when a grass-fire had been through, I thought to myself, 'I'll just have a bit of a look up on that hill and see if I can find any trace of the O.T. settlement.' So I climbed up and had a poke around and I came across the remains of what would have been the original blacksmith's shop. There were horse-shoes lying around and bullock cues; properly made ones, not just the cues we used to make do with up in the Gulf by cutting old worn-out horse-shoes in half, but properly made cues with the edges turned.

The old wagons that they used building the O.T. line had heavy wooden wheels with a steel axle and hub-fitting which slipped into the hub of the wooden wheel. It was tapered, with a pin where the wheel was slipped on, and would have been packed with bullock fat. There were a lot of these axles lying round in the bush around Roper Bar, in gullies and wash-aways where wagons had been abandoned and left to rot. They were about six to eight feet long and were ideal to use as anvils for shoeing. You could jam them in the fork of a tree or set them up on a stump, and the tapered section was just the right shape to fit a horse-shoe over, to shape it or expand it. You could poke your shoe up through the slot where the wagon-pin went and turn the heels in and get the shape required. I set some of these wagon-axles up as anvils at all my mustering-camps around Urapunga, wherever I could get them in with the blitz. They were ideal for shoeing on camp.

The wreckage of the paddle-steamer *The Young Australia*, wrecked in 1872 while carrying supplies for the building of the Overland Telegraph Line.

Courtesy Professor Harry Messel, University of Sydney Research Team, 1971

Originally Urapunga was known as Paddy's Lagoon, owned by a family called Warrington-Rogers. You can still see some of the posts of the yards they built, good big posts over eight feet high, but the lagoon has dried to a clay-pan surrounded by dried-up river gums and paper-barks. Old Duncan told me he could remember as a little boy when the lagoon was so deep they could swim horses across but that a 'proper big flood' came down and filled it with sand and mud. In that flood the Warrington-Rogers had to swim for their lives to the top of the hill. They spent about six or seven days waiting for the water to go down. All they managed to save was their sulky. They took the wheels off and floated it to high ground. Kate Warrington-Rogers is regarded as one of the greatest woman pioneers of the Northern Territory, known far and wide as an excellent horsewoman and a crack shot. She overlanded cattle from the Roper to Camooweal while her husband stayed on at Paddy's Lagoon running the place.[2]

There is a little bush cemetery on Urapunga with about six or seven graves. One is the grave of Harry Warrington-Rogers. In the Births and Deaths Register for Palmerston – old Palmerston, not the new place – his death is registered as 'Paddy's Lagoon, Roper River, February 1902'. On the same page is 'Aeneas Gunn, Elsey Station'. In the Births section are recorded the births of two babies born to 'Bet Bet', who gets a mention as the

Little Black Princess in *We of the Never Never*. For the first one the Place of Birth is given as 'Paddy's Lagoon'. For the second one it is 'Urapunga station', so that's when the name must have been changed, about 1916. Harry Warrington-Rogers' grave has a cast-iron railing around that has been badly damaged, probably by some old buffalo itching his backside.

There are several other graves. One is a Chinese lady who was a station-cook, and as far as I know the others are a couple of children. In the late 'seventies I had to dig a grave for my old mate Stan Norgren. I was going to put him right next to Harry Warrington-Rogers but when I got down a bit I struck bones and a skull. Some other poor bugger was already buried there. No name. No stone or anything. So I filled it in again and moved over a bit.

I became very good friends with the police constable at Roper Bar and his wife. Graham Chung was a part-Chinese chap, a very decent man. He is dead, now, poor fellow. But he and I were good mates during my early years at Urapunga. The first Wet that I was there Graham and his wife told me to bring my swag over and camp under the police station house. They knew the bark-hut was very leaky and miserable. The police-station house was on high-blocks, beautifully situated, over-looking the river, with the residence upstairs and the police-station offices downstairs. I was glad to take them up on the offer.

There is a lot of history around Roper Bar. The original police station in the Roper River area was at Mount McMinn, about seven miles along the road. It was named after the chief surveyor of the northern section of the O.T. Line. The police camped there and had a big mob of horses and some black-trackers to tail them. They were mainly rounding up lepers and keeping an eye on the blacks.They say leprosy came into the Top End with the Chinese coolies that were brought in to build the railway line to Birdum, the original name for Larrimah.

There were different policemen at Roper Bar during my time – two years seems to have been about the longest stretch they were expected to put in. I got on well with them although sometimes some young fellows sent out from Katherine were not what you could call too bright. A couple of rookies turned up home one day and told me they were a search-party looking for an old man believed missing. I thought to myself, 'Oh, yeah!'

A bit later, the sergeant in Katherine rings me up – he used to come out here fishing a bit and was a mate of mine. He said, 'Ray, I've just got a message on the police radio. Do you know which way those two young fellows went? 'I said, 'Well, I don't know where they are, but I can track them down.' He said, 'Would you mind going out after them? Apparently they've got two flat tyres.' So I said, 'Righto.' So I threw a couple of tyres in and away I went. I found them, and I said, 'Having a bit of trouble, eh?' They had a bit of a grumble about 'No-one put the bloody spares in.' I thought to myself, 'Well, you'd be a useless couple of young buggers not checking to see!' So anyway, I helped them put the spares on and gave them an extra one for good measure. I said, 'No hurry, but when you get back, can you send the tyres out to me again? OK?' and I said, 'Well. You right now?' 'Yeah. We're right!' they said,

The original police lock-up at Roper Bar.

grunting at me; no thanks or anything. I thought to myself, 'Well bugger you!' and away I went.

Next day, Andy McNeil rings up again! He said, 'Ray. Those boys are in trouble again!' I said, 'What's wrong now!' He said, 'They're out of fuel!' He sounded as though he was scratching his head a bit! He said, 'Do you think you could find them?' I said, 'Yeah. Righto!' So I shove a couple of twenty-litre drums of fuel on. And I found the young fellas way to hell up the Jalboi, fishing! I said, 'God! You fellows are never out of trouble, eh!' One of them said to me, 'Look! There's no need to come the bloody smart Alec!' I thought, 'Oh, yeah.' But I let it pass. I said, 'Have you got a funnel?' He said to me, 'What! Didn't you bring one!' I said, 'No. But I've got a syphon-hose here.' And they're standing back watching me balance the drum on the side of the truck. I said to them, 'For Christ's sake! Give me a bloody hand, will you!' So I siphoned the two drums of fuel in for them and away I went home.

A little bit later I saw them coming back along the road. I stopped them and said, 'Hey! You haven't got to worry about that old fellow you've been out looking for. He's sitting down in his camp.' They said, 'Oh! Won't we have something to say to him!' I said, 'No! You leave him alone! That poor old bugger's just been out doing a bit of prospecting! He comes up from down south every year! He doesn't ask you lot to come chasing him round. And when he does go bush he can find his own way back without making a bloody nuisance of himself!' That settled them.

About six weeks went by and I rang Andy McNeil up in Katherine. I said, 'Those two bright boys of yours! I told them there was no great rush but I wanted them to send those three tyres back.' He said, 'What! Haven't they done it yet!' Oh, he was savage. He said, 'You'll get those tyres back today! And, bloody oath! Won't I tear strips off the young bastards!' I said, 'It's OK, Andy! There's no rush. Just get them to chuck the tyres on the back of a truck that's coming out this way sometime.' But if I hadn't rung up about it those two young fellows wouldn't have even had the decency to do the right thing!

At times there were a few wild parties around the Roper Bar police station. Blokes working out bush would come in for a bit of a break. And one night one of them is lying there on a Cyclone stretcher and it's a hot, sweaty night and he's just got a pair of jocks on. The others get a thong and they tie it on to his old fella with a long piece of string. And then they get the thong and they keep dragging it across his face and he'd half wake up and slap at it and then he'd go back to sleep again. And this goes on for a bit. And after a while he wakes up and he says, 'You bastards!' and he grabs the thong and he pelts it as hard as he can. Well, I never saw a fellow leave his cot so quick! He's out the door following that thong for about the next twenty yards, speed-galloping!

And Keven West was telling me; one fellow, he's lying there drunk as a lord and his mates get this Yale lock and they get his old fella and pull it through, gently, gently, and they lock it up! He's still out to it and they all go away! And they take the key with them! And later on, this fellow comes to. The lock's starting to get a bit tight on him after three or four hours! And when the others come back to camp, he's got the shot-gun! And he says, 'You bastards! Come on! Where's the bloody key!' And no bugger can find the bloody thing! He's saying, 'Get that bloody key, Mate! Or I'll blow you bastards out.' And one of them says, 'That's right! The key's in the glove-box of the truck!' and he gallops over and gets the key and unlocks him. And he tells them, 'Just as well, you bastards! I'd have shot the lot of you!'

The original corrugated-iron lock-up is still standing; just two cells, four paces by three; a couple of vents at the top and bottom of the walls, and a heavy steel door with a grill. It can't have been much of a joke waking up after a bender and finding yourself in there, all the drunks in together. It must have got a bit on the warm side.

A couple of police trackers had been there for many years before they came to Urapunga. Duncan Yappanala and his wife Doreen, and Roy Kulakundu and Sam Thompson. Sam had an Aboriginal name but he preferred to be known as Thompson. His wife Una was a lovely old lady. She used to sing in the church choir and her voice would over-ride everyone else's. Sam was one of the best trackers in his time.

When the Duracks were travelling their stock through to the Kimberleys in the 1870s, they struck a very dry time. Drought set in by the time they got to the Roper. They pushed on to what is now Urapunga, and set up camp about eight or ten mile further up the Wilton valley at a place later called Farrer's Crossing. Dan Farrer was an old-timer who took up Mainoru in the early 1900s. When he came down to The Depot, as they called Roper Bar then, to collect his supplies, he would bring his wagons across the Wilton at the rocky bar, which is how it got the name Farrer's Crossing. There are descendants of Dan Farrer around the Roper area today. They have mostly intermarried with the local tribes' people.

At the Roper River in 1872. Some of the men who built the Overland Telegraph Line; workmen on left; Mitchell & Todd on right.

Courtesy South Australian State Library

The Duracks set up camp at this crossing and they put the wet season in there[3] holding their cattle in the valley of the Wilton. The cattle were that bloody poor when they got there they never moved for a month. Once the Wet came on they couldn't shift. No fences, of course, but that Wilton valley has big mountain escarpments and with the river in flood it was a pretty good place to hold the mob. They could ride out and pick up any stragglers and turn them back towards the river again. And then after the Wet was over and the cattle had put on a bit of condition, they packed up and headed off for the Kimberleys. The site of the old Durack camp – a couple of fireplaces and some piles of rocks – can still be seen out on the bank of the Wilton. There's also the grave of a young fellow named Sherringham that went off his head with fever and the rum and shot himself. He was left to look after the cattle while the others took a sick fellow named Urquhart back to the Roper Depot to get help for him. The isolation must have got to him.

The river is beautiful at Farrer's Crossing. The water drops over a rocky bar, all flat ledges of slate. I never saw it dry in all my time. Above the bar it is one continuous waterhole right back to Elu gorge, ten miles up, where the Wilton comes through about five miles of high gorge. They call that place Quirindi. It is so narrow that when we were shifting horses through there to muster further up the river, they would have to walk along in single file. There wouldn't have been more than six or eight feet between the river's edge and the escarpment. Lovely water all the way through – long deep pools and then you get a set of rapids or rock pools. You can only get a boat through in the Wet. One policeman we had there at Roper Bar, Peter Watton, was the adventurous type and he liked to take a boat through when there was a bit of fresh coming down. That gorge is not the head of the Wilton. It comes down from further up north. Those mountains are the Arnhem Land boundary; thirty-three thousand square miles of it. And I tell you what, in the days before I put in that fence I'd always brand that area early! Once you get the storms, all those clean-skin cattle would come down there out of Arnhem Land!

Sam Thompson, a valued tracker at Roper Bar police station, who showed Ray Fryer to the location of Tommy Roper's grave so that a memorial plaque could be placed on it. Sam was not only an important tribal elder but also a committed Christian and church warden. Ray valued his integrity and friendship.

Young Dan Farrer – he would be the third generation of the Farrers that owned Mainoru – showed me Sherringham's grave. I said to him once – must have been going on thirty years ago – 'Do you know anything about the grave of that young fellow that shot himself at Farrer's Crossing?' He said, 'I'll take you there.' He showed me the Duracks' campfire, a circle of stones, about five feet across, with smooth pieces of river stone that had been carted up. They call that stripey sort of river stone 'laterite'. It's not actually the best stone in the world to build a campfire. It can explode with a hell of a bang if it has water trapped inside it. None the less, there was this big, well-made fire-place and you could just imagine the Duracks all standing around while the quart-pots boiled and the beef cooked, planning when they should start to move out for the Kimberleys.

About fifty yards away on the edge of the timber there's a rough cairn of river stones which is almost certainly young Sherringham's grave. Dan Farrer would have known more about where the Duracks had camped than anyone else. In about 1988, when the government were starting projects to commemorate the Bicentenary, I went up there to Farrer's Crossing by Bell helicopter with a committee that were going to put in a memorial cairn with a brass plaque to the Duracks, but nothing ever came of it.

At Roper Bar are the graves of some other old timers. Most of them would have died of malaria, or fever, as it was known in those times. They are buried just opposite the crossing. One headstone was C.H. Johnson. It had "Speared by blacks, 1876" on it. He was one of a party of three that reached the Roper in 1876. They went down the river to have a drink and the next thing they were attacked. One was speared in the leg, one in the face and Johnson in the back. The other two stayed with Johnson until he died and then they took off.

The Police Inspector at Palmerston, a bloke named Foelsche, sent a detachment under Corporal Montague to bury Johnson's body and 'to have a picnic with the natives'. Rough justice was Foelsche's idea of handling things. They buried Johnson at the foot of a big old tree, and knocked the bark off and carved his name and the date he was killed. But over time the tree was washed out in floods and fell over. Someone before my time had cut the stump out and brought it up to the front of Roper Bar Police station. But it was splitting apart so Graham Chung and I mixed up some cement and Cobb and Co'd it together, and tried to make the inscription readable again.

They reckon that Foelsche was a tough bastard. There's a story told that one time he's in dress uniform for some flash turn-out; might have been the planting of the first pole of the O.T. line. And he's trotting past all these ladies and gentlemen and his horse gives an enormous bloody fart. And keeps on farting. Brtt! Brrt! Brrt! The way they do. And Foelsche calls out, 'Sorry about that!' And one of the Palmerston wags calls back, 'That's OK! We thought it was the horse!'

The grave of John Urquhart, the bloke the Duracks brought in to get help for, is across on the other side of the river. The headstone has been damaged and repaired but it is a wonder it has survived at all because some very big floods have come through over the years.

One year – it must have been about 1976 – we had fourteen foot of water over one end of the air-strip.The police-constable, Peter Watton, brought his wife and their two little children, Nicole and Daniel, across the river in the police-boat so that the Police Air Arm could come out and evacuate them to Katherine. I went back in the boat with Peter to the police-residence to salvage what we could. His wife had just had time to grab a few photos and things. There was over six foot of water inside the house. I was walking around on tip-toes and could just keep my mouth above water. You could feel the pressure of the water against the side of the house and I thought to myself, 'Christ! If this thing lifts off the stumps and goes down the river, we're goners!' But we did what we could. After, when the water went down, I brought my pump over – the one I used to quench the buffalo with on the trips up to Darwin – and set it up on the back landing, and Peter and I and about six or eight blackfellas helping, we kept sloshing that water around to keep it moving to pump all the silt out. If it had settled there would have been ten to twelve inches of mud right through.

Another grave at the old police-station is Tommy Roper's. Tommy was the first Aboriginal to be given a full pension. When we wanted to put a plaque on the grave I had a hell of a job getting any of the blacks to show me where it was. Aborigines won't talk about anything to do with death, and won't say the name of anyone that's died. The most they would do was poke their chin out a bit to indicate the possible direction. To them it offends the spirits to talk about them and they come back and stir up trouble. But then, even my Mother used to say, 'Speak well of the dead.' I found where Tommy was buried through old Sam Thompson. Old Sam was very much a Christian. He told me, 'That Tommy Roper grave. I show you.' And took me to this bit of a depression in the ground out in front of the old police station. We put a slab and a brass plaque on it.

Tommy was a police tracker for forty-odd years. He was involved in the capture of a wild blackfellow by the name of Tuckiar who speared a police constable over on the east coast of Arnhem Land, towards Gove. South of there is the Walker River which runs into Blue Mud Bay. The local blacks killed some Japanese beche-de-mer fishermen who were working in the area. So the constable and the tracker from Roper Bar were sent over to investigate. When they were asleep in their swags this Tuckiar crept up and speared the constable. The tracker escaped and brought the news back to Roper Bar.

A police-sergeant set out, taking Tommy Roper. Tommy tracked this Tuckiar down and they arrested him and brought him back for trial. The slab we put on Tommy's grave reads;

ROPER TOMMY
1876-1948

Erected in July 1985 by volunteers and former members of Roper Bar Police Station in recognition of almost forty years service by Police Tracker Roper Tommy. His service included a celebrated patrol in Arnhem Land with Mounted Constables Bill Johns and Jim Kelly in 1910. During this patrol they crossed and named the Mitchell Range after Government Resident S.J. Mitchell. Tommy was a member of the ill-fated patrol to Woodah Island in 1933 when Constable Albert McColl was fatally speared by Aboriginal Tuckiar.

Tommy was the first Northern Territory Police Tracker to be granted a full Federal Age Pension. This resulted from the untiring efforts of Chief Inspector Jim Mannion who took up his cause.

Leichhardt's 1845 expedition crossed the river at Roper Bar. The river is deep from here to the coast, fifteen to twenty feet, so it is the first place he would have been able to cross. There is a stone monument to the expedition – must be twelve feet high – in red local stone which was erected in 1945 by the army. Someone pinched the original plaque but the replacement reads,

> To commemorate the expedition of exploration
> Led by Ludwig Leichhardt
> Which crossed the Roper River at this bar
> On the 24th October, 1845.
> The crossing was made by the good will
> Of the Aboriginal owners.
> Among Leichhardt's party were two Aboriginal guides from New South Wales
> Charles Fisher and Harry Brown.
> This plaque was unveiled in 1966 in place of the original
> Which was unveiled on 24th October 1945 on the cairn constructed by the
> Northern Territory Military Force.

Roper River Mission was set up by C.M.S. – the Church Missionary Society, sometime back in the 1890s. Four missionaries came around from Cairns in a lugger and came up the river and set up camp. They can't have had much in the way of gear. But they got around amongst the Aborigines and got a few to come into the mission and then they sent those first ones out to bring in others. They started growing fruit and vegetables and feeding people and gradually got Roper River Mission on its feet. Then they branched out and started Rose River Mission and Oenpelli and Anurugu on Groote Eylandt. But it must have been a hell of a job. For years they lived in bush huts. All the old photos show these missionary fellows with beards and long white trousers, in front of their bark houses. Their rations must have been pretty light on. There aren't that many overweight missionaries.

There were about a thousand blacks living at Roper River Mission in my time. At first there were regular ministers there all the time; Percy Leske, Barry Butler and his wife Margaret, and Kevin Geirkus, but as the church started to get a bit short handed, a minister would just turn up from time to time to take a service. Finally Michael Gumbali, a full-blood Aborigine who had trained down south and was fully ordained took over 'running the stock-camp'. It could be a bit of a larrikin show at times. He'd be in his nice white vestments preaching away and he'd get a bit worked up because not many were coming to church, and he'd switch to blackfella talk, and let fly at them! But no matter who didn't show up, old Sam and Una were always there.

The mission used to try to make Christmas Day a big event for them all. They'd have a little black piccaninny for the baby in the manger. They always asked me to go over and I would make the effort. The missionaries were very good to me when I first arrived. I had to depend on them when the tides were low and the boat was due. They would let me unload on to their landing. It was better because I could

Ray Fryer and Bluey Ellis at the memorial to the Leichhardt Expedition of 1845, which crossed the river on the way north at Roper Bar Crossing. The remains of the historic police station can be seen in the background.

back a truck right to the wharf and unload straight off with the crane. So I would go to the services at the church and Michael Gumbali would say, 'It's very good to see the Urapunga team here.' And I'd be the team! Me and a couple of old blackfellas. I'd say to Old Duncan, 'Come on, Duncan! We gotta go long that church!'

One of the missionaries used to have an old slide projector and he would come over to Urapunga and show slides to all the people. One of Duncan and Doreen's kids, a little fellow named Sammy, a nice little bloke, he'd be about six or eight at the time, used to come looking for a drink of lolly-water or a biscuit or something. And this night the missionary was showing all these slides, and he's explaining them. He showed them a picture of Jesus, and he said, 'Now this fellow here, name-bilong him Jesus. And him riding ass. Ass him all-same donkey. Him going ass longa that place name-im Nazareth.' And the story goes on and on. And afterwards when Sammy came looking for his drink of lolly-water, one of the Shell fellows that was staying over with me, said to him, 'Well, did you have good pictures tonight, Sammy?' And Sammy says, 'Yairs. Good one!' And this fellow says, 'What them pictures about?' And Sammy tells him, 'Oh, him 'bout man name-bilong-im Jesus. Him bin riding long arse long donkey. Him bin go longa Mataranka, but me not know time him comin' back!'

Ken Mason was the Anglican Bishop of the Northern Territory at the time. He started out as one of the Bush Brothers up there. One day, I saw this fellow trudging up the road through the dust towards the homestead, and I thought, 'I wonder who the hell this is coming!' And when he got a bit closer I saw that it was Ken. I said to him, 'What's up? Have you broken down?' And he said, 'No! I just baptised my car!' I said to him, 'What! Where abouts?' And he said, 'Oh, I just drove it into the crossing down there!'

The crossing of the Wilton on the way to Roper Mission used to be tidal. The salt water never came that far up but it used to push the fresh water back, and make the crossing too deep for a sedan. It was OK for four wheel drives and trucks. I said, 'Come on. We'll go back down and unbaptise it!' So I took him back down, and got a rope on to the front of the chassis and snigged him out. Oh, it was a mess! Water right through, over the seats and all! So I towed him up to the homestead, and got underneath and drained all the oils and fuel and flushed it through and let it dry out for a while. Then we put a new battery in and hit the key and away she went! I thought the starter-motor would have packed it in with all the water and everything, but, no, we got him going and away he went! That's the power of prayer for you!

Christenings at Roper Mission were a bit of a one-off. Aborigines like to name their babies after some event or some important person. If Scuthorpes' Buckjumping Show had been to Mataranka or Katherine, sure as eggs there would be a rash of kids named Scuthorpe! We had one, Robin John Scuthorpe!

And Old Duncan decided he was going to be christened – he must have been in his late sixties at the time – but he wanted to be a proper Jesus-man. They did the ceremony down at Flat Rock waterhole on the Wilton. I thought they were going to drown the poor old bugger; pushing him right under. Afterwards he got up on the rock and wanted to make a speech but everyone was talking and carrying on, after all, it was a big occasion. But, Oh! Didn't Old Duncan get cranky! He couldn't make himself heard. He said, 'Listen! You mob! Now! You hearim me talk! Melike talk long yu long Jesus! Orright! Now! Shut your bloody mouths and this-fella Jesus, 'im make you good-fella tru!'

One time this young gin was having a baby up in the camp. She was having complications and the old gins came down to tell me. So I went up to the camp to see if there was anything I could do. This is about 2 o'clock in the morning, of course. Always the way! Anyway she had the baby eventually. And a few days after she comes down to the house and she says, 'Maluka. Me like namim this baby Rayfryer. You been proper good long we-pella.' I said to her, "Oh, that's alright, Judy! Don't you worry about that! But, look, suppose you call him Henry. Henry's a good name!' So off she went, happy! But how would you be! A little fellow getting around the flat with a name like 'Rayfryer'! I ask you! Those gins would sometimes say, 'Sposim' you put handle in my tomahawk. Me like.' But no way in the bloody world, Mate! No way!

Sometime in the 1980s, the government took over the running of Roper River Mission. It was getting too much for the church and they didn't have the staff any more. The police station at Roper Bar was closed down and shifted to Roper River Mission, which by that time was known as Ngukurr. It wasn't long before the Aboriginals put a claim on the original police reserve, about a hundred square miles, where the mounted police used to spell their horses. The land was granted to them as an Aboriginal reserve. Not long afterwards the original police residence was burnt down. There's not much left of it today, just the concrete house-stumps and steps where it used to be. So now, the old cell block and a couple of graves are all that are left to show where a very historic police-station once stood.

1 Nicholson, Ian, *Via Torres Strait*, p.264. '...the Omeo, accompanied by the Tatarua and PS Young Australia steered for the Roper River to discharge their cargo at the Leichhardt Bar depot, 60 miles upstream...but the Young Australia unfortunately struck a rock in the river and sank.' See Appendices A and B

2 Miller, Lilian Ada; *The Border and Beyond*, p.89. 'She (Kate Warrington Rogers) buried her only daughter on Urapunga Station on the Roper.' Ernestine Hill (The Territory) believed that a young son of the Warrington Rogers had been buried at Urapunga. The only headstone in the station cemetery on Urapunga is that of John Warrington Rogers, aged 51. But Ray records elsewhere in his story that he had found other human remains when digging the grave of his friend Stan Norgren. Perhaps the grave of one of the Warrington Rogers children was never marked. Kate Warrington Rogers lived at Camooweal for three years before her death. Her remembered account to friends there of having lost a daughter while at Urapunga is more likely to be the correct version.

3 Durack, Mary. *Kings in Grass Castles*, p 244 'The Roper depot, among thick tropical trees and creepers on the riverbank, had the unreal quality of a stage setting. A supply schooner was anchored among the mangroves and the crew, Chinese, Aboriginal and Malay, was lounging about the little timber and angle iron shanty....The Duracks pitched camp at McMinn's Bluff about seven miles upstream. It was a miserable camp, for the intolerable heat, ceaseless rain, mud and mildew played havoc with the men's morale....John Urquart was by this time so ill with fever that they hurried with him back to the depot hoping to catch the schooner for Darwin and medical aid. By the time the boat arrived however the good old bushman had shot himself in delirium. When they returned to the camp they found that young Sheringham, likewise maddened by malaria and rum, had put an end to his misery in the same way.'

nine...

'GETTING ON MY FEET'

The New Homestead; The Airstrip

After a few years, I was was starting to get on my feet a bit and I decided it was time to begin work on putting something decent in the way of a roof over my head, so that Betty and the kids could come over in the holidays. I stuck to the same site because of the view across towards the ranges, looking out towards Knuckey's Bluff. The sandstone escarpment caught the light at sundown and turned red and orange like a Namatjira painting. Another consideration was that the position was a good height above flood level. One hell of a lot of water comes down those big rivers in the Wet. You always had to have that in mind.

During the previous couple of Wets I'd put in the time making bricks, using cement and cement-moulds. I'd get about a hundred done and then I'd get sick of it. Then after a bit of a spell I'd make some more. There was a big mob of steel poles that had been brought in there for the construction of the Overland Telegraph, once they woke up to the fact that eucalypt got white-anted as soon as they put it in the ground. Those steel poles were manufactured in Adelaide, in three sections; the top section with a spike where the insulator was fitted. There were stacks of them, just dumped. I managed to procure some of them to use as rafters in the construction of the roof and supports for the verandahs.

There was a chap named Parfit, a retired furniture-maker, camping on the river. He and his wife were travelling around the north. I got talking to him and he agreed to stay on and help me build the place. So he was the builder; I was his off-sider! I took my orders from him. And I paid a couple of blackfellas to be off-siders with me. That was our builders' team. I sent round to Cairns and got roofing-iron and steel and cement brought round on the barge. It took us six months to put the place up. The living room was thirty feet by twenty, with six big pedestal fans; bedrooms, all with ceiling fans; big kitchen; all slate-tiled floors; verandahs floored with slate flagstones from the river, with a room on one end for my office and a radio-room. Where the steps went down to the garden I put in a nice smooth slab of concrete with the imprint of a fern leaf in it. Every visitor we ever had thought it was a fossil! In the kitchen there was a Raeburn slow-combustion stove, and, later, when the highway was put through, and it was easy to get L.P. gas tanks, I upgraded to gas.

Old Duncan's wife, Doreen; a lovely old lady, very neat and tidy and clean, used to work in the house and cook for us. She and her daughter Hannah and the others used to come up every morning, showered and clean, with fresh dresses on and their hair all sleeked back with California Poppy. You'd hear them laughing and giggling away. Doreen was very capable in the kitchen; she would put the beef on to get it started and make the bread. She was an excellent bread-maker. She'd use that Drybalm yeast. You put it in a container overnight with a bit of water and it brews up, then you mix it in with the flour, and cover it with a cloth and leave it somewhere warm near the stove. When it starts to rise you knock it down a couple of times and stick it in the camp oven or the oven. That's how we always made our bread. I could make a decent enough fist of it myself. All the members of the Yappanala family worked for me. They were very fine people.

With those big old slow-combustion stoves I would at times put on a good roast myself and tell the girls to keep an eye on it. When it was done they would move it into the warming oven, then all you had to do was to put on the vegetables and you've got a decent sort of a feed to come in to. Whoever was at the homestead at the time, pilots, pastors, health visitors, school inspectors, visitors from down south, we all ate together; one long table. No-one went without a decent feed; the whole mob of us sitting down together. No flash tucker, but plenty of it.

Rosellas grew wild all round Roper River Mission. There was a Sister there, Sister Edna Brooker, from New Zealand, a lovely lady. She had spent years of her life with the Church Missionary Society. I said to her, one time, 'Do you mind if I pick some rosellas? My mother used to make a lovely jam from them. I don't know how she did it but I'll work it out.' She said, 'If you get the sugar and the bottles, I'll show you how to make the jam.' So she showed me and that was how I learned jam-making! There is nothing tastier than rosella jam, especially on freshly-cooked damper or bread not long out of the oven.

The homestead had a verandah all round for coolness but at times it was so hot at night you couldn't sleep. The temperature remained in the mid-thirties most of the year round but during the Wet the humidity could be 100%. And I thought of the old Coolgardie food safes we used to have at home at Tabletop when I was a kid. They worked on the principle of water trickling down the sides and evaporating. They kept butter and milk reasonably well for a day or so even in the summer. And I thought to myself, 'Well, there's all this water in the river here.' And I couldn't see why the same principle of water being evaporated wouldn't work just as well to cool a house. So I sent down to Queensland for a couple of those big Knocker lawn-sprinklers – the sort that swing round with a long arm. I installed them on the roof-capping and connected them to a big overhead tank. There were no gutterings round the edges of the roof and when those sprinklers were switched on the water trickled down all the way round the outside of the verandahs. It knocked the heat right out of the roofing-iron and dropped the temperature inside the house by ten degrees.

Professor Harry Messel, the crocodile research specialist from Sydney University, was one of the Atomic Research mob and he had also done a lot of research on solar energy. He gave me a lot of advice about putting in a hot-water system, so I

Urapunga homestead in the 1970s from the air. The abattoir is out of sight on the right hand edge. The beautiful Wilton River is below the left hand corner. The homestead was built on this ridge to be above flood level during the Wet.

had one of the earliest solar hot-water systems in Australia. It was made up of tubes – they called these tubes 'evaculators'. They collected the heat. The water moves down through the centre of them. With the climate we had up in the Top End – the temperature gets up round thirty-eight and forty – the water used to almost boil in the holding tanks; enough to blow steam. I used that black polythene piping. Because I'd put the sprinkler system on the roof of the house I installed the poly-piping backwards and forwards over on the roof of one of the outbuildings. From there it was connected into a holding tank and from there into the hot water taps in the bathroom and kitchen. There was never any shortage of hot water.

To set the place off a bit, I fenced off a fairly wide area around the homestead with a post and rail fence with wire-netting underneath; quite nice-looking, and put in lawns to keep the dust down. Round the back was just barbed-wire with wire-netting.

Once I had finished building the homestead I started work on a machinery shed, saddle shed, fuel shed and chook yard and so on. And during the Wet when there was no cattle work to be going on with I did the garden. I put in shade trees and fruit trees; six mangoes – a couple of Bowen Specials and several other varieties. They did very well. And years later I met one of the fellows who had been kids there and he said to me, 'By Chrise, Maluka! You could run!' and he told me that one time I had caught a couple of them up in the mango tree pinching the fruit and chased them and booted their backsides! I wouldn't have minded if the fruit had been ripe; but they were just knocking down the green ones for the hell of it! Young buggers!

Members of the Yappanala family, the redoubtable Doreen third from left. Her daughters, Hannah, second from left, and Hazel, third from right, worked in the homestead, and could be heard 'giggling and laughing' in the early mornings. Doreen worked in the kitchen and was 'an excellent breadmaker.'

I fenced off an area for a vegetable garden. In the hot months of the year you could grow no vegetables whatsoever, but once the Wet came and there was a break-down of the heat, ordinary vegetables like pumpkin and sweet potato did well; and those long beans and also that big guirda bean, which grows over a trellis. You pick them when they are young and they are like a marrow. If they get away from you they go to fibre and turn into a big sponge that you can use for scrubbing. The pumpkins were trained up over the chook yard. We always had plenty of pumpkins to go with the corned beef.

We could grow tomatoes in the cooler months but come the heat they would go to jelly. They would form, half grow, but then break down. April, May through to September, things would grow but after September it was too hot. But when the garden was in full swing in the cooler months we would give any amount of surplus to the house-mob, Old Doreen and Duncan and their families, to take back up to the camp and share round.

I put in any number of fruit trees; oranges and mandarins and Mediterranean limes – they are little fellows, yellow, about the size of a plum. They make a lovely drink with water and ice. One problem we had with fruit trees was that white-ants used to get into them. To fix the bastards I used to drive a crow-bar down into the ground beside them and pour dieldrin down – which is completely banned today – but that was the accepted way you treated white-ants then.

Another thing that grew very well were granadillas; they grow on a vine over a trellis. Very nice eating; We had passion-fruit, the yellow kind, not the purple one. And on the drainage ends, where the laundry water and house water ran out, we grew bananas and paw paws. A couple of old fellows, Tommy Malauwi and another old fellow used to look after the garden but you had to be on them all the time to tell them what needed doing.

The hardest job was to keep the piccanninies away from the garden. The fence might keep out the stock but not the piccananinies! They wouldn't even wait for the fruit to ripen. If they felt like helping themselves they would just go for it!

I put in a proper chook-yard. Old Doreen and Hannah used to feed the chooks and collect the eggs.The old gardener-blokes would rake it out every now and then and spread the chook-poo on the garden. There are no foxes in that Top End country at all, but the native cats, you had to watch out for them. They would kill the hens just for the pleasure of it. And goannas would come and steal the eggs. You've got to shoot them when you see them. And those big black-headed pythons would come and take the hens. They'd sneak into the hen-coop at night and grab a hen and strangle it by stretching it out to twice its length. They have what is called an articulated jaw which means they can stretch it out around anything they want to swallow. The old hen would be going 'Scrark! Scrark!' and all the others singing out 'Ged-dark! Ged-dark! Ged-dark!' wondering if it was their turn next! You'd wake up and hear the racket and you'd grab your shot-gun and race out and shoot the bastard, or take a big stick to him.

Those pythons, if they swallow a hen, it is like a big football in them and it buggers them up for making a quick getaway! Or they find they can't get back out the way they came in, and they are poking their head this way and that trying to get through the wire. So you give them one good whack and they've had it. But if they managed to get away, say I was out in the stock-camp, they'd slide off and find a hollow log and sleep it off. One hen would do a black-headed python about a month. The blacks didn't need too much telling to track them down. They reckon that python-fella; he number-one good tucker! The old gins hated them. They said they could 'steal'im piccanniny'.

With the river being so close there was never any shortage of water so I had lawns right round the house and planted shade trees which I got from Parks and Wildlife; African mahogany, tamarind, palms and bougainvillea, crotons and ferns. I had big pots full of bougainvillea hanging along the front of the verandah and a hedge of white bougainvillea out the front. One of the visitors we had said it was like a Botanic Gardens. One of the trees was a henna tree. I used to gather the berries and give them to the Rural Heath sisters to rinse their hair. They loved getting them. There was an Indian curry tree which produced beans. Two doctors, Dr. Thenarajah and Dr. Ramakushna, came every month to treat the Aboriginals and anyone else around the place that needed attention. I had a room set up on the end of the verandah with a collapsible examination couch and other gear such as bins and stools for their use. When these two Indian doctors were due I used to pick the curry-beans and put them in the cold room ready for them. Oh! They were pleased to get them! They looked forward to it.

The verandah at Urapunga homestead had plenty of beds. Anyone who came was made welcome. The floors were flagged with beautifully smooth river slate. The sign reads "The Bushman's Rest. Pull up a stump and have a yarn".

In one part of the lawn I put in an ornamental well with a monkey-tail pump and when friends' kids came they would pump it up and down and watch the water pouring back into the well. Sometimes I'd put detergent in it so they could make the bubbles foam up! They thought it was great!

I got a company, Gorries and Cole, well-known drillers, from Alice Springs, to sink a bore.The fellow who handled the drilling couldn't read or write. But, by God! He was magic on a drilling rig! They had put a bore down at Roper Valley and they also drilled for the mining companies in the area. Before they came I gave the possible site for the bore a bit of thought, just going by the lie of the land where a slight valley came down off the hill as the most likely spot. When the drilling-plant arrived I said to them, 'What do you reckon?' This fellow had a look around and he said, 'I reckon it's as good a place as any. They had a powerful new rotary-percussion machine – spinning and hitting at the same time, all worked off a big compressor. They went straight through the shale rock and sandstone and hit the stream. First try! The second-hand casing for the bore came from Western Mining, a bit of a mystery operation in the Roper area. No-one ever seemed to know what they were drilling for.

There was some talk about it might be industrial diamonds. There were traces of diamonds in some of the creek-beds.

All through that country you find gem-stones; chrysophraze, a milky green stone, beautiful; they call it Australian jade, and on V.R.D. tiger eye, like lightning in a stone. As for agate, you can pick it up anywhere. And ribbon-stone – the best comes from Anthony's Lagoon – there are miles and miles of it there. When they were putting the road in, the grader would push it up. And amethyst; when I was clearing the Arnhem Land fence-line with the 'dozer I could have got a Toyota-load of amethyst that the blade pushed up. I chucked a fair bit of it in the back of the ute and took it back and put it in a heap at the back of the house. Any visitors that came I'd say to them if they wanted a bit to take it. And I ended with only one piece myself as a paper-weight!

We had been pumping our water directly from the river but in the wet season you were pumping a lot of mud into your tanks as well and you would have to drain them and get inside and shovel out the silt build-up. But once we got the bore down we had clean water all the time, house and yards. I built a six-foot chain-wire fence around that bore to keep the piccaninnies out.

I built a long shed for a work-shop with old six-inch bore-casing that I bought from around the district for the posts, sixty feet long and the full length of a truck in width so they were all parked under cover; a work-shop at the end and six bays about ten feet wide. A dirt floor at first but as I got a bit more money I concreted it.

I built a very nice meat-house to hang the beef and keep the salt-beef. It had a galvanized-iron roof and over the top of that was another roof thatched with spinifex, with a false roof over the top to shade it. The floor was ten foot square and concreted and the walls were slate-stone up to two foot six, and above that was screen-wire. The roof extended well out over the sides to shade the walls. There was a bench along one wall and a rail along the other where the beef was hung. In one corner was a cask for the salt beef. It was a big wooden brewery-vat with bands around that I got from an old bloke in Darwin. I had two of those kegs and they were used alternately. When one cask was finished it was hosed out and cleaned to keep it sweet-smelling.

Beef makes its own brine when you are salting it down in a keg. I used salt petre, about one tablespoon of salt petre to a hundred pounds of beef. Once it is in the keg you have to check it after the third day. You take the meat out and boil up the brine. Any blood that is in it comes to the surface as froth about the consistency of thick gravy. You skim this off and throw it away. You might have to repeat the process a second time three days later. If you don't get the blood out of the brine like this the meat goes off.

We salted three parts of the beef and a lot went to the Aboriginals. At first I had an old Electrolux kerosene fridge and it was never used for anything else except fresh beef. But those old kerosene fridges played up a lot. If they weren't smoking they were freezing. You had to watch them all the time or you could lose the lot.

What you didn't have eaten by a week or ten days you might as well throw to the dogs.

There was a set of gallows out in the yard but most of our killing was done out in the paddock. When we wanted a killer one of the men would push a small mob of cattle up under a tree. There'd be another fellow up in the tree with a rifle. When the cattle wandered along under the tree, to catch their attention; he would go, 'Hrr!' The cattle would look up, and he'd get a clean shot at the killer from about ten or twelve feet. It would drop in its tracks. Wouldn't know a thing. The others would gallop off. The men would bleed the carcass and bone it out and throw the meat on to a pile of green boughs in the back of the Toyota. You'd do this late afternoon because the meat had to be hung overnight. I had a wire strung across between two trees for the purpose. Later on I built a gallows and put a cold-room in.

We killed about once every week or ten days, depending on how many people were around the place. I fed my men on beef all the time; them and their families. I'd kill a beast for the camp. I'd get some cuts that I wanted and they would keep the rest. They mainly grilled it. Everything was just chucked on the fire. A bit of sand and grit didn't seem to worry them too much.You would hear them grinding away! They never were ones to make stews or curries or roast beef. They would just cook on the coals. They never left anything. All the beef-bones and rib-bones they could get, all sitting down around the fire at night, piccaninnies and all, chewing on bones. That was the way they lived. They were a healthy mob the Welfare Department told me. They were pleased with the way the camp was running.

I built a saddlery shop, two rooms, with a verandah front and back, with accommodation for the saddler, Stan Norgren, though he usually had his main meal with us over at the house. Middays, if he felt like it he would come and have lunch which was usually just cold corned-beef and salad.

I got a contract builder to come in and build a decent school for the kids at the far end of the lawn. They played on the lawns in the garden. I built a new ablution block with proper toilets. You couldn't have them using those old pit latrines. It was bad for their health. So they had a new ablution block with two showers for the girls on one side and two for the boys on the other side and a breeze-way laundry area with two sets of tubs and a copper and an electric washing-machine in the centre. The old ladies who came from the camp each morning to look after the school kids' clothing thought they were made! Better than flogging the clothes up against the coolabah tree, they reckoned!

The first power plant I had there was a DC plant run off a bank of sixteen two-volt batteries which made up thirty-two volts, charged off a petrol-driven motor, which I would charge at night to keep the lights going. It was for lighting only. But later I put in a 240volt diesel Southern Cross generator which ran continuously and which I would turn off at night about ten o'clock and start up again at about four in the morning. If we were away mustering and there was no-one at the homestead it was left off. But once we had refrigeration we more or less had to run the plant all the time. There was no mains power in the Roper district but later on when I had my abattoir there, I built a bigger power station with bigger generators. Eventually

NTEC, the Northern Territory Electricity Commission, took it over and they provided all the upkeep and I bought power off them. It was costly but it was a more efficient way of handling the power situation and I never had to worry about it.

Ray built the airstrip himself, cutting and burning the timber, then by dragging a discarded steel wagon tyre, smoothed the surface. Later it was further upgraded by the Department of Civil Aviation so that medical aid could be provided to the Urapunga Aborigines. Once the Urapunga air-strip was fully licensed 'as many as seventeen planes a day' called in.

I have always had a hell of a lot of admiration for those old fellows – the Buchanans and Costellos and the Duracks who overlanded cattle in the early days, taking up land and carving properties out of wilderness. I sometimes get the feeling I was born in the wrong century. I would have liked to have lived back when a man could take up new land and make something of it – starting in from scratch and working his way up.

But I have to admit there are a few advantages of running a place these days. Steel posts make putting in a fence-line an easy matter by comparison with having to go out bush and cut and split timber posts. Another modern advantage is black polythene piping. It is light and easy to handle and you could trench it and run water for miles if you wanted to, to the citrus trees and gardens, and the machinery sheds. Anywhere you wanted water to you could have it. It is a huge asset, that black poly-piping; and a hell of a lot easier than screwing the old galvanized stuff together, length after length; this galvanized stuff is was heavy to handle and it gets that hot in the sun. And the freight on it costs the earth. With poly-pipe you just run her out wherever you needed it and there was a hell of a lot you could do with it in a short time.

When I first went to Urapunga there was only the government air-strip at the police-station at Roper Bar, where Connellan Air came in once a week. All I got was my mail. I couldn't afford the freight on perishables.

But once I started to get a bit of money together I decided that I would get in some equipment and put in a licensed aerodrome on Urapunga. There was a good gravelly flat a couple of hundred yards out from the front of the house, looking over towards Knuckey's Bluff, but it had a bit of timber on it. So I bought a little old second-hand Fergie petrol tractor. I hitched a long wire cable to the front of it, and I had a ladder, and I'd climb up the ladder and fix the cable to a tree as high as possible so as to get more purchase on it. I would dig out round the bottom of the tree a bit, then I'd hop back on the Fergie and give the cable a long steady pull. When the tree came down I'd snig it off to the side. When I had a decent sort of pile I'd put a fire into it. I did this the full length of the strip until I got it cleared; and all the trees on the approaches at both ends.

And to level the strip I dragged old steel tyres, old wagon tyres that I found out bush, up and down till I got it smooth enough. I ended up with the strip cleared to forty-two hundred feet long by three hundred feet wide. The actual landing strip was a hundred feet in width. I marked it either side with tyres painted white. Later on, because Urapunga had Aboriginals and they had to have Aerial Medical services, the Department of Aviation came and put a surfacing of heavy gravel on it to upgrade it to an all-weather strip. So then it was available for any medical evacuations that were needed or any other emergencies. From then on it was a fully licensed aerodrome and got a lot of use. It got that way we had aircraft coming and going all the time.

And a funny thing! One of the old chaps who was working on the grader died a few years later when he was doing a similar job west of Alice. It was the middle of summer and they had just had a heavy fall of rain so the roads were out and no-one could get out or in. So they took all the beer out of the big camp freezer and doubled him up and fitted him in. It was a few days before anyone could get through and they reckon he was as solid as a rock by then! Well, he would be! Poor old bugger!

The Shell company put in a refuelling depot for us, and down south they got the idea of having these flying safaris around Australia. The rivers were what attracted the tourists. They would fly in and park on the airstrip and go camping along the river. It was the barramundi fishing they came for. Some people used to come back every year. Some came two or three times a year just for the fishing. I got to know a hell of a lot of people from all over Australia.They thought we were the genuine outback, and they wanted to experience it for themselves. I've seen as many as seventeen aircraft on our strip at the one time. There was an old DC3 that used to come in for one of the mining companies and even a Fokker Friendship. They were fairly new in those days.

One night we had a Dutchman there. He'd been with the RAAF during the war and he was telling us about a time he got into a dog-fight over the English Channel. Afterwards he'd been interviewed on the BBC, and he was telling them, 'There was one Fokker on the right of me and another Fokker on the left of me. And I looked up, and there was another Fokker right on top of me....'At this point the BBC interviewer said in a nice calm voice, 'Perhaps I had better explain to the listeners that a Fokker is a type of aircraft.' And this fellow says to him, 'Yes, That's right. But on this occasion I was thinking of the *other* kind!'

Then, about 1974, Thiess Brothers constructed a more-or-less all weather road through from Katherine. Shell could then deliver fuel, which gave us a bit of cash flow. But that refuelling depot was a bit of a hassle to maintain. Someone had to be there all the time in case a plane flew in. If you are advertised as a refuelling depot and they plan on coming in there to get fuel, well, there has to be someone there to do it. You couldn't have planes landing and there's no-one there. It wouldn't have been the right thing. So there wasn't any money in it; it was more in the way of providing a service. But then I would often be able to get a lift up to Darwin if I needed to go up, so it was handy from that point of view.

If we had to do an emergency evacuation at night we used to park vehicles at the end of the strip, with their headlights on, and others along the sides; every hundred yards. That was the way the pilot liked them to be spaced, so he could judge his landing. Later, the Department of Aviation provided landing-lights which were filled with diesel and had a wick. They didn't look much from the ground but apparently from the air they were OK. Even so we still placed vehicles with their lights on at both ends of the strip for any night landings.

Once we got on our feet, I got a Cessna 206 on cross-hire from a bloke in Darwin called Steven Styles. You have it on permanent charter from them. We had that Cessna for about seven years. Before my father's death in 1948 I had got up twenty-eight hours of solo time towards my pilot's licence, flying a little old Victa Air Tourer trainer; made by the same company that made Victa mowers. It had one stick in the middle where both hands, instructor and trainee, could fit; and you both had a set of pedals. Those Victa Tourers were an Australian design but made in New Zealand.

But after Dad died there was probate to be paid so I couldn't afford flying lessons and I had to let them drop. So I employed a young fellow, Laurie Shaw, a commercial pilot, from down Windorah way. He had just completed his pilot's licence and he was keen to get his hours up. He stayed with me for three years. When I needed to fly across to Tabletop – you can't fly over the Gulf in a single-engine – you've got to stick to the coastline; we would cut over Borroloola, refuel and grab a sandwich at Normanton, then head across to pick up the Greenvale line and follow it down till we sighted the old chimney at the Argentine and from there picked up the strip at Tabletop. I had an old mate, Bob Mackenzie, managing my part of things there for me; a very decent bloke and a good friend to me. I've always been very grateful to him for the good job he did. The flight over took about seven or eight hours. In a twin-engine job, a Beech Baron, it was only six hours, because you can cross the Gulf a bit higher up. We did this trip about two or three times a year.

About twenty-five years later the phone rang and this voice said, 'How you going?' I said, 'Good! How about you?' This voice said, 'I just rang up to thank you.' I said, 'Thank me?' He still didn't tell me who he was. I said, 'Well, righto! You rang up to thank me. But what for? Who the hell are you?' He laughed and he said, 'Laurie Shaw! And I've just been made Chief Pilot for Cathay Pacific!' I couldn't have been more pleased. He was a very nice fellow. And he started off flying a 206 with me!

We had a regular radio sched. with O.P.R. – Outpost Radio – Darwin. We had two scheds. a day, one at seven o'clock in the morning and another one at four in the afternoon, but, naturally, in an emergency you could call up any time. Then everyone else would stand down until you got your message through. The routine was that they would announce before the scheds. started who they had traffic for. They would say, 'We have traffic on hand for…' and name the places. We always tried to listen in to see if there was traffic for us. Our call sign was Five Sierra Alpha Lima. You would say, 'VJY Darwin this is Five Sierra Alpha Lima Urapunga standing by for traffic.' If they had traffic they would give it to you otherwise they would say, 'All clear, Five Sierra Lima Urapunga, standing by'. It was good to know we had communication. Later on they changed our call to Eight Sierra Roma Kilo.

Once, during a heavy wet season, the Air Med plane was coming in for a routine medical. The pilot was taxiing in and he overshot the edge of the parking bay. Even with all the rain we'd had the strip was good, and if he had turned around in the parking bay he'd have been alright because it was heavily gravelled. But he ran off the edge, and down she went. Right over, one wing touching the ground. I had plenty of jacks but you can't jack an aeroplane, so you're buggered! So I drove up to the camp and I got all the blackfellas. And we get about eight or ten of them under the wing. And I'm telling them, 'Righto! Stand up! Lift with your shoulders!' And I'm in there with them getting my back into it. And we get her up; get her up; get her up. And we chuck bits of wood and planks under it. And we kept doing this till we got her upright. And then, of course, the bloody nose-wheel, it's still stuck in the mud. So we all pull down on the tail and get the nose to come up.

All the blacks are as happy as hell! Covered in mud! Laughing and yak-ai-ing! Everyone's giving everyone else advice. So then we get her upright but when you go to push her forward the nose-wheel would bite in. So I said, 'I think we'll have to take her out backwards.' So I get a couple of long ropes and tie them on to the back wheel, and we're all on the ropes, yelling, 'Come on! Pull! Pull! Put your back into it!' And, steady, steady we got that plane back on to the airstrip. You could bet your bottom dollar they'd have made a big corroboree about it up in the camp that night. They'll be dancing that one for years! Getting the Docta's Plane out of the Bog!

After the war a chap named Eddie Connellan started up Connellan Airways and once we got our strip registered Connellan started coming in. One of the pilots was Sam Calder. During the war Sam used to fly Beaufort bombers and later he was in the Federal government for the Liberals. Another Connellan pilot, Christine Davies, was a very nice lady. She would deliver our mail and have a bit of a yarn to us. The blacks had a very good opinion of Connellan Air. One day a tourist landed there and he said to one of them, 'How far from here to Mainoru?' The Aboriginal looked at him and said, 'S'pose you foot-walk, it three-fella day. S'pose you go long yarraman (horse), one day. S'pose you go long Connair; You *there*!'

The medical plane came in every two months, with a doctor and a couple of sisters. They would fly down from Darwin and generally get to Urapunga about nine o'clock in the morning. I would take a Toyota down to the strip and bring them back and we would all sit down on the verandah and have a cup of tea. Then we'd ring the school bell and all the people would come down from the camp, all spruced up for the occasion, and the school kids would be brought down, and everyone would sit out on the lawn waiting their turn to be checked out. They would do the clinic in the room on the end of the verandah. It was like a holiday for everyone; a big excitement. Anybody that was really crook they took back to Darwin with them. On alternate months Mobile Sisters came by vehicle to follow up on any instructions that the doctors had left.

It was remembering the Coolgardie safes, similar to this one at Tabletop, which were cooled by evaporation, which made Ray devise the concept of installing sprinklers on the roof on Urapunga homestead, which "dropped the temperature inside the house by ten degrees."

We had a big medical chest at the homestead which was kept under lock and key. It was provided by the Commonwealth Department of Health, with all the standard medicines and antiseptic creams and antibiotics. There were some restricted drugs that were locked in a separate compartment, and not to be administered by anyone except under doctor's orders. Each time the nurses came around they went through the chest and anything that was out-of-date they would either take back to Darwin or give to me to incinerate.

At any time when anyone got hurt or was sick we could call up on Outpost Radio and they would connect us through to the doctor. We would tell him the symptoms, and he would advise us what to give them or what to do for them. I can't speak highly enough of the Northern Territory Medical Services. They were marvellous.

Leprosy was once common in the Roper area but there haven't been any new cases for quite a few years. We had a few cases at Urapunga. One old girl had lost a leg after she was burnt in the fire and another one had deformed hands. Leprosy affects the nervous systems in their hands and feet and they have no feeling in them and don't realize when they are picking up boiling hot billy-cans or standing on hot coals. They get shocking burns. When I first went there, the Roper Bar police-constable used to do patrols up into Arnhem Land trying to track down any cases that hadn't come in for treatment. They were sent to East Arm outside Darwin, but now there are modern drugs like avlosulphone and they don't have to leave their own area, which is very important to them. Most of the leprosy up there was the tuberculoid type which isn't so infectious, anyhow. The man who did a lot of work with leprosy in the Top End was Doctor John Hargraves – he was very highly respected right across the North.[1]

Sandy blight was always a problem. Flies would get in the kids' eyes – you'd see them with four or five flies lined up along each eyelid and not even bothering to brush them away – and that spreads the germs from one kid to the next. Properly, it is called trachoma but the blacks call it 'ply-bite'... 'Piccaninny long-me gottim ply-bite'... The medical sisters would leave a mixture of olive oil for the mothers to rub around the kids' eyes to keep the flies away but not many of them ever got around to doing it. Those gins could be a bit rough and ready on the mothering side of things. They'd had 'ply-bite' as kids themselves and didn't see it as a problem.

Every so often a team came round checking the Aboriginals' eye-sight, going round all the stations in turn. To test the old people who couldn't have understood an ordinary eye-chart they had cards with circles with a gap in them. I would hear them saying, 'Now which side does this gate open?' The younger people and the school-children were tested in the ordinary way. The team would stay with me at the homestead for a couple of days and test the whole camp. Old Hinkler Daiwanana was about ninety and they kept him fitted out with glasses as thick as glass bottles! You'd see him getting around, looking this way and that, very pleased with himself.

We'd also get visits from a mobile dental unit. It was completely self-sufficient with its own power-plant and water-tanks, with one section for the dentist and one for the dental technician, like a normal dental surgery. There was another section like a kitchen where they could knock a feed together, but at most of the stations they visited, the station would have been pleased to provide them with a feed and accommodation. Whenever they came to us they were always well looked after. They checked everybody out, whites and all, making sets of teeth for anyone in the camp who needed them. They would be at Urapunga a week or ten days.

It was marvellous, the health care that the government gave to outback people in the Northern Territory. It didn't matter if you were black, white or brindle. If you needed treatment you got it. The Health Department people who came to Urapunga seemed to love their work and it was a pleasure to have them turn up. And I don't mind telling you, in the early days, it was a welcome sight to see a few white females turn up on the place.

Coastal Patrol used to come in from time to time in an aircraft called the Shrike Commander. The Darwin lot would do up around Arnhem Land and down the coast to Borroloola. The ones from Townsville were Neptunes. We would see them regularly down in the mouth of the Roper, coming in very low. They would fly over, take a look at the Toyota, see my hat and think, 'He's not a sampan boy!' They must have spotted a few illegal vessels because every now and then the cops from Katherine would go down and round up a mob of illegals out of the mangroves. From time to time the Shrikes would come in and refuel. Strangely enough, two or three of the crews were all-female. And good luck to them! There's no strength needed to fly a plane.

A friend of mine from Darwin often used to fly down and stay overnight. He was an inspector for the Northern Territory Electricity Commission. One time I said to him, 'Have you ever seen the Ruined City?' He said, 'No. I've heard of it. I wouldn't mind having a look at it.' So we flew out on the eastern side, zero-one-zero, about thirty-one mile. So there we were, flying around, backwards and forwards, and he's getting more and more absorbed. And then we headed right up the top end of Urapunga to look at a mob of cattle I had up there. And all of a sudden I looked at the fuel gauges – the two gauges on this little 172 – and I said, 'Hey! Are those bloody gauges right?' Both them were on empty.

'Hell!' he said, 'We'd better get back! Where's the straightest line! So I pointed it out to him and he swung the plane around. After a bit we picked up the Urapunga airstrip away in the distance. He lined the thing up and came in and made a normal landing, no problems at all; taxied down the strip and swung round. And at that very moment the bloody engine cut out! No need to switch it off! Completely out of fuel! Bone bloody dry! I thought to myself, 'Christ! How lucky can you get!' Which only goes to show you've got to keep your mind on the job in hand! And when you go flying around looking at things, make sure you've got plenty of fuel!

1 Leprosy in the Northern Territory; Northern Territory Medical Service; Darwin; 1968. The tuberculoid form of leprosy attacks the peripheral nerves. It is regarded as being less infectious and is treatable with the drug avlosulphone in tablet form.

ten...

'A RIVER FULL OF CROCODILES'

Harry Messel and Crocodile Research

The Roper was full of crocodiles. There are crocodiles all through that country, both salties and freshies. If you see a croc lying on the mud with his tail straight back, that's a saltie. But a freshie[1] will get up on a log, and when you disturb him he dives. Splash! Any big splash you see, nine times out of ten it will be a freshwater fellow. He'll dive straight into the water when he sees you coming. The old saltwater fellow, he suns himself parallel to the water, and he goes in silently.

Saltwater crocs used to come right up to the Bar. The earliest recorded attack on a European in the Territory was in the 1880s at what we call the Barge Landing. Two of the OT workmen were fishing in a dinghy and one of them had his leg hanging over the side. A croc got him. And some time early in the 1900s an old woman was taken when she was swimming across the river in the same area. Crocs live to a good age so it was probably the same one.[2]

They say that east of Elsey there are saltwater crocs in all the big lagoons and channels. An old bushman told me once, 'A man would have to be mad to swim in any of these billabongs in the Top End!'

Saltwater crocs will move overland from lagoon to lagoon. One time, when the BTEC Scheme was on, we were out shooting brumbies, as well as cattle, in some of my back country. We were knocking some buffalo on a ridge between two billabongs and the pilot said he would have to go back to the airstrip and refuel. Ted Easten, one of the DPI – Department of Primary Industry – blokes up there, said to the pilot, 'Rather than just hang around, to fill in time while you're gone, we'll walk up over the ridge, and you can pick us up on the other side at the billabong.'

So we were going up this ridge, and suddenly, out of nowhere, comes this bloody old croc – a big salty; a square-headed fellow – galloping down towards us! Talk about scramble! Fellows dodging round rocks trying to get the hell out of his way! But the croc was trying to get out of our way as much as we were trying to get out of his! All in among these rocks! He would have been a good fourteen foot! The billabong on the other side had dried up and he was migrating across. I have heard of stockmen out mustering during the Dry who have come across the carcasses of

Aerial view of the floodplain adjacent to the upstream section of the Roper which provides the variety of habitat favoured by crocodiles for breeding. Smoke can be seen from the Aboriginal burning-off fires which ensure green regrowth early in the wet season to facilitate hunting.

Courtesy Professor Harry Messel, University of Sydney Research Team, 1971.

crocs in the grass that have perished whilst travelling overland from one waterhole to another.

During the seventies, Professor Harry Messel from Sydney University set up a crocodile research project in the Northern Territory, based at Urapunga, to do a study of the croc populations of the south-east coast of Arnhem Land.

I had a friend, Hughie Roberts, an ex-R.A.A.F pilot, who became a commercial pilot flying all over Australia; he brought Harry Messel up one time, and Harry said to me, 'Hey, Guy!' – he was American; everyone was 'guy' – 'This would be the ideal place to set up a crocodile research project.' He could see the potential of it; our own air-strip, good communications and deep enough water to bring his research ship, the 'Harry Messel' right up the river and moor off our bank. They had their own plane and pilot. Next thing builders started arriving and putting up a decent set of accommodation units and a shed for his boats and equipment.

The research team used to come up a couple of times a year. They had topnotch boats and equipment and gear. The 'Harry Messel' was about sixty foot long with a draft of about six foot, very suitable for either coastal or river work. There was accommodation for six on board. As well as the crew there were cameramen and technicians. Besides Harry Messel there was Professor Gordon Grigg and Dr. George Vorlicek and a mangrove specialist chap named Graeme Wells. You would never pick these fellows for University professors. They'd be getting around in shorts and thongs, with their bellies hanging out over their trousers, just like ordinary blokes. The skipper was a retired sea captain by the name of Bunny Warren and the engineer was Ian Onley. The deck-hand was a bloke named Wally Gill. They used to come across from A.I.M.S. – the Australian Institute of Marine Science, just south of Townsville behind Cape Cleveland. They'd go up through Torres Strait, around the tip of Cape York, across the Gulf and come up into the Roper.

Urapunga made a good base for their work because of the big flood-plains we had there which had the different habitats that crocs like to move in and out of. They might be nesting in the big lagoons at the beginning of the Wet but by the end of the Dry, food gets light-on and they start moving back into the rivers. If they don't build their nests early enough at the beginning of the Dry the eggs hatch more slowly, or they might not hatch at all. It takes anything from about eighty to a hundred and twenty days for the baby crocs to start coming out. You generally see them, hatchlings, they call them, by the end of October. But, if we had a dryish Wet the water level might drop, and the occasional old fellow will get isolated up in the lagoons and have to sit it out until the following Wet. There's generally a bit of tucker with all the bird-life, and maybe even a feral pig or a young buffalo coming down to wallow.

The team did most of their work of a night-time and if I could get away I'd go out with them. They used a sixteen footer with a de Haviland Trojan engine. There'd be Harry Messel, Gordon Grigg, the photographer Bill Green, the engineer and me. They had the river marked out into three mile sections with reflector beacons on the trees and we would do one section a night. We'd leave home just on dark. Bill Green would be right up the front with a big spotlight run off a bank of batteries he would charge during the day. We'd poke along, up and down the night's section, and Bill would have this big spotlight trained along the banks and the water's edge. A croc's eyes glow red in the spotlight and most of them would be lying along the edge of the shallows. Harry would pick the times that the tide was just right; too high and you miss half of them up in the vegetation. It didn't seem to make much difference whether the tide was on the make or dropping, or what time of night it was, numbers were pretty much the same. He reckoned that we could count on seeing about sixty or seventy percent of what was there. When we spotted one, Bill would cut the motor back and we would idle to within about fifteen feet of him. Then Harry would record its size and exactly where it had been spotted. If they were in the water with only their eyes showing that went down as 'Eyes only', with a rough estimate of what length it was. They were mainly interested in getting an idea of the crocodile population of the Roper. They weren't all that interested in the freshies but if we saw them they made a note of them.

Harry was surprised at how many freshies we saw in the salt water stretches of the river. He reckons it was probably because in earlier times there would have been more salties in the downstream parts and they are aggressive buggers and would have seen the freshies off. As the numbers of salties dropped with shooting and drownings in fishing nets the little freshies got cheeky and started coming down into the tidal parts of the river. At the same time you've got to have it in mind that the old saltie is just as happy to come up into the fresh water. I've seen big fellows up to ten or twelve feet within a couple of hundred yards of the bar, and campers swimming and fishing there.

We'd work right through the night, doing different sections each night, for about six hours, working our way down river. After six or eight hours of this we'd be glad to get back to the homestead and have a clean up and a feed and a camp.

To snare the crocs they'd set long, narrow box-traps on the bank. They'd shoot a wallaby to bait the trap and set it where a wallaby pad came down to the water's edge. The old croc would crawl in to get the carcass and the trapdoor would drop behind him. Built across the rear deck of the boat was a platform where all the scientific work was done. The croc was winched on to this and secured by two steel half-hoops on hinges, something like those steel locks they drop across a railway line to close the track. One was dropped across the thick end of the tail, and another one behind his shoulders. Once these were in place they would put a twitch around his snout and tie his tail down because that's where most of the power of a croc is. One swipe with that and you'd know all about it. When they were working on the little freshies they would just use a bit of inner tube like a rubber band around their snouts.

But those big salties; their teeth would be up to three or four inches long. Sometimes you see them lying along the bank with their jaws wide open and a mob of little birds – those little sand-pipers – picking their teeth for them! So they would make sure his jaws were well and truly twitched together before they started work on him. They'd measure him and look for any injuries and estimate his age and so on. Each croc was given an individual code name, such as 'Charlie Number Three'. Then a solar-powered beeper was attached to his head, to keep track of him. Every beeper had a different signal that ran off a micro-battery inside.

There is a big rough barnacle knob on the back of a crocodile's head and that was ground down and flattened off. Then they would screw a plate on and bolt the beeper on to it. Once that was attached to the crocodile's skull, wouldn't there be some fun getting him back into the river! By this time he was well and truly stirred up! But generally, the best way to get him back into the water was just to stand well clear and let him go for it! Didn't he get a shift on! He'd be over the side that bloody smart! Just a splash and he's gone!

The team had their own aircraft based at Urapunga and they would fly around locating crocodiles by these beepers to see how far they had moved over the years. They kept a record of all the data of croc movements on the plane and they could see how far each one had gone. They found that, generally speaking, your old croc is very territorial. He pegs out his own territory and that is where he stays. He will see off any intruders.

Certain crocs would do a lot of fighting and the beepers would get ripped off. Then they were trapped again and another beeper was attached. And there were also rogue crocs. One time, there was one fellow they hadn't seen for twelve months, north of Maningrida, and, on this particular day, the survey plane happened to be out a bit wider than usual with its instruments on, and it picked up the beeper of this croc about halfway between New Guinea and the mainland! And within a couple of days he came right back into the Liverpool River at Maningrida where they had trapped him. Back to his base camp!

An upstream section of the Roper showing the northern bank, which is part of Urapunga station.

Courtesy Professor Harry Messel, University of Sydney Research Team, 1971.

The Sydney University Crocodile Research team came to Urapunga for a good many years and I got to know Harry Messel very well. He was a very fine man; very dedicated to his work and I always enjoyed his company. When the team finally pulled out they left me a decent sort of a shed they had built in the grounds for their research work. They said it was a gesture of appreciation from Sydney University for the help I had given them over the years.

There were always crocs about. One wet season there, I could hear this old creamy mare that I had, whinnying outside. I thought, 'What the hell's going on? What's she whinnying like that for?' And I walked out on to the verandah. And straight away I could see blood pouring from her flank. She had three great rakes across her belly and half her guts were hanging out. She must have gone down for a drink and when horses go down for a drink, they're snorting all the time: 'Brrrff. Brrrff'. The croc must have got her off-guard. They can come right in on an animal without making so much as a ripple.Then they surface at the last moment. Bastards of things that they are! And here she was, whinnying, and coming over to me. She must have thought I'd be able to do something to help her. I caught her, and I stroked her down. And I told her, 'You poor old bugger!' She was a quiet old thing, too! She put her head against me, as though to say, 'I'm in a bad way!' But there was nothing I could do. I went up and got the rifle and shot her. You can't

do anything for them when they've been ripped open like that. But I'll never forget the way she was whinnying and coming towards me

I said to the blacks, 'Hey! Don't you fellas go swimming down there! There's a bloody big croc hanging about.' The crocs would get out of that strong-running current in the Wet and come up into the gullies. Not long after this I saw this big old croc not far below the house. I thought, 'You bastard! You're the one that killed my mare!'

The blacks told me, 'You kill'im finish, Maluka! Him grab one piccaninny for sure! Maybe one of them women!' So I grabbed my .303 out of the truck. I knew the blacks were right. He would take one of the women or kids if I didn't do something. I put a shot into him just behind the shoulder, a heart shot. Oh! Didn't I enjoy doing it, too! Mongrel bastard! But a funny thing, eh! He slid down into the river and I wasn't so sure I'd got him. But then, later, the tide changed and up he came again, dead, with his jaws wide open. Kept doing this for a couple of days; a big, puffed-up floating thing! Going up and down; up and down with the tide!

A nine foot (three metre) saltwater crocodile, Crocodyllus porosus, basking on a mud bank in the Roper River.

Courtesy Professor Harry Messel, University of Sydney Research Team, 1971

Graham Chung, the copper, said to me, 'You wouldn't credit it, but there's a bloody croc, dead and stinking to high heaven, cruising up and down the river! I'm coming up the river the other day and here the bloody thing is, coming along at me with its jaws open!' So I told Graham what had happened. I said, 'Yeah! It's been up here once or twice, too! It's coming up and down on the tide.' So he said, 'Well, we've got to get rid of the bloody thing out of the river, or do something with it!' So the next time it came up we got a rope on to it and dragged it up on to the bank and burnt it. Graham reckoned it had been coming back to haunt me for my sins!

There'd be times there when you hold up a mob of cattle on the river for a dinner-camp. And you'd hear them bellowing and you'd walk over to the bank to see what was up. And if you'd stand there you'd see a croc. They float up. They hold themselves perfectly level. A croc, he can surface and he can go down without a ripple in the water. The only thing you see is these two big knobby eyes. They stop and hold themselves still.

By Christ, they used to frighten me, those crocodiles! I didn't like taking cattle across those rivers up there. There were only certain places you could cross and your common sense would tell you there would be crocs about, trying to pick up any stragglers. We used to push the cattle hard, to get them across. There was no loitering. And I can tell you I wasn't on the tail of the mob when we hit that river! And if ever our camp was on the river for the night, by gee, there was no way in the world I would go dipping into the river to get cleaned up! I would tie a rope on a bucket and chuck it in and haul in some water and take it up the bank well away from the river's edge as quick as I possibly could. I never gave them any chances.

A friend of mine, George Booth – he was born and brought up in the Gulf near Normanton – he says that the Aborigines can sense when there is a crocodile around, in much the same way as you can sense when there is a thunderstorm building up. They can sense the change. George says one night he was fishing down at the river with a couple of friends, when all of a sudden he got this feeling; a feeling of there being a change in the atmosphere around them. He said to his mates, 'Don't make a noise. Don't say anything. Just roll over quietly into that bit of a gully behind us.' So they did this and they lay there watching. Within a few minutes this old croc poked his head up out of the water just where they had been fishing and where the carbide light was still burning. George reckons that croc swung his head from side to side looking this way and that as much as to say, 'Now, where the hell did those buggers get to!' and then he disappeared again. If George and his mates hadn't moved, that croc would have grabbed one of them.

I have seen cattle that have got themselves bogged going down for a drink that have been grabbed and taken by a croc, but for the most part up there in the Top End, cattle get a bit cunning; they seem to know when there's a croc about. There was one time when I took a semi-load of bulls from Tabletop up to Urapunga – two year old fellas, good breeding stock. And we turned them out into the paddock. Being from Hervey's Range, they didn't know anything about crocs. They were just going into the river, standing up to their brisket, the way cattle do, when they wanted a drink. The crocodiles got most of them.[3]

Georgie Booth's father took a thoroughbred Percheron all the way from Mount Isa to their place on the Gulf intending to breed from it. It no sooner went down to the river for a drink than a croc grabbed it. But horses from the Top End develop some kind of a sixth sense about them. If they know there is a croc around they will be snorting and sniffing and not wanting to go near the water. That was a pretty good indication that a croc was in the area.

Urapunga homestead is approximtely half a mile up the Wilton River from where it junctions into the Roper[4]. One day, a young lad named Jimboy came racing up to the homestead yelling, 'Boss! Boss! You come! That boat! Him bin turn over! You come quick!' There are rocks where the river turns a bit and that was where the boat had capsized. Jimboy was sobbing and telling me, 'All them kids gone! Mother and Father gone! Baby Alastair him die finish!'

The boat had hit the rocks and the force of the current had tipped it over. His mother and father and all his brothers and sisters had gone into the river and the little baby had been washed away. They had all got back to the bank but there was no sign of the baby. So I raced down to the river and there they all were on the bank, screaming and shouting and carrying on; 'Oh! Alastair! Him die finish! Him gone in the water down the river!'

I said to them, 'Well, don't just bloody stand there! Spread out down the river! Run down along the bank! He might have washed up somewhere down there! Keep looking!' We all spread out. I didn't think there was much hope, but we had to do something, even if it was only to find the poor little bugger's body so the crocs didn't get it.

There was a lot of fresh coming down, and, out a bit, there was this big old she-oak washed over in the current. And with the force of the water the boughs were going up and down in the flood, and I looked and there's the baby! Jesus Christ! Here's this little bloke – I don't think he would have been much more than ten to twelve months old – and he's hung up in the branches going up and down with the current! Not hanging on, just lying on it!' I yelled out, 'Here he is! He's here!' I off with my boots and jumped in to try to get to him. But the current was too strong. It grabbed me and washed me down a couple of hundred yards before I could get back to the bank.

I got out and raced back up. The old father, Tommy Mulawai, had got to the spot. He was an old man but he was a pretty good swimmer. He jumped in and after a couple of goes he got to the baby. He grabbed him by the arm and swam back with him. He gets him out on the bank. The little fellow was as good as drowned, but the old man gets him by the legs and shakes him and shakes him, up and down.

I said, 'Hey! Not so rough! You'll end up killing the poor little bugger doing that!' But he kept on shaking him and shaking him and then, all of a sudden, he started bringing up water. And then he starts to squeal. And Old Tommy says, 'Him orright now!' But then he stops squealing and goes all limp again. And Old Tommy says, 'Oh, Poor fella! Him die! Him die pinish!' And he picks him up and starts shaking hell out of him again. All the gins are crying and wailing, and I'm saying to Tommy, 'Hey! Take it easy! You'll bloody kill him!' Anyway, he started breathing properly again and crying away. I tell you! It's the best sound you'll ever hear! And they're all laughing and crying and crowding round and wanting to touch him. And they're hugging him and kissing him. Then they all troop off back up to the camp. And that little fellow survived and he's a grown man now. Old Tommy had about ten kids in all. Urapunga was pretty good breeding territory, not only for cattle!

A 'freshie', a freshwater crocodile in a tidal gully of the Roper. 'Freshies' can be found in both fresh water and salt water reaches of the river. 'Salties', the larger saltwater variety are often found in freshwater sections of the river and in freshwater lagoons across the Top End.

Courtesy Professor Harry Messel, University of Sydney Research Team, 1971

The other big river on Urapunga was the branch of it, the Wilton, which has its headwaters somewhere just below Manigrida. These rivers come down for three hundred miles through Mainoru to junction near Urapunga homestead. By the time they get down to Urapunga they are pretty big, and in the Wet, you get biggest mobs of water coming down.

Having to cross these rivers when you were mustering before the Wet set in could be a bit of a problem. You could get caught and at times we used to have to make a boat to get our gear across. It's an old bush method used by drovers and ringers. I learned how to do it from my father when I was about fourteen or fifteen years old, mustering on the Walsh at Tabletop. You pull your packs off, and you get your camp tarpaulin and double it over. Then you get three pack saddles – sometimes four – and stand one on its end, and three upside down, about the centre of the tarp. You flip it up around the pack-saddles and tie both ends and throw the sides back in over the pack-saddles, which makes it look a bit like a boat or a canoe. You put your packs and your swags and gear in, and you get whatever ropes you've got on the pack-saddles, or halters or surcingles or anything like that, and tie them on at the front. Then one fellow swims across the river and pulls it and the other blokes swim alongside to keep it stable while it's being pulled across.

A horse when he is swimming, his head and shoulders are out, but the rest of him is underwater; he is more or less sticking out of the water from his withers to his neck. You see a bit of his rump but not much. So if you swam the pack-horses with the packs on, everything inside them would get soaking wet. So that's the reason you have got to unpack them and make a boat.

If the current was very strong you would have to be a bit careful but generally you got it across and kept your swag and your tucker dry. Then you swam all your plant across and packed-up again and headed off. Sometimes we would have to do that a couple of times a day, but it was the only means of keeping your swags and tucker dry, so you had to get on with it.[5]

One time, when we were out mustering, three blackfellas and myself got caught on the wrong side of the river. I saw this bad weather coming on so I sent the plant on ahead to make camp but by the time we got the cattle to the river she was running a banker. Oh! She was coming down! And it's coming on night-time and we've got no swags. No tucker. Nothing! Luckily one fellow smoked so we got a fire going, putting big logs on to try to get a bit of warmth. And it drizzly-rained all night. On the second day I thought, 'Bugger this!' and we grabbed a little-fella weaner. All we had between us was a pocket knife but we scruffed him and cut his throat and butchered him. We cut steaks off and slipped into a decent feed and hung what we couldn't eat in the smoke. We didn't know how long we were going to be stuck there. No such things as helicopters in those days!

By gee! When that river dropped after about four days didn't we move! We had to take those cattle way up the river and get them on a big bend and push them in hard to swim them across. By God! Wasn't I glad to see the other side! And if you asked me if I was worried about crocs when we were doing all this, I can tell you, 'Too bloody right! Worried about them all the time!' And when you are crossing cattle, even when we were out mustering, you push the mob in, and get in after them quick in case there's a croc waiting for the last man or the last beast! I got over those rivers as quick as I could. I hate the bastards!

One time, I got this message from Graham Chung over at Roper Bar. He said, 'How are you off for tucker?' I said, 'Oh, all right. Enough to get me through the Wet.' 'Well, I'm glad to hear it,' Graham says, 'Because I've had this call for help from up the Neimann River there. Birdie Timms has run out of supplies and she's got nothing to feed the children.'

This woman's husband used to go away every Wet. He'd leave her there at the station, her and the kids, and go up to Darwin. He reckoned he was involved in trying to get the export cattle market up and running. But every year he pulled the same stunt! I've never struck such a mongrel bloody act! He seemed to think he was one of these film-bloody-stars; leaving a woman and kids on their own like that. No supplies got in for them. Nothing!

So Graham brings the police boat round to Urapunga and we load it up with everything we think a family might need, and we head off down the river. We turn south along the coast and pass the Cox. Then we try and pick up the mouth of the Neimann. Rain and mist. Can't see a thing! What with fog and the bloody rain, and Graham being about as much of a sailor as I was. All we knew was how to start the outboard.

There are a lot of little creeks along that part of the coast, and the Neimann's not very big. We nudge into some of them, and I say to Graham, 'I don't think we're in the Neimann, Mate.' We'd go a bit further and turn round and come back. We're cold and wet so we get these body-bags – the police always have them – and we get inside one each; cut a couple of holes for the arms and feet. You zip yourself up. They keep you dry!

Eventually we found our way up the river and we came to the Archers; four rocky knobs all exactly the same-looking. Leichhardt named them after the Archer Brothers in Queensland who'd given him some backing for his expedition.[6] A crocodile-infested looking place! Pandanus hanging right out over. We're pushing through. And it's drizzly bloody rain and getting dark. But we got to their landing and there's the lady from the homestead and the kids waiting. The boy, he'd have been about twelve and the little girl about eight. And all they've got to carry everything is a bloody old wheelbarrow! Her husband would have taken the only reliable vehicle away! So Graham and I man-handle all this stuff up to the homestead; drums of flour, tea, sugar; dehydrated vegetables, a drum of powdered milk, all on our shoulders. All the stuff to keep that family going through the Wet.

We had to do that same thing more than just the one year! That mongrel used to go to Darwin for three or four months at a time leaving his wife and kids like that! He'd tell his wife, 'I'll be back! I won't be gone long!' And, poor little woman! She'd believe him! After the third time Graham Chung said to me, 'If I don't go to Darwin and grab that bastard and give him the greatest-ever talking to! I'll have him that way he won't be wanting to pull this stunt again!'

The river was full of fish. At first we used to pay for a tag and we were allowed to net our own, just for personal use. You get two tides a day in those rivers. It was all fresh water where we were, but the tide used to back the fresh up for about forty mile. We'd go down on the incoming tide and stretch a net across, and when the tide dropped, pull her out. You'd get five or six big barramundi every time. Later Fisheries closed the river as far as Roper Bar for netting. But there were always plenty of fish for line fishing. Harry Messel was dead set against any more fishing in the Roper. He reckoned it would wipe the entire barra' population out. He wanted a complete stop put to it.

After one wet season, up on the top boundary between us and Mainoru – after the floods of course, there was plenty of fencing to do – this blackfella was sent to fix up the fence on one of the holding paddocks. But after a while he turned up back again. The head stockman said to him, 'What the hell are you doing back? Aren't you supposed to be fencing?' 'Oh, yeah, Boss!' he reckoned, 'But I got big-fella fish!' The head stockman said to him, 'You're not supposed to be bloody fishing! You're supposed to be fencing!' The blackfella said, 'You get that Toyota and you come! You see this big-fella fish!' So they get in the Toyota and they are driving down, and the head stockman says, 'By Christ! This will want to be a bloody big fish!'

But when they got there, here was this bloody great barramundi! A hell of a size! They weighed it later back at the station and it was eighty-four pound! That's heavier than a bag of sugar!

The blackfella said that what happened was that he was working away and he heard this noise, flop, flop, flop. He told them, 'By Crise! I proper fright! I think him crocodile coming get me! And I look around, and this proper-big bloody fish

The Sydney University Research Team tagged each of the salt water crocodiles they trapped with a solar-powered tracking device. Ray says "Once it was attached to him, wouldn't there be some fun getting him back into the river! The best way was just to stand well clear and let him go for it."

Courtesy Professor Harry Messel, University of Sydney Research Team, 1971 coming down!' The barra' was coming down over the rapids where the water was very shallow, working its way down. He reckoned, 'So I got that crow-bar and I spear him!'

That barramundi was taken back to Mainoru homestead and put in the cold-room. It was the biggest barramundi anybody had ever seen! They've got photos of it hanging on the wall; 'World's biggest barramundi. Speared with a crowbar.'

A big prawning concern built a base with a refrigeration plant at the mouth of the Roper, where it widens out into the Gulf. The trawlers used to come in there to unload. The prawns were freighted south by road to Perth. A chap by the name of Deiter Januska – he was from Czechslovakia originally – took on the job of managing the place. He had been a crocodile shooter before but he was also a trained refrigeration engineer so he was the ideal man for the job. But the company found that for months on end no trucks could get through because of the Wet. So they closed the base and built a big barge called the *Roper K* which used to go out and pick up the catch from the vessels that were working out in the Gulf.

Like Urapunga, the prawning boats were connected to VJY Darwin, Outback Radio, and I would get calls from them at times – I didn't know these people personally but we got to know each other by name. And being at sea and living on fish all the time they used to get hungry for beef. So they would call me up and ask if I could swap a side of beef for prawns and bugs – Moreton Bay bugs – a seafood delicacy, and fish. There was no money exchanged. The *Roper K* would come up the river to the landing where there was a bit of a log wharf which used to get washed away every Wet. Big refrigerator trucks from Perth would back down to the landing. They had a crane to lift the boxes out on to a conveyor belt straight into the trucks. When they opened the hatches the cold blast would condense like smoke and you would think the whole boat was on fire. I would hand the beef over to them to put in their freezers and they would hand me over the seafood. We had so much that after a while I got that way I couldn't look a prawn in the face!

During the Wet, blokes that used to work at Port Roper down at the mouth of the river would come up to Roper Bar. There were some very nice fellows among them, but for the most part you could say they were mostly the alcoholic type. They would come up to Urapunga and say to me, 'Any chance of sitting-down here, until the fishing season starts?' And I would say, 'Yeah. Righto. But I'm not paying you anything! If you want to come and camp here and give me a bit of a hand around the place, well, you're very welcome!'

And one night, just on dark, one of these fellows came to me and he said, 'Which one of them lubras up the camp could you recommend?'

Well, didn't I up him! I told him to get to hell! I told him straight, 'Look! They are decent people and they have strict laws! If you go bloody sneaking round up up the camp you could end up with a spear in your back or a knife in your guts! And good enough, too! Now get your gear and clear out of here before I put my boot up your backside! That will take your mind off that caper for a bloody long time to come!'

One time, one of the young Aboriginal women up in the camp was in childbirth with a baby and it was in breech position and she couldn't deliver it. The old women came down to the homestead and told me,

'That young gin, she close-up die-finish!' They didn't want anything more to do with it. Aboriginals are pretty down to earth about death. If an old person is about to die or if someone is sick with a fever and looking a bit dicey, they think nothing of moving them out of the camp and taking them out bush and letting them get on with it. They'll sit back a little way and wait until it's all over. They don't want anyone to die around the huts. It brings bad spirits around. And they will never live in a place once someone has died in it. No way! So these old women had washed their hands of the whole thing. The girl was going to die and that was that. They just wanted to see the back of her.

Well, I knew nothing about delivering babies so I thought I would get her down the river to Roper River Mission. I had a twenty-one footer but the motor was out of commission so I got on to Graham Chung over at Roper Bar Police Station, and he brought the police boat around. It wasn't big enough to accommodate the stretcher but I had a ten foot dinghy. So we put the stretcher on to it and lashed it securely and rigged up a bit of shade over this poor girl. She was moaning and then she would lie still for a while and we would think, 'Well! That's it! She's had it!' She was pretty well all in.

We started to tow her down the river, but with the motor of the police-boat churning up the water the dinghy started yawing from side to side. And she started screaming. And I'm thinking, 'Oh, my God! What can we do!' I was no doctor and nor was Graham. All I knew about was calves and foals, but I had pretty good knowledge about them. That was the extent of my midwifery! Graham said, 'All I know about delivering babies is to get them out as quick as you can!' So we did what we could. So we're going down the river like this, twenty miles! Before we could get to the mission the baby started to come and she had it right there in the boat. I took off my shirt and wrapped it round it and put it on her chest. It was still hanging by the cord! And talk about blood and guts! A terrible sight! What worried me was that it might have been choking or not able to breathe, or something like that. But, God! When you think of it, nature is marvellous, isn't it!

When we got to the mission I jumped out of the boat. There were some young kids hanging about at the landing, and they were looking, looking! I'm yelling at them, 'Go and get Sister Brooker! Get Sister Brooker! Quick!' And they were saying, 'Who that? Who that lady?' and one started strolling up the road. I thought, 'Jesus!' So I raced up the road myself straight into the hospital. I said, 'Quick, Edna! Quick! We've got a girl down here; she's just given birth! We've got her in the boat!' So poor old Edna and I, we're running down the road and the other sister's following along behind with towels and medical gear.

After that I just stood back and let the sisters get on with it. Graham and I carried the stretcher up to the mission and took her into the hospital ward. Then didn't a big run-around start!

We went out to the kitchen and got a cup of tea .Which we needed! Later on Edna came and told us that the mother and baby were both doing well. Graham and I shook hands on it. We reckoned we'd made a decent fist of bringing that baby into the world. No worries, Mate! There was nothing to it!

1 The 'saltie' is the large salt water species, Crocodyllus porosus; the 'freshie' the smaller, freshwater Crocodyllus johnstoni. 'Freshies' can live in salt water, and previously smaller numbers of them sighted in the salt water environment were possibly the result of the former larger population of the more aggressive C. porosus.

2 Searcy, Alfred, *Adventures Ashore and Afloat*, George Robertson and Co., Melbourne, 1911, quoted in Messel, H, et al, *Surveys of Tidal River Systems*, Monograph 12, Pergamon Press, 1980.

'It must have been midnight when we were all startled out of sleep by a heart-rending cry. For a moment we were silent, dazed with fear.Then someone asked, 'What was that?' One of the men forward, noticing a blanket hanging over the side, looked closer, and cried, 'Good God! Salim has gone!' Glancing over the side we saw that the water was greatly agitated and at the same instant, up through its swirling, glittering surface shot our comrade as far as his waist. He gave an appealing cry, his eyes glittering with terror; then, throwing up his hands, uttered a blood-curdling scream – the anguish of death – and was seen no more. The tragedy had taken less than a minute's time. Silenced with horror, we stared at the fatal spot. In his sleep, the poor fellow must have thrown one of his legs over the side of the boat, which had been seized by the alligator, and by it he had been dragged into the river.'

3 Almost a century earlier the Durack party overlanding cattle to the Ord River had a similar experience of crocodiles, which at that time were known as 'alligators'. Durack, *Mary Kings in Grass Castles* p.241 "Four horses had been taken on the Robinson and while camped on the Limmen several beasts, wading deep as cattle love to do, had been taken. One cow managed to shake herself free and struggle out, badly torn by teeth and claws, and was afterwards affectionately known as 'the alligator cow'.

4 Leichhardt, Ludwig. p449. *Journal of an Overland Expedition in Australia*. About four or five miles from the last creek, which I shall call Hodgson's Creek in honour of Pemberton Hodgson, esq. – the river divided into two almost equal branches, one coming from the northward and the other from the north-west by west. I named the river from the northward the Wilton in honour of Rev. Mr. Wilton of Newcastle, who kindly favoured my expedition. About three miles above the junction of the Wilton with the Roper, we again encamped on the banks of the latter, at a spot which I thought would allow our horses and cattle to approach in safety. One unfortunate animal, however, slipped into the water and every effort to get him out was in vain. I watched by him the whole night . At high water we succeeded in getting him out but he began to plunge again and fell back into the river. I found a tolerable landing place about fifty yards higher up; but as I was swimming him up to it he became tangled in the tether rope, rolled over and drowned.'

5 Byerly, Frederick.(Ed.) *The complete Jardine Expedition Journals*, page 102. 'A raft was made with a hide capable of carrying 400 lbs. weight. It answered admirably and everything was ferried over in safety, till the last cargo, which nearly cost the life of one of the party, Cowerly, who being unable to swim, had to be taken across holding on to the raft, and was therefore left to the last. All went well until within 30 yards of the bank, when, whether from trepidation induced by visions of alligators, or from an attempt to strike out independently, he succeeded in upsetting and sinking the raft, which was with some difficulty, got to the shore.'

6 Leichhardt, Ludwig. *Journal of an Overland Expedition in Australia*. p.433. Oct. 13th. '...following the river and heading several salt water creeks prolonged our journey very much and rendered our travelling difficult and fatiguing. High rocky hills formed deep declivities into the river. We had to ascend them and travel along their summits. To the southward were four remarkable flat-topped cones of sandstone, which appeared like a plateau cut into four detached masses. These I called the 'Four Archers' in memory of my excellent hosts, Messrs. David, Charles, John and Thomas Archer, of Moreton Bay.' Charles Archer was later to discover the Fitzroy River upon which Rockhampton stands today.

eleven...

'MUSTERED, BRANDED AND TESTED'

The B.T.E.C. Scheme; The Cattle Crash; The Abattoir; Pleuro.

During the war years Urapunga was owned by a chap named Jimmy Gibbs. He came on to the place after the Rogers family. Jimmy used to see a lot of a mounted mob, the North Australian Observer Unit, known as the Nackeroos. They were along the same lines as the New Guinea Coast Watchers. Their job was to keep an eye open for anything that might be coming in on our coast.

I used to get visits from some of these old Nackeroos, quite elderly by then. They would turn up at home to look around for their old camps. I'd take them out to look for them. We would climb up a hillside and see a pile of rocks where they'd had an observation post, just a few rocks thrown together up in the hills that they had made for a bit of a defence. They were pretty rough old camps! Some of the Urapunga Aboriginals had been with the Nackeroos and were glad to see them turn up again. All these old blokes would be shaking hands and laughing and remembering the war years.

A good mate of mine, Rob Whelan, from outside Pentland, was in the Territory during the war, with the Second Fourth Independent Company, something along the lines of commandos, except that Independents were larger units.

Rob is the quiet type, but he can make you laugh! When his group finished their training they were convoyed straight through to the Territory. The heat was so intense that the trucks were vaporizing so when they got to Banka Banka they pulled into the staging camp there. It was midday and they were given two bottles of beer each. One was hot and one was cold. Rob reckons the hot one was just as good as the cold one.

At Katherine they pulled up and made camp just down from the Low Level. There was very little food available for the army because Darwin had just been bombed. They had seen civilians heading south, at Elliot. They were issued with a bit of bully and biscuits, and Rob and his mates are thinking, 'What! And this is cattle county!' They decided, well, there were plenty of cattle tracks about, and where there were cattle tracks there must be cattle, and they'd knock off a killer, so away they went. They couldn't find the mob and when they got back to camp they were in strife because they hadn't let the lieutenant know what they were up to. Next they're up before the Company Commander because he hadn't been told either. But next thing they're called back up again. The lieutenant says, 'Right! Here's your orders! You chaps go and find a killer.'

So out they go and they find a mob and they think, 'Well! Three hundred blokes. That's a lot! We won't have one killer. We'll have two!' and they knock over a couple of bullocks. They butcher them and take the meat back to camp. The sergeant-cook says to them, 'Where's the bloody undercut?'

And Rob says to him, 'Undercut, Serg. What's that?' The sergeant says to him, 'You bloody drongo! It's here! Just under the ribs!' And Rob says to him, 'Oh, Gee, Serg. I don't know much about that kind of thing. I'm afraid that bit might have got thrown out with the carcass.' But that night their section had the best ever feed down on the river bank!

Rob's Independents were spread right across the Territory from the mouth of the Roper to the Victoria River. Later they were sent up to the islands and Rob subsequently won the Military Medal. A very fine man, Rob Whelan. He is the great, great grandson of Sir William Hann who formed Maryvale station in the 1870s.

At one stage I was advised by the army that I would be getting a visit from one of their officers and could I help him in any way possible. The chap that turned up was Les Hiddins, 'Bush Tucker Man', on television. Les told me that his orders were to examine the area and learn what he could about bush tucker and survival skills to teach stranded air-crews and army-patrols. Les spent a fair bit of time with me there on Urapunga, throwing his swag on the verandah, and more or less making it his base.We were always pleased to see him. He was a terrific fellow and got on well with everybody. I introduced him to some of the old ladies – they were the experts on bush tucker – and they'd climb into Les's Land Rover and away they'd go out bush.

They showed him how to poison fish in the waterholes with certain leaves off a shrub they called 'fish-poison bush'. You find it around billabongs and gilgais; a green bush, not much more than six or eight feet. They'd rub the leaves between their hands and throw them in the water. Next thing, all these little fish about an inch and a half to two inches start coming up gasping. The women wade in and scoop them up and throw them on the coals to cook. They scrunch them up bones and all. 'Fish-poison' leaves don't actually poison the water; just take the oxygen out of it. That's what brings the fish to the surface.

They showed Les how to wade in and grab freshwater turtles and cook them in their shells on the coals. Les said he couldn't hack cooking them alive the way the old women did; he would try to put the poor little buggers out of their misery first. They showed him how to dive for water-lily roots and to roast them, and grind them into flour. And how to feel around under the rocks to catch tcherapin.

They taught him that the seeds of the pandanus are edible and that, at a push you can chew the fleshy part at the base of the leaf, also how to suck paper-bark and grevillea flowers for honey. They showed him how to spot bush-potatoes and bush-onions and how to dig out sand-goannas. The valleys up along the Roper were like a supermarket for bush tucker if you knew where to look. Back last century, when Leichhardt's expedition was going through, and they were getting light on for tucker, they watched what the blacks ate and copied them.[1] In his journal Leichhardt often mentions the well-worn foot-tracks his expedition came across leading to lagoons and billabongs, and the middens of mussel shells they saw.

Those old ladies knew about 'bush soap'. There's a black wattle that gets bunches of soft browny beans. If you get them and wet them and rub them between your hands they froth up like frog-spawn. I've used it myself.

Another bush food is the bark of the chidwood tree. They bash the bark off with the back of an axe and underneath there's a stringy substance. They dig in with their fingernails and strip it up, then chew it. But what I can't understand is how the hell the blacks know all this? It must have taken thousands of years for them to work it out.

So the old ladies shared all their bush knowledge with Les. Every morning they would all pile into his vehicle, all laughing and yak-ai-ing out to one another, and away they would go. They loved Les and loved spending time out bush with him. Les gets on well with everyone and he had the happy knack of getting on with the old people of Urapunga as though he was one of them, like a long lost son. He would squat down on his hunkas and share the food they'd cook up on the coals and really relish it. You'd never see a fellow smack his lips like that man over a bloody witchetty-grub! Les is one of those blokes who can make people feel they matter. He's got a way of making them feel that what they have to say is important. Les made it plain to these old people that when they were out bush they were the boss of it all and he was doing all the learning. It made them feel pretty good about themselves. But I reckon it was the hat that got them in!

After this Les started bringing groups of chopper crews and air-crew to Urapunga for survival training. They were flown in and they stayed at the homestead long enough to get the feel of the place and have some basic lectures. Then they were taken out bush and dropped off at a billabong or a creek and had to spend up to about a week surviving on what they could scrounge up for themselves. Each man was issued with a pack of cards with photos of the different sorts of bush tucker that could be eaten and what to avoid, the 'cheeky-fella' ones. Over the years we saw quite a bit of Les. Besides these official trips he used to turn up once in a while to get in a bit of fishing. It was always good to see him. He and I became good mates.

I was just starting to make a go of things when the cattle crash of the early seventies hit us. The main cause of it was America and the Argentine undercutting our prices. They were selling to countries that had been our markets at low rates we couldn't compete with. Our beef used to go in cartons to a big American company in Chicago, International Packers. They dropped our prices so low that you could hardly make a living. We were lucky to get fifty dollars a head for a beast whereas before the crash we had been getting anything from $200 to $250. But you had no alternative but to keep selling. Some money was better than no money. And then the Katherine meatworks closed!

Katherine had been our outlet after we stopped walking the cattle through to Elliot. When Katherine shut down the only thing we could do was to pay big freight to truck them south. You were worrying whether you were going to make anything out of them at all. At night I'd be lying there wondering what the hell I could do; thinking, 'Christ! Will I ever get my head above water!' Then I'd remember my Dad and Mother and the hard times they had. They never had a pot of cash when they started off at Tabletop. Dad would do a bit of droving and with the money he would put in some more fencing or add another room on to the house or some other improvement, and gradually he worked the property up. And I don't think there was a happier couple than Dad and Mother; or a happier family.

So I knew I just had to keep on. A chap by the name of Robert Bright started up a small abattoir, Meneling Meatworks, at Bachelor, south of Darwin. I used to sell bulls to him. He would pay us about $50 to $70 dollars a head, but it cost me twenty dollars a head to get them there. So that was another knock. There wasn't much money coming in at all.

But you had to sell so I had to get them to another meatworks. I started trucking by road-train to Cape River meatworks outside Charters Towers. After I had paid the freight and a commission to the stock agent I ended up getting $10 a head. Which never even paid my mustering costs!

So I decided to take my cattle across to Wyndham. I'd leave home about four in the afternoon and get into Mataranka that night. An hour and a half up to Katherine and then refuel. That was one hundred and eighty-seven miles. Drive through the night across to Wyndham, three hundred and sixty miles, and get there about ten o'clock next day. And if there was ever such a thing as being tired! I'd pull up, get out and check the cattle, walk down the road a bit and turn round and run back. I always had a tank of water on the side and I'd get some and throw it over my head and give my face a sluice. And I'd open the windows – even though it was hot air blowing on my face. But if I ever found myself getting drowsy, cattle or not I would pull over and might have half an hour or an hour's camp. The cattle would stand steady. I'd get to Wynham, unload, have a shower at the meatworks and a bit of a camp, then turn round and head off home. I'd drive through the night to Katherine. I always had my swag with me and I'd have a camp at Katherine and then head the hundred and eighty miles home. A three days round trip; eleven hundred miles. It was the only way to get a bit of money coming in. I could take twenty-two bullocks, or twenty cows and I would get around $150 a head for them, so that was $3000. It used to cost about $500 for diesel.

Then I decided to tender to the Department of Works for a contract to put in grids on the main roads. I had the moulds, board-frames that you bolt together and pour the concrete in, from when I had put the grids in on Urapunga. I bought a back-hoe for the job. I had another bloke helping me, a friend of mine, a bloke named Eddie Clark. He had been an electrical contractor and he used to come into the Roper area to do maintenance for the Aboriginal Welfare Department.

He'd always stayed with us. Eddie said to me one time, 'You know, I'm fed up with crawling around in ceilings putting in wiring. The heat really knocks you! I'd like to get out and do something else for a bit of a change.' So I said to him, 'Well, chuck your job in and come and work with me!' We put in grids down as far as the Murranji station turn-off at Newcastle Waters, out along the Roper Highway, and down Malapunya way. We also got contracts dam-sinking and fencing. It was money to keep us in food and a bob in our pockets but there was nothing in it to keep on with maintenance on the property.

Another thing that helped me to get through the cattle crash was a slate mine I opened up at the top end of the Wilton valley. A Chinese chap, Ernie Chin, a very good friend of mine, came to me and he said, 'I tell you what; you go into Katherine and peg that slate lease out. If you don't, I will! There's money in that slate.' So I pegged it out and that slate mine helped to keep the place going during the recession and kept the tucker-bag full!

I had a partner in it because I couldn't see my way clear to be doing it on my own. We employed two fellows. I bought an old second-hand excavator and loader and put a fair sort of a road in. We had to be able to get semis in to get a loading out. There is a lot of slate in that area. The table we had on the verandah at home was one example, sixteen foot long and four foot wide; so smooth that people used to think it had been polished. I used to say to them that I would give it to anyone who could lift it! That's the size we used to try to mine for. We'd sell a piece like that for $200.

The Queen's adviser on building and architecture, Lord McAlpine, heard about this slate and he came over and talked to me about it. He said, 'Yeah. I'll take twenty ton a time.' He was in the process of setting up a tourist complex in Broome, and everything he built there was done with slate from Urapunga; hundreds of tons of it. He was the best customer we ever had. You would get an order from him in the mail for so many tons and the cheque would come with the order! Even before you had the bloody stuff loaded on the truck! The greatest Pom I ever met!

You had to think on your feet to survive the cattle crash. Old Stan told me that during the crash of the 'thirties when he was helping muster on Nicholson they were bringing cattle across the river. The head stockman had a .303 and he was blowing the bulls out one after another as they were coming up out of the water, they had so little value.

There was one old fellow up in the Top End. He wasn't getting anything for his cattle, so he went to the bank and talked it over with the accountant; said he had an idea to go in for the tourist side of things; put some weekender accommodation on his dam where the people could come out from Darwin to do a bit of swimming and fishing. And things started looking up; a bit of money started coming in and he's sitting back in the traces enjoying a bit of cash-flow for a change.

Then one day he thinks to himself, 'Suppose a bloke ought to go up to that dam of mine and make sure she's holding.' So he grabs his hat and whistles his dog and jumps in his old ute. And he drives up into the hills. He gets there and he can see all these young women in the water swimming and none of them has got a stitch on. They spot him and they swim out to the middle of the dam and start yelling; 'Go away, you horrible old man! If you've come up here to perv on us you're out of luck! We're not coming out of the water until you push off! So go away!'

And this old bloke, he pushes his hat back on his head a bit, and gives his backside a bit of a scratch, and looks thoughtful. He chews on his baccy for a bit. Then he calls out to them, 'Aw! That's alright, Ladies. Don't you worry about that! I didn't come up here to look at you lot swimming in the nuddy. I only come up here to feed me crocodiles!'

I always felt that the crash would end and that things would come good, and eventually they did. I started getting on my feet again. Though they reckon it got that way that there were these two blackfellas drinking in the bar in Katherine. Two cattle men come in and one of the blackfellas says to the other, 'Come on, Mate! Drink up and let's get out of here before these two bastards start putting the bite on us!' That would have been about the size of it at the time, too!

I was running seven thousand head of cattle on Urapunga at this stage. The Territory is good breeding country, but we never got what you would call really fat bullocks. You can't fatten a beast there in a short time. If you want fats you can't beat that Inland Mitchell grass – or Downs Mitchell, some call it – that you get further south from us. It's got the protein cattle need to fatten. But, none the less, some of those old piker fellas, six or seven years old, that had been hiding out in the gullies and back country till we caught up with them, they had a bit of condition. They were fat.

When I first went there, there were more scrubbers than controlled cattle, until I put in decent paddocks. Then in the late 'seventies the B.T.E.C. Scheme was brought in to eliminate brucellosis and bovine tuberculosis. Anything that wasn't in a controlled paddock had to be shot to stop the spread. They used to come out with helicopters –'gasoline cowboys' we used to call them – and they would fly round with a case of ammunition and blast out everything they could, bulls, cows with calves, anything they saw outside of the controlled area. We got about seventy dollars a head compensation. I'd go out with them at times to shoot a few brumbies. Because I had put in a lot of fences the upshot of it was that Urapunga was declared T.B. and brucellosis free and given a licence.

To get a clearance for T.B. you had to have everything mustered, branded and tested; kill a certain number and take blood samples. The stock inspector would come out from Katherine and he'd take samples of every beast we killed back into Katherine to be tested. So we killed regularly, twenty beasts from here, twenty from there, all round the property until finally we got a full clearance. Once we had that clearance it meant we could start selling cattle down south. I was trucking away about six or seven hundred head a year; in double-decker road-trains. It is unprofitable for trucking-companies to run single-deckers; it costs no more on fuel for a prime-mover to pull double-deckers. On the days when the road-train came in everyone from the camp would be at the yards to watch. It was a big occasion.

And one time up at Gunn Point, outside Darwin, I'd seen this abattoir and thought to myself, 'They seem to be doing alright. I wouldn't mind having a go at something along those lines.' I thought I might be able to sell direct to the interstate market. I was told to go down to Peter Severin's place outside Alice Springs to see how his was built. It seemed to be suitable to what I had in mind so I got the plans and started work.

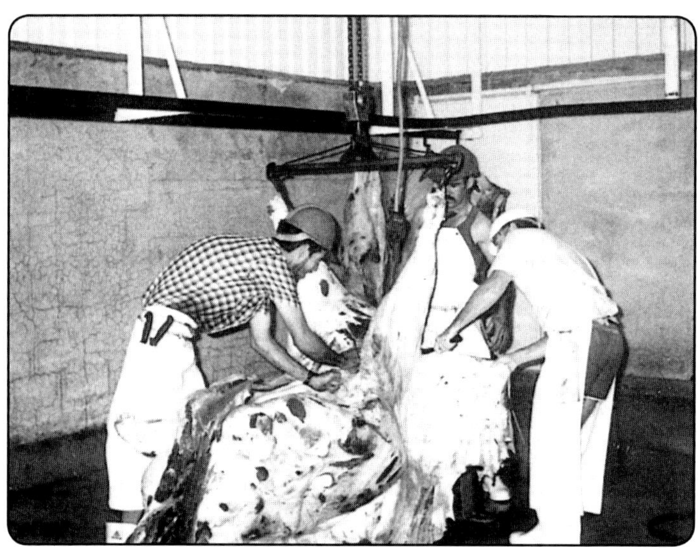

Slaughtermen skinning a carcass in the abattoir at Urapunga.

We built it all out of cement blocks, high, with a ramp for the cattle to come up. There was a knocking-box where they were all brain-shot individually. We might kill ten one day, twenty another day. Once they were shot and fallen there was a trap-door and the carcass would come on to a rack. If they hit the floor they were condemned. There was an electric winch which ran along on a high steel beam. A chain went around the leg of the carcass and it was hoisted until it was properly bled. We might do them in batches of two or three and just keep them hanging there and bring one along on the pulley as we wanted it. From there they were gutted and skinned and quartered with an electric saw, then put into a chiller for twenty-four hours. The meat was then boned and packed into cartons which were snap-frozen ready to be trucked south.

It cost me a fair bit to get all this built; about $80,000 to $100,000. All the equipment had to be top quality; refrigeration plant, tiled surfaces on the walls, stainless steel work benches, hot and cold water, fans. It had to be up to Northern Territory Health and Safety standards. The surrounding area had to be kept grassed and watered for dust control. In the end it worked out to be profitable, but a hell of a lot of work to cover the outlay. I employed a slaughterman and a boner and a couple of

Brunette Downs cattle feeding on the carcass of dead beast, a cause of the disease botulism.

what they call slushies who used to do a bit of skinning, and wash the floor and clean up. They were good blokes. I got them by word of mouth and some of them would come back year after year. Our season lasted from about May to October. I had to build accommodation for them on the place, of course.

The abattoir was a half a mile away on the western side of the homestead, down-wind from the prevailing easterly. All the gut and offal was carted away in a trailer and dumped into a pit and covered. D.C.A, the Department of Civil Aviation, wouldn't allow us to burn it because the smoke would have attracted too many hawks over our airstrip. The offal had to be covered every day. The blood and water was pumped out with sludge pumps through a big poly-pipe into a fenced-off area on the flat. The green grass that grew there was fed to the horses. There was no value in hides so they all went into the pit as well. I offered the hides to a company in Darwin. I said I didn't want anything for them, that they could just come down and take them. But they told me there was no money in it.

I was licensed to sell anywhere down south; New South Wales, South Australia, Victoria. The refrigerator trucks used to come in and leave a wagon. I had a blast freezer and I'd pack this Fridgmobile truck and send it and they'd back-load a freezerful of goods for Darwin and then on the way back they would come out and drop the empty off for us. I'd have the spare truck packed and ready and away they'd go. We kept this up, killing up to twenty or thirty a day, all through the season. But once the Roper came down at the beginning of the Wet we'd have to stop. Then, it was a matter of waiting until the trucks could get in and out again the following April.

In my early days at Urapunga we had to maintain a constant programme of inoculation against pleuro. I was aware of it from early on, because even at Tabletop we always had to be on the look-out for it. The Gulf used to be very bad for pleuro pneumonia, and a lot of store cattle used to be brought down from places like Vanrop and Miranda, to Dotswood, which Tabletop bordered, and with us being on the stock route, we had to be very wary that we kept it out of our herds.

If you found a sick beast you shot him. You didn't bleed him in the normal way that you do when you are killing for beef. You would skin back the hide and cut the ribs back to get at the lungs. This was so that you could collect the virus that was needed for the inoculation programme. You had to be very careful not to get blood mixed in with it or it would send the virus off. You would be as careful as you could and bail it out with a pannikin. Then this fluid was used for inoculating the herd.

The method we used was called 'needle and seton'. The needle was something like a large packing needle with a flattened point with a groove in it. And for the 'seton' part, you cut up pieces of wool about an inch long. You soaked them in this virus, hooked them up and poked them into your needle. Then you separated the hair on the tail of the beast and shoved the needle with the 'seton' in. That gave him a slight dose of the pleuro, which gave him immunity.

There would be times when as a result of doing this the tail of the beast would start to rot. You could always tell which ones were affected. The tail would be dead-looking and hanging down. Sometimes it would be a bit screwed up, like a possom tail. I have seen tails like that rot right off where they go up into the rump. What you did then, if you had them in the yard – or if you were out bush you would throw them – you got your pocket knife, and you kept digging it into the tail until you've got good fresh blood coming out. You took the tail off; generally at the next joint above where the fresh blood had showed. You cut all the rotten stuff away. Later on you would see all these old stumpy-tailed things getting along in the mob. It didn't seem to affect them much, though it didn't leave them much to switch the flies away with! Today you seldom seem to hear of pleuropneumonia. The inoculation programme seems to have it wiped right out.

Another disease you have to watch out for right across the north is botulism. Cattle get it from eating the carcasses of cattle that have died. It tends to happen in a very poor season. Once it seemed to be a disease that was confined to coastal country, but I have seen it right up through the Barkly, through Anthony's and Walhallow and Brunette – all through there – cattle with hunks of gut and hide hanging out of their mouths. You will see them standing around a dead beast chewing away and when you disturb them they run away with a bit of hide hanging out of their mouth! As soon as the carcass bursts they will eat it; eat the flesh and chew the bones. Or you'll see one with its mouth open like a shark with a bit of bone jammed in its throat. If you don't get it out they starve to death. We used to pull them down and get a bit of wire or rope and hook it round the bone. Then if you tie it to a post or a tree, it will jerk the bone out with its own weight. Botulism bacteria lives in anything rotten; rotten hay, or stinking horse-troughs. If I find a dead beast I drag up a heap of dry timber and chuck it over it and burn it. These days you can inoculate against botulism with a once-a-year shot. I usually give it in the loose part between the shoulder and the neck. But burning any dead carcasses you see is the best way to control it.

At one time a fellow that was living at Urapunga for a while was Rod Ansell, a bit of a character. He was down the Daly River in a flood once and his boat sank and he was up a tree for about six days, crocs all round watching him, until a chap by the name of Luke McCall rescued him. Rod and his wife Joanne had a place called Melaleukah out on the Arnhem Highway. They used to fly into Urapunga to refuel so we got to know them fairly well. During the BTEC Scheme the authorities shot all Rod's cattle out and paid him $70 a head compo for them, which sent him broke. The bank foreclosed and he was told to get off his place, which turned him into a bit of an outlaw. He went up to Darwin and got involved in a shoot-out with the coppers near Noonamah. He and one of the cops were killed.They made a film about Rod called *Crocodile Dundee*.

Ray (at right) and Dr. (now Professor) Gordon Grigg on the airstrip at Urapunga.

We used to have a lot of visits from religious groups. The Salvation Army padre, Major Vic Petersen, used to fly an old Auster. He was always having problems with the thing. He'd land somewhere way off the beaten track with the motor cutting out or some other difficulty but he was never discouraged. He'd take it all in his stride.We'd put some fuel in his tank and off he would go again! Once he ran out of fuel coming into Katherine and tried to land on the main road. He hit the table-drain and smashed himself up pretty badly. Wrote the old Auster off, too!

Then the Catholic priest would turn up or the Anglican Bishop. They were all very friendly. One night the Australian Inland Mission padre was showing films. He used to bring this heavy old projector and stand it up on a table out on the lawn. For the screen we'd hang a sheet across on a heavy wire. All the blacks would come down from the camp. They'd bring their pillows and blankets and make a little camp for themselves out on the lawn to watch the movies, some religious ones, some documentary ones. One night in the middle of this, along came a snake, a big fellow, about six or seven foot long. Straight from nowhere right through the crowd! Well! Wasn't there a scatter on! Gins and kids going in all directions, screaming. But then some of the men got after it and killed it. After that they all settled down again as though nothing had happened and 'Hilary Conquers Mount Everest' and 'The Snowy River Scheme' could get going again.

When Aboriginals got the right to vote in the 'fifties we started getting visits from politicians of every creed and colour. They'd fly in and walk up to the camp and go into the school and say good-day to the kids. One bloke sent out cartons and cartons of potato chips to be handed out to the camp as they came in to vote. And another one was telling them, 'Now that Mr. So-and-So. Him very nice fella. But me very nice fellow too. So I tell you what. You give him two-fella vote! You give me one-fella vote. You put numba two next name bilong him. You put numba one next name bilong me. Orright?' The camp didn't have much idea what was going on. It was all 'bull-shit nuthin' as far as they were concerned.

One old girl lines up in the queue on voting day. The official is looking up the names in the book, and he says, 'No, I can't find your name.You mustn't be on the roll.' He is trying to be really helpful, and he says, 'Your name is not on the paper. Are you sure you been vote before?' And she tells him, 'Ah, Crise! Cause me bin bote! Me bin bote down that river long Roper Mission! Come back long bote too.'

The following election they sent a team who handled it better. They had worked out a system of photos of all the candidates, and they gave each Aborigine a stick as they came up. They would say to them, 'Now, which man you want? You show me. You point.' And the Aborigine would poke the stick on to the one he liked the look of. And the official would say, 'That is Mr. So-and-so. Is that the man you want?' And the Aborigine would say, 'Yair. That my man.' This became known as the Stick Election. Since then the people who were children when voting rights came in have grown up and they have all been to school and got a bit of education, so they can handle it better.

Some people get a bad impression of Aboriginals because the only ones they see are hanging round the pubs. They don't have any contact with the fair dinkum Aboriginal. When you talk to people like old Duncan – the intelligence of him, and his outlook on life, or old Sam Thompson. He had such dignity and so much wisdom and know-how in that head of his. When it's all boiled down, the outback of Australia was built up to what it is today by people, black, white and brindle. You have to give credit to old fellows like Duncan Yappanala and Sam Thompson. They were very great men. Very nice blokes. And down in Canberra when people present people to the Queen I think it would be a credit to us all to have someone like Duncan or Sam presented to represent their people and the work they have done getting this country on its feet. And as for old Doreen, she might just look like a little old thing, but by God! She is a great lady in her own right!

1 Journal of an Overland Expedition in Australia; '...large vine-bean which pounded and boiled for several hours, made a porridge, very satisfying...'(p.451) 'remains of freshwater turtles were frequently noticed in the camps of the natives...'(p. 470) '...gathered and ate a great quantity of yellow figs...'(p. 478) '...greatest number of flying-foxes...shot sixty-seven, which served for dinner, breakfast and luncheon, each man receiving eight.' (p. 477).

twelve...

'STAN NORGREN'S STORY'

The Saddler of Urapunga

I had a saddler on Urapunga for a good few years, an old mate, Stan Norgren. Stan was a decent old bloke; a man in his sixties whom I met in New Guinea. When the Europeans were starting to get out of PNG I said to him, 'Now, Stan, I'm thinking of looking around for a place in the Northern Territory. If ever you want to finish up here you can always come and make your home at my place.'

During the war Stan had been in the army, in the 6th Divvie. He fought in the desert in Africa and later against the Japs in New Guinea. But before he joined up in 1939 he'd been a drover and a stockman in the Northern Territory. He'd had a tough life right from a kid. It was the Depression years, so as soon as he was old enough, Stan headed for Darwin, taking whatever sort of work he could get.

He got as far as Larrimah and took a job on a property as a stockman. They were out mustering one day, and Stan went after a breakaway bullock. His horse hit an antbed and rolled with him. His hip was smashed. There wasn't much in the way of roads in those days, so they put him on one of those old-fashioned railway pumpers – the sort where two men on either side swing on a heavy pump-handle to get her moving. No motor or anything, but those things could get along at a fair speed once you got them going. They got him up to Katherine hospital, but he was in such a bad way that they told them he would have to be taken on up to Darwin. So it was back on the pumper again to Darwin, another couple of hundred miles.

The Darwin hospital was just an old corrugated-iron place, open at the sides, and the matron used to keep chooks. These chooks would come into the wards and roost on the foot of the beds. It was nothing to wake up in the morning with a rooster on the foot of your bed crowing his head off. One night a stockman was admitted. The nurse was taking down all his particulars. When she said, 'Married?' this bloke reckons, 'Yairs.' The next question was, 'Wife's address?' This fellow scratches his head a bit and says, 'Well, I dunno, really. The last I heard of her she'd gone huntin' down the East Alligator!'

When he got out of hospital Stan did a few droving trips across the Barkly. He was working on Argyle when he heard that war had broken out so made his way down to Melbourne to enlist. This was in 1939 so he was pretty quick off the mark. He joined the 6th Divvie and got sent to the Middle East. They saw action in most of the desert campaigns, Benghazi, Mersa Matru, Tobruk; some of it pretty rough. Stan was a bren-gun carrier driver, but he didn't like to talk about it much. He would only tell you about the funny things that happened.

He said once when they were outside Bardia his C.O. said to him, 'Corporal Norgren, you're going to be my driver today.' So they were driving along, and the Germans are throwing a few shells at them. And this colonel is standing up there – with this little swagger-stick tucked under his arm – and he's saying, 'Carry on! Corporal! Go on further!' until they were right in the thick of it. Shells landing hell, west and crooked, all round them. Then this colonel says, 'Right! Corporal! I think we've seen enough now! We can go back! Carry on then!' And Stan reckoned, didn't he get to hell out of there! He said, 'God! That man was a dangerous bugger to work for! He had no idea of keeping his head down!'

Once, after they'd been fighting the Italians at Ben Ghazi there was a big church parade. The town was full of beautiful Italian women all going to the big cathedral. Stan reckoned, 'And us lot'd been in the desert and hadn't set eyes on a woman for months. So when the Sar'Major gave the order, "Roman Catholics! One step forward!" nearly every bugger stepped out smart! We all wanted to go to the big catholic church and get an eyeful of these beautiful women! There was hardly a bloody Protestant left!'

After Bardia the 6th Divvie was pulled out of North Africa and sent to Greece. By the time the Australians got there the Germans were pouring down from the north through Bolas Pass. The Aussies had no air-cover and had to retreat. The Germans had all the air-power under the sun and they used to strafe hell out of them. They'd be trying to get a bit of cover in the olive groves by day and retreating by night. They were pushed back down the peninsula to Athens where ships were supposed to be going to evacuate them to Crete. Stan was one of the last to get away. The destroyer was standing off the coast and they had to swim about a mile and a half out to get picked up. They headed for Alexandria but were torpedoed off the coast of North Africa.

Stan was paddling round in the Mediterranean for about thirty-six hours. I said to him, 'God! You must have been a pretty good swimmer!' He said to me, 'I'm not much of a swimmer. I done a lot of floating. I'd get the benefit of the in-coming tide and I'd swim like hell to get ashore. Then the outgoing tide'd be against me and it'd take me out again. But in the end I made it! My legs had just about given up on me.'

In Australia things were looking bad. The Japs were coming down from the north, so the 6th Divvie was called back. Their first run in with the Japs was on the ship on the way home when they came under attack by Jap fighter-bombers.

They got three weeks leave and were then sent up to New Guinea. Stan said as they were coming in to Wau in these DC3s, the Japs were dug in at one end of the strip firing on them. The next DC3 brought in a couple of 25 pounders, so that settled that.

Eighteen months after Stan Norgren's death Ray laid a concrete slab on the grave with a brass ex-serviceman's plaque, in the station cemetery at Urapunga.

They fought the Japs back to the Wondumi Gorge and down to Salamoa. Next they were dropped by parachute into Nadzab with not much in the way of preliminary training. They fought them back along the Markham Valley to Shaggy Ridge.

Stan got malaria and was flown down to hospital in Melbourne. He was discharged as medically unfit and came back up to the Territory and got the head stockman's job on Rockhampton Downs, north-east of Tennant.

After the war he saw an advertisement by the Department of Agriculture and Stock in the *Courier*, for a manager for a cattle and tea-growing research station they were starting at Kainantu in the New Guinea highlands. And that's where I met him. Stan was a very capable man; never had too much to say. But he had a vast amount of knowledge on many things. He should have written a book about his life.

When Stan came to Urapunga I put up a decent little place for him, with the saddlery shop at the back. He put in a nice little garden around it. He'd get me to get him a trailer-load of manure from the stock-yards. He would box up areas and put manure on them and let it rot in over the Wet and then dig it in. He grew tomatoes and cucumbers and rock-melons and those long skinny beans; they did very well.

Stan could turn his hand to many things. His health was buggered for stock-work but he did beautiful saddlery-work, and took great pride in it. If I said to him, 'Stan, can you sew a patch on this pack-saddle?' he would tell me straight, 'Look!

Will you get this into your head! Saddlers don't sew; saddlers stitch!' He showed me how to pack a saddle with spinifex. It does a top job. Spinifex padding will last in a saddle for years. It doesn't break down into powder like a lot of grass. A pack-saddle has got to have good padding; it takes a lot of weight.

Stan hadn't had much to do with his family since he'd left New Guinea but he had a daughter down south somewhere, and one son. The son was in the army in Vietnam. One morning I got this message on the two way radio that his son had been wounded in action. When I went down to his quarters to break the news I was worried how he would take it.

Brass plaque on Stan Norgren's grave at Urapunga station homestead. "Lest We Forget"

Stan was smoking a pipe on the verandah of his place, and I said, 'Stan I've got a telegram for you and the news is not too good, I'm afraid. Your boy Laurence has been wounded in action.' Stan shook his head and chomped on his pipe a bit. Then he said, 'Useless bugger! I spent five years in the army in the War and never got a scratch!' Then he smoked a bit more and said, 'But of course, I might have been lucky, eh!'

Stan used to get a lot of bad headaches but he put them down to the malaria in the war. The Flying Doctor used to come every four or five weeks to Urapunga to check on all the Aborigines, and while they were there they used to check all the whites as well. They had Stan on Mogadon for these migraines. And then one day the doctor took me to one side and he said, 'We're going to have to take your old mate away. He's got some sort of a tumour on the brain.' So they took him up to Darwin to do some tests. Later they told me that he wouldn't be able to carry on without injections all the time and that he'd have to go into hospital.

I said to them, 'Look, Stan's been a good mate of mine. Couldn't he stay on here?' They said, 'Who's going to give him his injections? They've got to be every four hours.'

Now I knew a lady in Katherine, a Mrs. Robertson. She had not long retired from the hospital. Her husband, Ted, was retired and they often used to come out to Urapunga to do a bit of fishing. I said to the doctor, 'Look. I'll get on to Mrs. Robertson and Ted and ask if they'd mind coming out and living here for a while.' The doctor said, 'Well, if you can get a qualified person to come out we won't have to take him away.'

So I went and told old Stan I'd arranged all this. He said, 'Don't let them take me to Adelaide, whatever you do.' I said, 'No way, Mate. I've got on to Mrs. Robertson. She's a nurse, and she'll be out and she'll take care of you.' Mrs. Robertson knew Stan well. She knew he might have three, maybe six months. I had some of those demountables on the place and I set up some nice accommodation for them. They were due out the following week.

Stan's grave, revisited by Ray & Bluey Ellis after many years.

And that night – I always used to go down and see Stan before I went to bed – though he had his own little place there, he'd always come over to the house for supper. I went out to talk to him that night, and we had a bit of a yarn as we usually did. Then I said to him, 'Oh, well. I'd better get going, Stan. I've got cattle in the yard there and I'll have to make an early start.' And he stood up. And he shook hands with me. And he said, 'Thank you for everything you've done for me.You've been the best friend a man could have.'

The next day, after I'd seen to the cattle, I said to the housekeeper, 'Have you seen old Stan around this morning?

Mrs Robertson and Ted are due out today.' She said, No, she hadn't seen him and that he hadn't come up for breakfast, either.

So I went down to Stan's place. I called out, 'You there, Stan?' No answer, so I went in. And, Christ! There he was, lying across his bed, dead. He must have thought things over and decided to end things in his own way. He'd got his rifle, sat on the bed, put it to his head and pulled the trigger. Then it came back to me in a flash, how he had stood up the night before and shaken my hand and thanked me for what I had done for him. Very formal, which wasn't usual. I realised it had been his way of saying good-bye.

So the first thing I had to do was to get the police over from Roper Bar. They took his body away to Darwin. I knew Lionel Parker, the Salvation Army padre, was somewhere in the area. I got on to Civil Aviation in Darwin, and they said, 'Oh, Yes. Lionel's in the air somewhere. We'll track him down for you.' They got in contact with Lionel and told him he was urgently needed at Urapunga.

And a friend of mine had our Cessna 206 up in Darwin getting it serviced. I said to him, 'Grab the Cessna and bring Stan's body down when they release it.'

I knew his daughter lived in Yeppoon near Rocky, because he'd had a Christmas card from her. So I told the copper at Roper Bar and he said, 'Right-o! I'll get on to the Rockhampton mob and they'll contact Yeppoon.' He came over next morning and he said, 'The Yeppoon lot have got on to his daughter, and she's going to contact the brother. They'll both be here.'

Within three days they were both at Urapunga. The daughter flew to Mt. Isa and got a bus to Mataranka and I went in and picked her up. And the son flew to Darwin and hitched a ride on the aircraft bringing the body down.

There was a bit of a cemetery about a half a mile from the homestead so I and old Tommy Mulawai dug Stan's grave. It had to be strictly six foot deep. Well, at the start, one would swing the pick and one would shovel and use a crowbar. The ground was that hard! We put water in it to try to soften it. But once you got down a bit, you're in your mate's road. You have to get out of one another's way. We only finished it just in time. The station people from round about turned up for Stan's funeral, and others came out from Katherine. Stan was well respected. We made sure he got a good send-off.

And about eighteen months afterwards I put a cement slab on the grave, and a standard ex-serviceman's brass plaque. There is a foundry down in Crookwell in Victoria that has the contract to do all the ex-service plaques. I sent down all the particulars and I told them to make sure they put some good strong hooks on the back to bed it into the concrete. Anybody trying to pinch it for the brass would have to get a ten pound sledge-hammer! I wanted to do the right thing by Stan. He'd been a good old mate of mine. Everyone of my kids has got a beautiful handmade leather brief-case that he made for them. Stan was a very decent bloke; a genuine Old Digger.

A very good friend of Stan's wrote this poem, and sent it to me.

Stan Norgen Remembered

Old Stan, the saddler, has passed away
We got the message yesterday.
No telegram, no written word,
And yet, we heard, we heard.

Our thoughts are now in other places,
Far from the city of vacant faces.
With harness, horses and cattle lowing,
By a fire's glow where the Wilton's flowing.

There's tales of cattle drives, and weather
Waxed threads and needles, the smell of leather;
The Barkly, Gulf, and the Warramunga
Shared with our saddler of Urapunga.

Buckles of brass and bridle reins,
Surcingles, saddles and hobble chains,
Awls and punches and greenhide strop.
It's a world apart in Old Stan's shop.

From the Roper Bar to the Castlereagh,
Station saddlers have lived their day,
Quiet rearguard of the generation,
The gentle men of the outback nation.

Don Naylor

thirteen...

'THE WILTON HILTON'

'Anyone Who Turned Up Got a Feed'

We got mobs of visitors at Urapunga, especially at Christmas. Friends would come down from Darwin and Betty and the kids would come over from Townsville. Old mates would turn up from down south. We more or less kept open-house. Everyone was welcome. We had stretchers along the verandah so there was always a bed. Or they would throw their swags out on the lawn for coolness. There was always plenty of tucker; nothing flash, but plenty of it. And at night we'd just sit out there on the verandah and yarn.

Once we had the airstrip in there were people coming and going all the time. A friend of mine, Keith Mason, made a sign to hang on the verandah; *'The Wilton Hilton'* ; a nice piece of work. Keith was a saw-miller so he knew a bit about timber. He retired to the Gold Coast, but he was an energetic bloke so he started organizing these round-Australia flying safaris; twenty or so aircraft. They would fly in, and camp on the airstrip under the wings of their planes. Of a night-time they would come across to the homestead for a bit of a yarn on the verandah. They were always interested in the chance to see a corroboree. Southern people don't know much about the Aborigines and they found it all very fascinating to see a real corroboree. Of course, the blacks would only put on a play-about-nuthin' one. There's no way they would have invited outsiders to a serious ceremony.

Outside the kitchen there was a triangular bell made from a piece of old angle iron, and when it was dinner time it got a good banging and anyone who wanted a feed turned up.We could seat sixteen at the dining-room table. There was no standing on ceremony. The food was put out and everybody helped themselves. I put in three transportable units, of five bedrooms each, for the Air Med people or any government officials or friends that came along. And after Professor Harry Messel and the Sydney University Research team pulled out they left me two blocks of demountable accommodation. Harry told me it was by way of appreciation for the help I had given them. I could always offer a bed to anyone who turned up.

People used to ask me if we got a lot of snakes around the house because of the lawns and the gardens. It wasn't really a bad area for snakes, and I used to say, 'Look, any snake looking for a drink has only got another hundred and fifty yards to get to the Wilton!' Though, there was one time when I knew this brown snake was around the house. I'd seen him a couple of times, and gone after him with a stick. But each time I missed the bugger. He'd be slithering on the tiles but he always got away from me. I didn't want to say anything to Betty. I didn't want to alarm her. She's doesn't have the best of health and hates snakes.

Once when the kids were little they brought in a snake they had found curled around a clump of grass near the horse-yard. They thought it was a nice snake and maybe they could have it for a pet. But it was a death adder. Death adders are pretty quiet sort of snakes but if it had turned nasty it could have killed any of them in a matter of minutes. It put Betty off life in the bush once and for all. So, when I knew this brown was around the place I got a decent sort of a stick and leaned it in the corner of the verandah. I said, 'Don't anybody shift that stick. I might want it.' For a few days I didn't catch sight of him, but I knew the bugger was about somewhere.

Then one morning I hear this hell of a scream, and it's Betty. She had got it into her mind to tidy out the linen press and she's taking out piles of towels and sheets and things, and stacking them on the table. In behind everything she comes across this old brown, curled up asleep. Well, I don't know who got the biggest fright, Betty or the snake! It came hurtling out over her shoulder. She's not slow going the opposite direction! Just by luck I just happened to be in the office that morning doing the books. But I had my stick handy and I caught up with his tail just disappearing into the ferns around the edge of the verandah. One good whack and I got him and chucked him out on an antbed. But, by and large, we didn't have much trouble with snakes.

Except one night there, Old Duncan comes racing down from the camp with young Sammy in his arms. 'Maluka! Maluka! Sammy bin bit by snake!' So I said, 'Well, for Christ's sake! Bring him in here and stick him on the table!' And I washed his foot and squeezed it and sucked it to try to get the venom out. Then I bandaged it up as tight as I could. I said, 'How'd it happen?' They told me that the snake was in Sammy's swag – which was out round the fire, like they always sleep. They never slept inside the huts, only in the Wet. It's in the Aboriginal's nature to like being in contact with the earth. And their belongings are just left lying anywhere about. The snake must have crawled into the swag during the day looking for somewhere dark to sleep. And when Sammy went to get in, it got him on the foot. I said, 'Well, for Christ's sake, go and find the bloody thing so we know what we're dealing with.' So off they went and they found it right enough. It hadn't gone that far.They killed it and brought it down to me. It wasn't a king brown or a down's tiger. They're the deadly ones. You don't get second chances with them.

I put him to bed on the verandah, and Doreen stayed with him, but then he was starting to get a bit woosie-looking and rolling his eyes, so I thought, 'Right! Get him to the mission hospital, quick!' So we raced him over – about twenty miles – and they gave him a shot of antivenene. In a couple of days Sammy comes home with a grin like a water-melon. He's a hero! We always had a soft spot for young Sammy. He was around the place a lot because he was one of Doreen's kids. You could say he came in for his fair share of spoiling.

Another time I was driving out along the Borroloola road in the old Toyota. I had a lot of spraying equipment on the back and I had put a reinforcement panel in the back of the cabin. And this bloody snake must have crawled in behind it and taken up quarters. I'm driving along and he must have found it a bit hot in there and suddenly he comes up the bloody steering-wheel and he's eye-balling me! Then he slides past and in under the dashboard. A big old yellow-belly. I thought he'd gone out through the back of the glove-box or somewhere, and I didn't think any more about it. Then, about a week later, bugger me if he doesn't front again!

Ray and visitors in the garden at Urapunga.

One of the blokes I had working for me, Rick Buckley, said, 'Can I borrow that old Toyota?' I said, 'Yeah, but there's a snake in there somewhere.' He said, 'Go on! Where?' I said 'I'm buggered if I know. He's up under the seat or somewhere.' So, anyhow, Rick and his mates are heading down to Port Roper at the mouth of the river, and up comes old Snake! Eye-balling him from the steering wheel! Rick and them all fly straight out! Let the bloody Toyota go! In gear!' And it takes off down the salt-pan and they're all chasing after it but they couldn't catch up with the bloody thing! It's trundling off into the distance! And the high tide's coming in, so it bogs itself! To the bloody chassis! It took us a couple of hours to dig her out. But we got her going eventually and no sign of old Snake. We think we've seen the last of him.

And a bit later, there's a fellow driving for Bill King's buses, and he came to me and he said, 'Can I borrow that Toyota? I want to go over to Roper Bar and pick up a few things from the store.' And I said 'Yeah. Righto,' and away he goes. And as he's driving across, bugger me if old Snake doesn't put in another appearance! He comes up between the two of them on the seat!

So this fellow rips up to the bowser at Roper. And he grabs the petrol-hose and he says, 'I'll fix the bastard!' And he pumps petrol in behind the seat and gives it a good dowsing. And out comes old Snake! But he's buggered, eh! When snakes get petrol on their scales they can't crawl. So he bashed it over the head. It was about four foot long; one of those yellow-belly tree snakes. But that snake, he must have been in the Toyota for a couple of months! I don't know what the bugger lived on! He must have been coming and going all the time. But, I tell you what! After that you wouldn't have wanted to be smoking when you were driving that Toyota!

Some strange things happened from time to time. One night during the wet season a helicopter came in. I had been half expecting him to turn up. It was a mate of mine who was working for Water Resources, checking out gauges along the Roper. And we were sitting out on the verandah after tea and he said, 'There's a Holden sedan back along the St. Vidgeon's road there. It doesn't look as if it's bogged. It's right in the middle of the road! The driver's side door was open. It was getting a bit late and wet otherwise I'd of landed.' I said, 'I'm buggered if I know who it could be. But I've got to go over to the Police Station in the morning so I'll mention it to Peter Watton, the constable there.'

So next day I went over to Roper Bar and I said to Peter, 'There's a car down the St. Vidgeon's road. The chopper pilot told me about it last night. It's not bogged. It's just parked on the road.' He said, 'That'll be right! I've just got a message through from Katherine. There was an old fellow left a note that he was going out to the Roper to top himself. Remember that old fellow who went past the other day when you and me were talking?' I said, 'That old fellow as clean as a Police Station?' He said, 'Yeah! That old fellow. That'll be him!'

So down the road we go, with the two black trackers. And here was this car, and sure enough, there's this corpse in it. He'd been there three or four days so you can imagine what sort of state he was in. So we spread a tarp underneath the driver's side door and managed to push him out. And when it fell on to the tarp the blackfellas, they laughed like hell. I thought, 'Well, you're a nice couple of bastards!' But I suppose because it was a whitefella it didn't worry them too much!

Anyhow, we rolled the body up in the tarp and loaded it into the back of the police wagon. But there was no way the trackers would get in the back with it! They said they would sit up on top!

And we threw an old tarp over the seat and I got in to drive. The battery was flat so he gave me a bit of a push-start down the road. And as I was driving along I see this bit of paper sticking out of the ashtray. I have a look at it, and it says, 'The first bullet wouldn't go off so I am going to have another go.' And here was this bullet in the bloody ashtray! The second one did the job alright!

Later on, we were told that this old chap had belonged to one of those strict religious sects and they had chucked him out for some reason or other. He must have decided there was nothing left in life for him. But I don't think I will ever forget having to go down and help get the poor old bugger's body.

*****

On the verandah we'd yarn about fellows we had known or what conditions in the cattle game used to be like in the old times and the changes that have come in. Anybody that got up out of his chair for a bit of a stretch, we would tell him, 'Yeah! And brew up another pot of tea while you're at it, eh!'

Once the all-weather roads were put in and cattle were trucked away to the railheads the old droving days were gone for good. Not only that, but with the live export market to Asia there was a bit more money around. In the old days things were pretty tough and Territory cattle weren't top quality. The earlier battlers couldn't afford to buy good quality bulls. At Urapunga I used to bring bulls in from Queensland every year to try to upgrade my herd. But now there are regular bull-sales held in the Territory, at Newcastle Waters, and Katherine and Darwin so there is good blood coming in. In the old days we used to talk about the Territory shorthorns, but today, the majority, maybe ninety-eight percent of Territory cattle are Brahman. The old shorthorn fellow, he's still galloping around out in the rough country, but less and less as the years go by. But Brahman bulls can be a bit slow off the mark. Whenever there are mickeys around, the mickeys seem to get more calves! The old Brahman bull, you'd see him camping around under the trees, snoozing, and there are the mickey-bulls getting stuck into the cows! You'd always get a percentage of mickey-progeny coming up in your herd.

As far as I am concerned the old days of the stock camp were the best. Today's ringers, they muster and put the cattle into a holding yard and then they go home! Nine times out of ten they drive back into the homestead, and there is a professional cook there putting on restaurant meals and there are air-conditioned quarters to sleep in. No-one watches cattle on stock-camp these days. They watch television! Sometimes they might muster a thousand head of cattle into a holding paddock and just take out the three or four hundred head at a time and put them in the yard and work them. And next day they go back into the holding paddock and yard another lot. They do this until they've cleaned the paddock out. But in the old times you went out, you mustered, and you were lucky if some of the yards had a windmill or a turkey-nest where you could get a bit of a clean-up. And you just threw your swag on the ground.

The old time ringer, he was far tougher. It was horse and man against cattle. There wasn't any of this chasing things with four-wheel drives, and quad-bikes and helicopters. Not that I'm against helicopters. They can flush stock out of rough country that you would otherwise have no hope of finding. But a man on a horse, he moves amongst his cattle, he steadies them and he gets to know them and they get to know him. They are quieter and better to handle for it. They say it's a matter of cost; that the industry can't afford the manpower and horses today. But, by God! Racing round in Toyotas and helicopters like these Gasolene Cowboys do today doesn't come cheap, either!

If you got some of these young fellows today and put them in a swag in wet conditions in half-drizzly rain, when your clothes are wet and your swag is soaked and your blankets are fly-blown…! Well, that's all we knew so we accepted it. But today, if you handed conditions like that to a young fellow, he'd be rolling his swag and heading off down the road into town!

Ray says, "When dinner was ready we would bang the gong. Anyone who turned up got a feed. Nothing flash. But good tucker and plenty of it" Ray made the dinner gong from a piece of angle iron.

In our day we just accepted that a man worked all the hours of the days that God gave. Daylight was for working, not lolling around feeding your face. You got your breakfast into you before sun-up and you worked until after sundown. That was what we expected and we were happy with it. It was a man's life. And it bred a certain type of man, tough and independent, and taking pride in the job.

Take old Johnnie Nicholas! He was that strong he could lift a forty-four gallon drum of fuel on to the back of a truck. I was helping him move a mob of cattle out to Payne's Lagoon once – just a small mob, three or four hundred, and he was ahead, driving the camp on an old blitz. I caught him up at a creek, and here he is with a forty-four gallon drum of fuel that had fallen off. He'd backed the blitz down into the bank to put it on. I said, 'Hang on, Johnnie! I'll give you a hand!' 'No,' he said, 'I'm right. This is the third time she's fallen off.' And he had been putting it back on his own! I called out to him, 'When we get up a bit further there's an old mine. We might find an old buggered-up fence and get a bit of wire to tie her down.' But, that man! Before I could get down into the creek to give him a hand, bugger me if he hadn't put it back up on his own! Rolling it up on to his knees! By God, he was strong!

And when Bluey Ellis was a young stockman, during the Wet when they were sitting round the station, they would have competitions to see who could lift those big old anvils the highest. They could get them up chest-high and that would be about the best they could do. What does an anvil weigh? Half a ton or so! They always had it stamped on them, on the soft part, so many hundredweight, quarters, pounds. But, by God, you'd have to have some strength to get one off the ground, let alone up to your chest! There were other bush games to test you out. One was to get down as if doing a push-up and with one arm, drop a matchbox out in front of you as far as you could reach. The next bloke tries to reach the matchbox and drop it further out. It was a test of strength and balance. But mostly, we'd fill in time breaking in horses, or doing a bit of saddlery to mend our gear. We were never bored. Didn't know the meaning of the word.

Bluey Ellis – his real name is George, but with red hair he always got Blue – has been a good mate of mine for many years. He was Western Australian and his dad was a shearer. When Blue was a young bloke he worked on Argyle, one of the Durack places. Then he worked his way around the Territory, fencing and droving. There wasn't a waterhole Blue didn't know. He ended up head stockman on Dunmara. Blue made his pile running a trucking business down New South Wales way.

Another old mate was Bill Wade. Bill and his brothers never wore boots; did all their stockwork barefoot! But Bill was a smart man with his hands! He built a replica wagonette, every bit of it by hand without any plans! Says he 'has the idea of it in his head'. Makes the wheels without any lathe, just shaving away at the timber for each of the spokes until they 'feel right.' The wagonette he built was the same as the itinerant schoolteacher's who used to come to Tabletop in the 1920s and '30s.

Peter Singh was very well-known as a drover and cattleman. His father was an Afghan and his mother was one of the Wadaman tribe from around the Katherine and Manbulloo area. He also had a touch of Chinee in there somewhere. But Peter was highly respected in the area, a very smart horseman. He never got 'Peter'. Always 'Sabu', from when he was a bit of a kid and a film called 'Elephant Boy' came to Katherine. The kid in it was called Sabu. After that Peter never got anything else.

The story goes that one time there, Sabu was contract mustering bulls over on Wave Hill and he had a truck-load ready to go into the meatworks at Katherine. The manager said to him, 'Hey, do you reckon you could get me a carton of Black Duck while you're in town?' 'Black Duck' is the nick-name for Swan Brewery beer. So Sabu says, 'Yeah. OK.' And he's driving along and he's thinking, 'Well, it could be late when I get into Katherine and the pub might be shut. I'd better pull over at Top Springs and throw that carton on.'

The pub at Top Springs was run by a lady named Ma Hawkes, a bit of a character. So Sabu pulls in and parks the truck. The bulls look like standing OK so he goes into the bar. There's about fifty ringers in there, all on the booze. Sabu says to Ma Hawkes, 'Could you give's a carton of Black Duck, Ma? I've gotta to get into Katherine with these bulls and you'll be shut when I come back.' She says to him, 'Well, I'll get you one, but you'll just have to wait your turn.' So he waits and then after a bit, when there's no sign of getting served, he says, 'Look, I've got to get on my way, Ma. Can you give's that bloody carton?' But Old Ma is still ignoring him and saying she's got her regulars to take care of and that he couldn't expect to come in off the road and push in.

So Sabu starts to get a bit annoyed. He can hear the bulls in the truck getting toey. Ma's still showing no sign of getting round to serving him, so he thinks to himself, 'Right!' He goes out, and he climbs into the truck, and he backs her up to the front of the pub. Lines her up with the door to the bar. And he pulls the gate open! And bulls start jumping out, left, right and centre! Straight into the bar! They're shaking their heads and snorting. And there are drunks and ringers and truckies going in all directions! Ma Hawkes is up on the bar singing out blue murder! They reckon there were ringers hanging from the rafters! The bulls end up knocking the side wall of the pub out and heading off down the paddock.

Sabu hopped back in his truck and went back to Wave Hill. The manager said to him, 'How'd you get on? Did you get me carton?' And Sabu said, 'Aw! I give them bulls to Old Ma Hawkes!' The manager said, 'What! What do you mean, you "give 'em to Ma Hawkes!" and Sabu tells him. Talk about laugh! Sabu was contract mustering at the time and only got paid for what he delivered to the works so he was only the one to lose out. He reckoned it was worth it to put the shift on the Top Springs lot!

Top Springs was a dipping point for movement of stock on three stock routes, Wave Hill, Ord River and Katherine. The Murranji Track came in there, across from Newcastle Waters. There were big yards and watering points. Stock had to be dipped, held for four days and then dipped again. So some pretty wild parties used to go on with the drovers and truckies and stockmen. Around the yard of the pub there were a lot of those hot chilli-bushes growing, and one time one of these fellows came up with the bright idea that every time a bloke downed a Bundy he had to chew on a hot chilli. So this goes on all night, seeing who can knock back the most rum and chillies. They reckon that when daylight came, here's a row of fellows with their strides down round their ankles, lined up along the edge of the trough cooling their backsides down!

But now there's a new highway, the Victoria highway, from Katherine to the Kimberleys, all re-aligned up on to the hard gravel country to get out off the black soil.The droving days are finished and now it's all done by trucking.

And of course, there were times when things went wrong and a man might get hurt. Someone knew a fellow who used to blow a waterhole for fish with carbide packed into a golden-syrup tin with a hole punched into the lid. The water just seeps in, slow, slow, and builds up enough gas, until all of a sudden she will blow!

Five or six feet of water in the air, and all the fish coming to the surface. Bluey Ellis was shearing with an Irishman years ago that used to dynamite a hole. He was a mean bugger and would only light a short fuse. One time this fellow lights the fuse and it blows before he can throw it. Blew both his hands off and his eyes out. But, generally speaking, blowing waterholes was not accepted. A good boss drover always considered the man behind him on the track.

"The Drover" Eddie Hackman's sculpture in the Drovers' Memorial Park at Newcastle Waters.

Eddie Hackman – he used to be manager of Dotswood, next door to Tabletop; he makes bronze castings of horses and stockman. He did the Drover memorial down at Newcastle Waters. A bloody beautiful piece of work! Eddie is a very well-read man and he will tell you that a good many of the old drovers mightn't have had much in the way of education but there was nothing wrong with their brains. At one time in the 'twenties the Carnegie Foundation sent a shipment of books to Borroloola. What with white-ants and dry-rot, most of them did a disappearing act. But for years some of them were turning up in swags out in the stock-camps. It would be nothing out of the ordinary to hear Tennyson or Longfellow being discussed around the campfire at night.

One fellow I heard of, Dusty Dundrovin; he and his missus were a well-known couple in the droving game. Bessie drove the camp truck and did the cooking. At one time Dusty starts to look a bit thoughtful. He's slipping a bit on the homework side of things. And he's heard that Air Med are due in at the station homestead. So he drives in to have a bit of a yarn to the doctor. The doc listens and then he gives Dusty the low-down. And Dusty says, 'Struth! Eh! You reckon!'and 'Go on!'

He jumps into his ute and heads off into Katherine. Straight into Cox's Stores! Gets himself a flash checked shirt, new moleskins, and one of them belts with big brass buckles. He gets a new Akubra, the sort with the narrow brim that verandah-bosses wear, and a new pair of RMW's, high-heeled jobs. Then he offs across the road to Top End Motors! Trades in the Chevvie on a brand new Holden Station wagon, latest model. Then he heads off back out to the camp. Bessie sees him coming and she goes out to see how he's got on. She takes one look at him getting out of this brand-new Holden in all this flash gear, and she says, 'Gawd! Dusty! What'ch done up like a flamin' sore toe for?'

And Dusty takes a big cigar out of his mouth and blows a couple of smoke rings, and he gives her a big grin and he tells her, 'Good news, Darl! That doctor, he's a smart bloke! Y'know what he told me! He give it to me straight. He says to me, 'Dusty. You're impotent!' And I says, 'Yeah? You reckon!'! And I thinks to meself, 'Impotent, eh! Righto! If I'm impotent, I'm gunna look impotent! The most impotent bloody bastard round these parts! Yeah!'

Now, that Colin Munro. He's on the ABC down in Sydney. God, he's a funny man! He reckons once he was interviewing this old bush lady, live, on air. All her life she's been a drover's wife, down the Strzelecki, across the Murranji. And Colin says to her, 'I hear that after your long life you are now confined to bed. How many years have you been bed-ridden?' And this old lady is stone deaf and she says, 'Eh?' So he yells, 'How many years have you been bed-ridden? And she says, 'Bed ridden! Gawd! Hundreds of times! And three times in a sulky!' This is going live to air! Colin reckons he came damned near getting the sack over it!

In my early days at Urapunga the Aboriginal Welfare Department used to send a big hand-out for the blacks at Christmas time; blankets and clothes and extra rations. But once they were all on Social Services that idea was dropped. So I always tried to put on a bit of a do for them. All the school children and their parents, and anyone else that wanted to come, showed up. I'd get a big order of party stuff sent out, bulk tins of lollies, and cartons of lolly-water and 'bizzakits'. And fruit and potato chips – they loved chips; all the stuff that kids go for. We'd carry a big mob of tables out on the lawn under the trees and all this stuff would be spread out on it and the kids would be looking and looking! And I tell you what, it was like trying to hold back a mob of perishing cattle back from water! When it was time for the party to start, well, talk about a rush! Those kids would swoop in and be grabbing lollies and biscuits and fruit and stuffing it down their shirts as if there was no tomorrow! And then, when it was all gone it was all gone! That was the Christmas party. I tried to make it a bit of an occasion; to make something a bit different in life for them.

And for Christmas a lot of friends would come down from Darwin, and the police-officer and his wife from Roper Bar would come over the river and any others that happened to be in the vicinity. Betty and the kids would be over from Townsville and I would cut a she-oak out of the river and put lights on it for a Christmas tree. I'd get a big ham sent out from Katherine Stores and boil it up in the copper. We'd have big shoulders of beef, and maybe a couple of sucking pigs and do them over a spit. At Christmas we made sure everyone was looked after and had a good time.

fourteen...

'THE BEGINNINGS OF TROUBLE'

Alcohol problems; Accidents; Urapunga Declared Dry

Once Aborigines got the right to drink, with full citizenship, well, it was the beginning of trouble in the cattle industry. And didn't we get our share at Urapunga! Alcohol! It's as if blacks have no resistance to it – in much the same way as they had no resistance to diseases like measles and whooping cough in the early days. Their physical make-up seems to be different from ours. Alcohol seems to be something they just can't handle.

And to make matters worse there were a lot of unscrupulous bloody whites quick off the mark to make an easy quid. Money-hungy bastards who didn't give a bugger about the damage they were doing to the blacks.

In the seventies, some blocks of land at Roper Bar were put up for auction. A Darwin concern, Escunzio's and Sons – building contractors in a pretty big way – migrants who had come in to Darwin and done very well for themselves, bought these blocks at Roper, and, unbeknown to us all, they built this 'shop' as they called it. Then they applied and got a grog licence. Holy hell! Didn't they cause some stir round the area!

Once the Aboriginals started going there and getting on the grog and then coming back to the camp full as ticks, Oh, God! wasn't there some fighting and screaming and yelling going on! The women would come crying to the homestead of a night-time for protection; 'Help! Maluka! Help! Him bin killim me finis! Help!' They'd be camping on the verandah, or out on the lawns, all the women and children huddled together, scared out of their minds. And there'd be fighting and yelling and bloody racket going on all night long in the camp. You'd get no sleep at all.

Then all the women and children started clearing out and going bush, which meant the kids weren't going to school. You'd see women with bunged-up eyes or swollen jaws where they'd been kicked and punched. The police would come and try to sort the trouble-makers out; locking up the worst of them.

Things got so bad that some of the older generation decided to move and make a camp of their own away from all the trouble. A group under Roy Kulakundu formed an out-camp called Budawarka. The government provided a truck for them to bring the kids backwards and forwards to Urapunga for their schooling. But when Roy died the whole thing folded.

Something had to be done so I went up to Darwin and had a talk to my friend, Ian Barker, the lawyer. I said to him, 'What the hell is a man supposed to do? It can't go on like this. They'll end up killing someone. And they're bloody killing themselves with the alcohol! They just can't seem to handle it.' Ian said, 'Well, there's one thing you could try. You could try to lodge an objection to Escunzio's licence. You might be able to get it revoked.'

So I put in an application – or rather, Ian did it for me – to appeal against Escunzio's grog licence. All the big business people around Darwin said to me, 'What do you think you're coming at! What chance have you got up against a big concern like Escunzio's!' I told them, 'Well, I don't know how it will turn out but I'm going to give it a go!' They said, 'You haven't got a snowball in hell's chance! Escunzio's got the money! He'll send you broke! Just let him be!' And I said, 'No way in the bloody world! If there's any chance of knocking his licence I will!'

So when the time came for the case and I went up to Darwin. Ian had got Michael Marice, a barrister-fellow, to take on my case. For my witnesses he called the Welfare Department, the church mob and the school-teacher. The case went on for days. They had me in the box for hours, questioning me and going into it. I just told the truth of what had happened, that it was wrecking the whole area, that the so-called shop was just a cover-up for selling grog, that the women were terrified and getting busted faces and heads and broken arms; that the kids wouldn't turn up for school, they were so frightened of the drunks. I told them it would ruin the whole Roper area if they didn't take the grog-licence off the store.

Escunzio's brought in a lot of big guns. How the 'shop' wasn't built for the Aboriginals. It was built for the tourist trade. They couldn't help it if the Aboriginals bought grog there. They were citizens and they had the right to drink, and all that kind of thing. The case was heard by Magistrate McDonald and the outcome of it all was that Escunzio's licence got knocked.

Well, wasn't I the worst bastard around! People from in town said to me, 'Aw! Now we can't go out to the Roper and buy a beer!' I told them, 'Look! If you want to come out to the Roper and bring your own bloody beer from town I'm not stopping you. But I'm not having my livelihood buggered up by a mob of drunks and a couple of money-grubbing shysters from southern Europe!'

So these Escunzio's got nasty and they brought in a Mafia hit man – I don't know whether they got him out from Italy or from down south, but Peter Watton, the copper, got word on the police grapevine that he was on his way out to do me over. Peter came over and got me, and he said, 'That lot from the grog-shop have brought this Mafia fellow out to get rid of you!' So he and I went over to the shop and Peter said to the Escunzio-character, 'I believe you have a bloke by the name of so-and-so here. You brought him down from Darwin in the early hours of this morning.' And this Escunzio scratches himself a bit and looks vague and says, 'Nah! I doan know nothin' about no man comin''. And Peter told him, 'I'm not joking now! You just produce the fellow that arrived here this morning or I will have the whole police force from Darwin right here!' And Escunzio suddenly remembers, 'Oh! You meana dat cousin o' mine!' And with that, this great ape of a fellow appears in the doorway! I'm six foot four but I'm telling you he was looking down on me! Anyway, the upshot of it was that Peter told him to get to hell out of the Roper area and get back to Sydney or wherever he came from or he would put him on a charge. And that was the end of it. I never had any more trouble from them.

Escunzio's sold the store and went back to Darwin. There wouldn't have been any money in it once the grog licence was revoked. It was only a cover for selling grog in the first place. After that things went back to being peaceful on the Roper. Of course, the Aboriginals still went to town and bought their grog, but it's the way with them that once they've got a load of grog on board they don't go far. They pull up under a shady tree and drink the lot. If they've got more money left they pool it and go back to town for another lot and do the same thing again and sleep it off until the money runs out. Then they come home and sleep it off some more and it's all over and done with.

After the highway was constructed from Mataranka out to the Roper a lot of the Aboriginals got themselves an old bomb. They'd go into Katherine and buy up all the old Falcons and Kingswoods and Holden Station Wagons. But they would get as far as Mataranka and get on the grog and were always rolling their cars. There were hospital cases but it was surprising how few of them got killed!

One lot of mine had this old Falcon and they were coming back out and they rolled it near Elsey. A couple of them were killed. Jacob, one of my best stockmen was in it. When he got back to Urapunga I said to him. 'By God, eh, Jacob! You're a lucky man you didn't get killed in that crash!' He just cheerfully said to me, 'Aw! Them fellas that got killed they was all up front. I was right! I was in d' boot!'

Another lot weren't so lucky. One night, my son David and I were at the homestead just talking on the verandah and this Aborigine comes running up and saying, 'Maluka! You come! Quick! Car crash finis out long highway! Plenty people killed. Plenty people hurt bad!' So we get in to the car and go to see what we can do.

Well, God Almighty! It was terrible. There's a couple of fellows lying dead. There's nothing we can do for them. But there's this one chap, he's got shocking injuries. His face, the entire skin of his face, was slit across and lifted up over his head like a cap. He must have gone through the windscreen. We managed to get him into the vehicle but all the way back to the homestead I had to use all my strength to physically hold him down – he was a big powerful fellow – to prevent him reaching up and grabbing at that skin on top of his head! It was like a cap sitting there and he was trying to pull at it.

We got on to Air Med and they come down and flew him up to Darwin. God knows how they managed to make a job of getting that face-skin back down and stitching into place! But that fellow is still alive and getting around in a wheel-chair to this day!

Another time I was coming out from Katherine at night, and getting out towards Roper police-station I saw a car, a Holden station wagon, all smashed up, all over the road. Those Holden station wagons, they would load them up pretty well. There might have been ten or twelve in it, all jammed in. There were people lying all over the road. Some walking around, just in a daze.

One old lady, she came over and as she walked past the headlights I could see she was a mass of blood; blood everywhere. She had one of those big old army coats on. She came to me and she said, 'Oh, Maluka! Maluka! Me gottim sore arm! Sore arm! Take me long hospital!'

I could see all the other fellows were coming good, so I grabbed her and I said to her, 'Righto! Get in!' and headed for Ngukkur. Got there after about half an hour or so and roused the nursing sister up. By this time the old woman's only half conscious.

The sister said to me, 'You'd better stay. We might need a hand here!' So we managed to get the coat off her and we found that she had the arm chopped off just above the elbow! No wonder the blood was flying! I don't know how she didn't bleed to death.

The nursing sister had her forceps and she's grabbing veins and clinching them off. I went and got the airstrip lit up and got the Air Med. plane down from Darwin and they flew her up to hospital. It wasn't that long after, about three or four weeks or so later, that I see her getting around the place, cheerful as a cricket, one wing cut off. As far as I know she is still alive today!

Another time, I was going into Katherine, and I see this Holden sedan sitting on its hood on the side of the road, wheels in the air. I stopped. It didn't seem to look right to me. I thought it might have been on the back of a truck and fallen off. All the oil was running out under the bonnet. I cooeed out to see if there's anyone around, and I'm scratching my head and wondering what the hell's going on and at last a lanky young blackfella comes up out of the grass.

I said to him, 'What did you do? Did you roll her over?'

'Oh, no, Mate.' He says, 'That thing unnerrneath, that prop-shaft. Him bin bugger-up finish.' He meant the tail-shaft. He said, "We got no jack, so we put him upside down to get that prop. shaft off.' I said, 'What are you going to do now?' He said, 'Aw! They bin take that prop-shaft. long Mataranka.! They can fix'im and bring'im back!' I thought to myself, 'Oh, yeah! This'll end up another wreck on the side of the road.' But when I came back that night she was gone alright! A big mob of oil there on the road where it had been but no sign of the car.

I saw that fellow a bit later on and I said to him, 'How did you get that car home? Snig him home, did you?' 'Aw! No!' he reckoned, 'We been tie rope long him and snig him little-bit long way. But him bin start! We gottim going! Him got that new prop-shaft. Him orright!'

Another time, Graham Chung, the policeman, had come over from Roper Bar, and we were sitting out on the verandah at the front having a yarn and a cup of tea. And a blackfella came up to the house and he was standing there. I said to him,

"What do you want, Mate?' He said, 'Do you reckon you can help me, Maluka' I said, 'Why? What's the trouble?' 'Oh,' he reckoned, 'That car, him bin tip over finish!'

I said, 'Yeah? He tip right over?' He said, 'Yeah, Mate. Him tip right up orright. Four wheel on top!'

Graham said, 'What the hell happened?' He said, 'That car, him bin tip over long river!' So we all hop in the police wagon and we go down the river and here's this bloody car, alright. She's well and truly upside down in the river.'

Graham said to him, 'What you been doing? You been drinking? You drunk?' The blackfella said to him, 'Nah, Constable! We not coming home from town. We going in!' As if to say, 'Come off it, Stupid, We wouldn't be drunk on the way into town, would we! Only coming home!'

So Graham said, 'Well, how the bloody hell did you tip her over like that?' And this other fella standing by, he said, 'Aw! Constable! That fella, him bin get there before he should've!' In other words, he meant he was going too bloody fast when he hit the bend!

Anyway, we helped them snig her out and get her back on her wheels. She was a bit worse for wear. But those fellows would have got her going again. They did some marvellous things with cars.

But the grog situation kept on getting worse. It got that way that there were grog-runners that used to come, taxi-drivers, bringing grog out from town. I was talking to one of my blokes one day and I said, 'How much do you pay that fellow to bring you that plonk?' And he gave a bit of a grin and said, 'Oh! Him bring'im $40 one-pella bottle! He orright!' He was happy about it! Thought the fellow was doing him a good turn!

And there were other whites, con-men, 'gin-jockeys', that would move in on the women around the district, even down at Ngukkur – which I couldn't understand the church allowing – and live off the women's welfare-cheques, taking advantage of them. I wasn't having any of that on Urapunga. I used to hunt the buggers! And the cops would also do their best to hunt them on their way.

To cap it all another big problem started when the kids got into the petrol sniffing stunt. It was as though they saw the men doing their brains in with alcohol and thought, 'Oh, Well, if the men can get on the grog we might as well have a go at this petrol sniffing.'

Out on the airstrip there was a heap of empty av. gas drums stacked up. And a mob of these kids would go at night time and tip them up and drain out what fuel they could get. There was a big old tarp that I used to chuck over these drums and they would drain the av. gas out into a dish and get around it like a lot of bloody kittens! Under this big tarpaulin on a hot day! By God, it used to flatten them! I came along there once and saw them and I thought 'What the hell's going on here!' Here's six or eight of them all lying karked under this bloody tarpaulin! Knocked right out to it! Lying there as if they were dead. I got a hell of a shock the first time I came upon them.

It got that way it was going on all the time. We used to have to lock everything up; keep all the fuel under lock and key. You couldn't have petrol around anywhere. Once they got the habit they just couldn't do without it. They'd get themselves into a hell of a state; glassy-eyed, staggering in their walking, stoned on their feet, shambling around. That petrol sniffing does considerable damage to the brain. But it was no use saying to them, 'Look, you've got to cut it out! You're doing your brains in!' You couldn't get through to them. The adults couldn't seem to do anything about it. The men didn't give a damn. They'd lost their authority with them. The women knew it was bad but they couldn't do much without the men backing them up. It got that way you couldn't leave your vehicle. Then, to cap it all, we get this directive from Welfare that you had to drain your petrol-tank at the end of each day's work!

At this stage we had a young lady teacher, in her early twenties, not long out of ASOPA.[1] She had her own accommodation, a mobile home provided by the Aboriginal Welfare Department, very nicely set up, all mod.cons, and everything, but I said to her, 'Look, Robyn, if you wish, come over for your meal at night and eat with us. You can't just spend all your time over there on your own. So she used to do this and she was a very nice young lady.

She came from somewhere down in New South Wales; Brown's Creek, outside of Bathhurst. And after she had been there a while she said to me, 'I've saved up enough money to put a deposit on a car. I want to buy one of those new Valiants! I want to drive down at Christmas time and surprise my parents. So, when you're going up to Darwin can I come up with you and pick one up?' So the next time I was going up she came with me and she gets this car. Well, it was something to her! Her first car! She was that proud of it! Polishing it and shining it and taking photos of it; a young girl with her first car. She'd worked hard enough to get it! Coming up to the Territory whereas a lot wouldn't.

And not long afterwards I happened to be away and when I'm driving back into the place I could see there seemed to be some sort of trouble. Some sort of riot going on! There were blackfellas swarming round, running about everywhere, yelling and making a hell of a bloody din. And there's Old Stan, he's got the 303! And the school teacher is bleeding and crying. I thought, 'What the bloody hell is going on here!'

Apparently it all started when this stranger-crowd of blacks turned up out of the blue and demanded that she drive them into Mataranka to buy grog! These weren't Urapunga blacks. Nothing to do with our lot. They were a mob that had lobbed in from God knows where, probably Ngukkur. They said to her, 'Well, s'pose you not drive us, we take your petrol. Your car got'im.'

The Valiants like the one she had were the first I had ever seen with the shiny flap over the petrol cap. And this lot got at it with a pinch-bar and busted it open, this brand new car! And she was screaming and trying to stop them and they smacked her round the head and knocked her down. She had blood pouring down her face.

Old Stan heard the ruckus from his quarters and he raced over to help her. So then they all turned on him and got stuck into him! An old fellow like that! But he got away and tore over to the house. He was looking for the rifle and he found it but he couldn't find any bullets. Which was probably just as well; the rage he was in. He was thinking to himself, 'I didn't fight all the way through the bloody war to put up with this! I'll take a few of them with me! Bloody hell I will!'

That was when I turned up. I jumped out of the vehicle and yelled at Robyn, 'Get inside your quarters and lock the door!' Stan is yelling at me, 'Where's the bloody bullets! Where'd you put them!'

With that about six, eight, ten – I don't know how many there were – started to get stuck into me! I kept on my feet for a bit but then I went down. They had rocks and sticks. At this stage I reckoned I was a goner. They just about had me. Too many for me. I was pretty sure they were going to end up killing me. They had me down on the ground with this bloody great rock over my head. I thought, 'Well, this is it!' But I rolled to one side and got to my feet and grabbed a stick off one of them and started laying around me. I would have flattened them with it if I could have got a swing at them. But just then the bloody police car turns up from Roper Bar! And it's my mate, Graham Chung. He didn't muck around. He ripped out of his car and pulled his pistol out and fired a couple of shots in the air. And didn't the bastards split!

I said to him, 'Jesus! Thank Christ you came! They bloody-near killed me! They were getting the rocks into me!'

Graham never let himself get too stirred up over things. He said, 'I was wondering where those fellows had gone! There was a couple of loads of them went past the police station and I thought to myself 'Hello! Where are you lot heading?' I thought I'd better follow them up in case there was some strife!' I said, 'Well, thank God you turned up or otherwise a man mightn't be here still!

We had to get the Air Med out for young Robyn. She was in a hell of a state, her head bleeding and her face swollen and she was shivering and shaking with shock. And poor Old Stan! His mouth was busted and he had a lump on his head like an egg! And talk about ropeable! He was snorting like an old war-horse! He said, 'I reckon I done enough for my country! A man's entitled not to have to put up with this sort of shit!' Oh, he was wild! Graham said to him, 'Put your rifle away, Stan! It's no use! You'd be the one who'd end up in clink!'

Another time we were doing some welding; Peter was home from Gatton and the school teacher, another Peter, Peter Adey, a very capable bloke and very helpful, were both giving me a hand. And suddenly, Sammy Duncan, from the camp, appeared in the doorway of the shed, and he was yelling out and singing out something to me. I couldn't hear him for the welder. So I went over and I said to him, 'What's the trouble?'

He said, 'One gin bin shot up long camp.' I said, 'What!' He said, 'You gotta come up long camp! I said to the other two, 'Hang on a bit. I've got to go up the camp. There's been some sort of trouble.' Sammy looked at me and he said, 'You come! You come f….ing quick! She gonna die!'

So I went up with him and I went in the hut and here's his wife lying on the ground. I rolled her over and I could see at once that she had been shot through the stomach and that her kidneys were blown out the back. She was in a hell of a state.

And just then I looked up and here's Sammy coming round the corner with a bloody shot-gun about to take a shot at me! So I swiped the barrel before it went off. He took off and I after him! I chased him around the back of the hut and, bugger me, if he hasn't got another gun there!

And, Jesus, wasn't I acting quick! I grabbed the gun and smashed it up against a bloody tree and buckled it. And there's a load of star-pickets stacked up beside the hut. He grabbed one and starts coming at me. So I thought, 'Jesus!' and I grabbed a picket as well, and I said to him, 'Sammy! Put that bloody thing down or I'll let you have this over the head!'

So he dropped the picket and ducked off around the front of the hut. There was a bench there and on it was a bloody old army jungle knife! He picked it up and was going to let me have it! And I'm saying to him, 'Sammy! Put the bloody knife down!' But he gets the knife and the next moment he starts to saw at his throat! The blood starts pouring out of him. And then he takes off and he's racing down the flat, pouring blood.

Just then the two Peters arrive in the bull-catcher. They'd heard the shot. I jumped in beside him and we lapped him down the bloody flat until he ran out of steam. I jumped out and grabbed the bloody knife off him and held him and we put him in the Toyota – he was bleeding pretty savagely – and as we drove back down along the strip, you wouldn't believe it, but an aircraft landed. It was a young fellow not long out of flying school and just got his licence. I said to him, 'Here! Can you take this fellow into Katherine! He's cut his throat and he's gone wild and trying to shoot everyone!' Well, this young fellow didn't want to know about it! He panicked. He said, 'I can't take him!' He hopped back in his plane and he was out of there quick!

And Peter Adey, the school-teacher fellow, he's got hold of Sammy, and wrapped his arms right round him. And I said, 'Don't let him go! He's still quick!' We raced back up to the house and I got on to VJY and called emergency. They said, 'What is the problem?' I said, 'Can you put us on to the police-station!' They said, 'Which one?' I said, 'Any one! I want to report a case here. Our own copper's away!' So they put me on to Darwin. And this voice says says, 'Who are you and where are you?' So I repeated what I'd said. And he said, 'What? You've shot a blackfellow and you've cut another one's throat!' I said, 'Aw, Look! Will you get it bloody straight! I'm telling you about a blackfella that's has gone off his head and shot his wife and cut his own throat! I've got him here now. He is bleeding badly.' He said, 'Well, you'd better take him to Roper Bar Police Station!' So I started all over again, telling him our own copper was away. And eventually it got through to him and they got the doctor on to tell us how to stop the bleeding.

And I'd had a look at Sammy and he hadn't cut his jugular through. He had only cut his windpipe and up into his jaw. And I got the old women from the camp to come down and we calmed him down a bit and put some of those big, wide stretch bandages round his throat until he looked like those Africans that bandage their necks.

And we rolled his wife's body up in her swag and brought her down. And I'm thinking, 'What next!' And would you believe it, if one of those A.T.King tourist outfits doesn't roll in! They are the ones that do bush safari trips round the outback. I said to the driver, 'Look, Mate. This is not a good time. There's been a shooting here and one of the blacks has cut his throat.' And some silly woman on the bus sings out, 'Oh! Whatever did you cut the poor man's throat for!' Oh! Christ!

Anyway, the Police Air-Wing plane arrived, with a very nice lady, Dawn Hayes, one of the Rural Health sisters, and she had a look at Sammy, and they loaded him on the plane and away they went. And about ten days later, back they came, with Sammy all sewn up, to do an on-the-spot investigation, and afterwards they took him back up to the lock-up.

Then there was an inquiry at the court in Katherine and he was remanded to the Supreme Court in Darwin two or three months later. I was called up as witness. Peter was due back at college, so I said to him, 'You'd better get out of the place!' So up in Darwin we are all booked into the motel. And, of course, I didn't take along any solicitors. As far as I was concerned I was just a witness, there to give evidence. But they had brought a QC up from Sydney and next thing, this fellow gets stuck into me! Sammy hadn't meant to shoot his wife, he didn't know the gun was loaded and all this bull-shit! It was all my fault! And this goes on and on. For a while there I was thinking, 'Christ! I'll be lucky to get out of here! I'll be going to Fanny Bay and Sammy going home!'

The trial went on for a couple of days and the upshot was that Sammy got fourteen months out of it. He only did a few months and they let him out for good behaviour. We were sitting at home on the verandah one day having a cup of tea and Jacob came down. He said, 'Sammy bin come back.' I said, 'Bull-shit! He's up in Fanny Bay doing time!' He said, 'No, Maluka. Sammy sit-down long camp now!'

So I thought, 'I'd better go up and see what this is all about!' So up I went and sure enough, there's Sammy, large as life! I said, 'What are you doing here, Sammy?' He said, 'They bin let me out. I good-fella now!' I said, 'Yeah?' He said, 'Yeah! I don't like shoot you no more!' This is the same Sammy that used to be in and out of our place all the time when he was a little kid, getting drinks of lolly-water and being made a pet of by all of us; the one I'd sucked the snake poison out of. I laughed. I said, 'Christ, Sammy! I should bloody-well hope not!'

So this sort of thing with alcohol meant trouble was always on the cards. You could be out mustering and if you were anywhere near the road and one of their mates came along in a car, they would jump off their horse and take off into town. Just leave their horse there! Saddle, bridle and all! There was nothing you could do about it. When they wanted grog they wanted grog, and that was it.

So I got on to Ian Barker, up in Darwin and told him about the way things were shaping up. He said, 'Well, we can try to have the place declared dry; no alchohol. And see how we go.' So he drafted up this application to have Urapunga declared a prohibited area for alcohol. It went before the court and was granted. I had these big signs made and put up on the road leading in. They made it clear; by law there was no alcohol allowed within one square mile of Urapunga homestead.

Faced with increasing alcohol addiction problems in the Roper area, Ray had Urapunga station declared "Dry". It was the first property in the Northern Territory to do so.

I wouldn't have alcohol on the place. I never drank myself. I promised my father before he died that I would keep away from the grog. Dad was a man who had never touched drink. He said he had seen too many lives ruined with it. I gave him my word and I have never touched the stuff. Never needed to. And I didn't want anybody bringing booze on my place. Urapunga was the first Dry Area in the Northern Territory.

At the homestead, as guests of mine, anyone that wanted to drink had to drink inside the house. They couldn't go down the river with grog or go driving around with cartons of beer. I wasn't having it. The rule applied to everyone, regardless of colour.

But didn't it stir a few people up! Some of them came on to me, not only the Aborigines, whites as well, that I had no rights stopping anyone's freedom. It was a free country, and all that. If they wanted to drink they should be able to drink. But I told them that I bought Urapunga to raise cattle and that was my livelihood. I wasn't going to be hunted off by a mob of drunks, black or white. And after a while it became accepted.

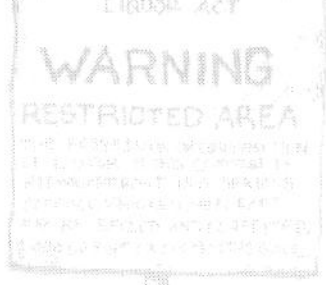

Or more or less accepted! There was one time there that I was bashed over the head with a steel pipe and woke up in the mission hospital. If you feel the top of my head there's still a groove right across the scalp you could lay poly-piping in. They damn near stove my skull in. I was over at the mission store and a fella just came up behind me and gave me one bloody great clout with this half-inch water pipe! He didn't want any 'white bastard' coming to their place 'causing trouble'! The mission had a shop there and I used to go over and pick up a ute-load of fruit and veggies out of their garden for my lot; pumpkin and water-melon and oranges and all that for the kids at the school, and I'm leaning over the counter yarning to the mission-fellow and that's all I remember! Just this bloody great whack on the head from behind! I was in hospital there for a couple of days. I couldn't walk straight; buggered if I could! And I was that dizzy, and seeing double for quite a while. Since then my sense of balance hasn't been as good as it used to be but I find that wearing a heavy-soled riding boot is a help.

And you wouldn't believe what the mission-fellow said to me afterwards? 'You'd better not come over any more. We don't want any more trouble.' He warned me that the blacks at Ngukkur resented me for having clamped down on grog in the area. The men, that is; not the women. It is the women who will take over the leadership role from the men one of these days and they will ban grog in all the communities. They can see what it is doing to their men and young people. Those old women, they're the ones with the savvee! And the traditions. The men are losing the old skills; just boozing themselves silly. On the grog all the time. But the women are still hanging on to the knowledge of the old ways. They will be the ones who will get the men straightened out, if anyone can. I have a lot of respect for those old women. If anyone can put their foot down about alcohol and get the men off the grog it will be the womenfolk.

One day I was coming back in the Toyota from catching bulls, and I saw a car coming out from the camp and driving straight across the airstrip. I didn't let anyone drive across the airstrip because of breaking up the surface. I used to make everyone go round. So I took off after this fellow. He saw me coming and he off! He had a faster vehicle than me, a Holden Station wagon. I was in the old blitz. I could see then that he was one of the bloody grog-runners that used to come out bringing out flagons of plonk on to the place. So I thought to myself, 'I'll catch this bastard!' He was a migrant fellow that had a taxi in Katherine, making a pile running booze to Aboriginal communites. So I after him! And I'm getting his dust! He was gaining on me till he comes to the Roper. The water was running across the bar about ten or twelve inches deep. He must have hit it at a hell of a bloody rush and swamped his motor.

And by this time I'm right up him! I come flying over the dip and he's right in front of me on the crossing, stalled! I hit the brakes, but the brakes on the old blitz weren't up to much. You had to pump them five or six times. On the slippery wet cement I rammed into him. Right into his bumper! Must have been a fair impact because his back window flew clean out! Right out onto my bonnet! He spun sideways, broad-sided forward and ended across the bar with one wheel hanging over the edge.

We both got out and we're standing in the water and he's waving his arms and shouting 'You could'a killed me! You breaka da car!' and all this. And he said, 'I'm gonna go to the poliza!' I said, 'Well, you'd better be in a bloody hurry because that's just where I'm heading myself!'

So I drove up to the cop-shop, on the bank not far up. I said to the copper there, 'I just slammed into a bloody grog-runner down there on the bar.' He said, 'What'd you do?' I said, 'He'd been delivering bloody grog to the blacks' camp and he wouldn't pull up when I went to stop him.'

And he said, 'Oh, well. Sit down and have a cup of tea. We'll go down and see him in a bit.' And we're sitting there and suddenly this car goes tearing past and it's him! He'd got the thing going somehow. And Peter said, 'Oh, that's good. That'll save me a bit of paperwork! I'll ring up Mataranka in a minute and they can nail him when he goes through!' And later we went up the camp and found all these flagons that he had brought out so we had proof that he was running the grog alright. When the case came up they knocked his taxi licence off him.

I can honestly say that I did my best for the Aboriginals on Urapunga whenever I could. For the government to put money into improvements for the people the land had to be owned by them. So round about 1980 I cut off one square mile from the Urapunga lease to allow the people to own it. They called it the Rittarangu Community. Once they had that in their own right the government upgraded the housing to very nice little cottages with a verandah at the front and with space for lawns and gardens around. They put in a generating-plant and street lighting and a supermarket and a health clinic. They built a school with separate teacher's accommodation, very modern with everything spick and span; all carpeted; lawns all round and plenty of playground equipment, just like any school you would see in town. The kids had a uniform, navy-blue shorts or skirts and a red shirt with Urapunga School on the pocket.

1 Australian School of Pacific Administration, Sydney, where Patrol Officers and teachers were trained for service in the Northern Territory and Papua New Guinea.

fifteen...

'THE WRITING ON THE WALL'

Land Claims and Stirrers

In 1988, the year of the Australian Bi-Centenary, the Northern Territory Government approached all the Top End properties and asked them if they would donate a certain number of cattle for an old-style droving trip through to Longreach. The cattle were to be sold and the money was to go towards the Stockman's Hall of Fame to commemorate the droving days. They wanted a mob of twelve hundred head of steers to be walked across the Barkly. So each Top End property got a few head together to make up this mob.

The big send-off was at Newcastle Waters and they had half the RAAF there to put up big flash marquees and to do the catering. The day before the event all the big nobs from Darwin and Canberra started turning up.

I'd sent a good mob of bullocks so I got an invitation. I thought I might as well go along and catch up with some of the old-timers I expected to be there and have a bit of a feed. So after the speeches and the meal were over I'm looking around for my old mates, but I couldn't see any of them. I thought, 'Where the hell *is* everybody!' so I went outside looking for them. I saw old Clarrie Pankhurst and Emily and Edna Jessop, Edna Zigenbine and the others. I said to them, 'Aren't you mob going to go and have a bit of a feed? And they all looked at one another, and Edna said, 'Oh, yes! We've got plenty of tucker down in our camp.' I said, 'No. There's food provided. It's all catered.' They said, 'We don't know anything about a feed. We haven't been invited. What are you talking about?' I said, 'There's a big show going on down there for the Drovers' Send-off. I was looking round for you but I couldn't see any of you.' They'd known nothing about it! Hadn't got a look-in! So that's the way things go! Here's all the politicians and big brass with their nose-bags on and into the tucker and there's the genuine old drovers down on the bank of the creek! So much for the Drovers' Send-off! [1]

The Boss Drover for this Last Big Cattle Drive was Pic Willet. He was called 'Pic' because when he was droving as a little fellow they used to call him 'Piccaninny' and the name stuck. So Pic was in charge of taking this mob through from the Top End to Longreach. The people organizing the whole shebang used to bring in groups of volunteers who wanted to be able to say they had taken part in Australia's Last Great

Cattle Drive. By the time the cattle reached Longreach they'd had a few different fellows poking them along. But Pic and his team were doing all the real work. The volunteers would have been mostly on the tail, getting the dust.They used to be taken out by bus to join the drive then taken back again at night to a hotel, and fed up well under big tents. So she was an elaborate sort of a droving trip! At the end of the trip those cattle were sold at auction, on the fourth of September, 1988, and a cheque was presented to the Stockman's Hall of Fame. They brought very good prices. I was amazed at the prices we got for our lot.

A bit of an annoyance to me was that – I suppose a bloke shouldn't give a damn – but anyone who made a reasonable donation to the Hall of Fame was supposed to get a Life Membership. I don't know what happened but I didn't get so much as a bloody mention. The amount of cattle we donated was a very nice cheque but we never got so much as a thank you. Yet people who only gave a donation of a couple of thousand dollars got their names on the brass plaque. I don't know what happened to mine! They must have thought I was too much of an old bushie! I'm buggered if I know!

Then we started to get these stirrers coming up from the south, poking round trying to cause trouble between the blacks and the whites. One day I was working on a pump down in the machinery-shed, and I see a car drive in past the homestead and down towards the camp. I'm not taking much notice. But after a while I see this fellow up at the homestead, poking round the house with a camera, a big flash thing, mounted up on his shoulder.

So I went over and I said to him, 'How y' going?' And he just ignored me, just kept swinging this camera this way and that, filming. So I went up to him and said, 'What do you think you're doing?'

He stopped for a bit and said, 'I'm making this film of the difference between where the blacks live up at their camp and this homestead of yours.' I said, 'Why? What's the problem?' 'Oh,' he said, 'It's bloody disgraceful! That's why I'm here. You sit on your backside here like Lord Muck and you've got these poor blacks working for you like so many slaves. Taking advantage of them. I'm making this film so I can take it back and show the people down south the facts!'

I said to him, 'Look, Mate. I don't know what you're coming at but you've got no bloody right to be in my house! I think you'd better piss off!'

But he just ignored me. He kept on filming. Well, that was it! I grabbed the camera and pelted it out on to the lawn. I said 'You get to bloody hell out of here! Now! Grab your bloody camera and get going!' And I said, 'You know, Mate! The likes of you bastards coming up here, all you're trying to do is big-time yourselves! These people here were happy and contented. They don't need the likes of you coming here to stir them. What would you city fellows know about conditions out here! Bugger all! You've never done a hard day's work in your bloody lives! Now get to hell off my property and be quick about it!'

I jumped in the Toyota and went over to Roper Bar and saw the copper. I said to him, 'I've just come over to tell you that I've had a bit of a run-in with some smart-Alec from down south. A flash-looking cove, all done up like a ringer; gabardine riding-pants, William's boots, Akubra; the lot! I found him poking round the house. I don't know who the hell he is but he was getting around with a bloody great camera filming the place. He said he was going to show them down south the difference between how the blacks and the whites live.'

He said, 'What did you do?' I said, Oh, I chucked him out! Told him to piss off ! Chucked his camera into the garden!' He said to me, 'Well, if he comes over here whingeing about it I will want to know what permission he had to be on your property in the first place. I wouldn't worry too much about it.'

These stirring-buggers were always coming around. One bloke that came along said to me that he was writing a thesis on Aboriginals for his university degree and asked me if he could stay around. I thought to myself, 'Oh, well. He's not doing me any harm.' So I said to him, 'Well, you're not throwing your swag up in the camp. You can stay here with me.' He said, 'Oh, I've been sort've invited.'

I said, 'Look! I've told you! You are welcome to stay here but I don't want any whites hanging around in the camp. It's not our place.' Because there was a certain type of fellow that liked to move in on the gins and take advantage of them. I wasn't having it.

This fellow didn't seem to be a bad poor sort of a bugger. He would go up to the camp in the mornings and sit around under the trees writing in a big notebook. I thought to myself, 'Oh, well, he's just poking around there. He doesn't seem to be doing any harm.' And after a while he left. Later I found out that he was one of the chief instigators of the Aboriginal Land Rights claims!

About that time there was a Land Claim Court held at Urapunga presided over by Justice John Toohey of the Supreme Court of the Northern Territory. They said they chose Urapunga because it was more or less handy to the area under dispute, which was the Limmen Bight area, all the coastal area from the mouth of the Cox to the Nathan. Urapunga could provide accommodation for the judiciary and the officials. We had a couple of big sheds there where they could have held the proceedings, but, no, it had to be out of doors so as not to make the Aboriginals feel at a disadvantage. So to make it more along the lines of an Aboriginal set-up I put up a bough-shed big enough for fifty people, under some shady trees, halfway between the homestead and the camp. Besides Justice John Toohey there were anthropologists and court officials and a lady with ear-phones, the court-recorder, to make sure that everything was going through OK on tape. The officials were the only ones that had chairs to sit on. The rest of us were sitting down in the dirt, blackfella style.

So we are all sitting there, all the Urapunga mob and blacks from near and far; some I had never seen in my life before. They had to give their cause why they felt they were eligible to claim some of this land. There was one chap there – he was pretty close-up white; quarter-cast at most – and he'd come from Hall's Creek. And the official fellow who was asking all the questions asked him, 'Well, if you come from Hall's Creek, why do you feel you have a claim to this Limmen Bight area?' He said, 'Aw! My grandmother, she was born here. And we Aboriginal people like plenty of fish in our diet so we all come over here every few months to catch fish to take back to Hall's Creek.'

And John Toohey said, 'Oh! Yes.' And he was asking him questions and examining him a bit. Meanwhile I am sitting down beside old Roy Kulakundu. He was a very well-respected tracker at Roper Bar. A very good man. And I'm looking at this quarter-cast-looking fellow from Hall's Creek and I thought to myself, 'I've been here a long time and I know the general run of the people, and I've never clapped eyes on this fellow before.' So I said to old Roy, 'Do you know that fella, Roy?'

Old Roy, he is scowling away, and he reckons, 'Nah! Me never bin lookim' long that fella bifor!' 'Well!' I said, 'Get up! Get up! And tell the judge! Tell him you don't know that person. Tell the judge you belong here. You've been here all your life and you've never seen that Hall's Creek fella before.' But he wouldn't get up. Aboriginals don't like to put themselves forward. They don't like to draw attention to themselves by speaking out. And I'm elbowing him and trying to get him to stand up.

And Toohey could see that I was egging Roy on and trying to get him to have his say. And he says, 'That man down there….; is there something he would like to tell me?' Now Roy was one of the tallest Aboriginals I'd seen. He'd be every bit of six foot four or six foot six; skinny as a wax match with the grease scratched off, as the saying goes. And he never could buy trousers long enough to fit him; you'd always see his ankles, and these long strides, tied in around the waist with a bit of a belt or a bit of rope. And he gets to his feet.

And Justice Toohey says to him, 'Now, is there something you would like to say to the court? What have you got to tell me?'

Well, Roy bent over, and he pointed at John Toohey, and he says, 'Eh! You! Mr. Judge! You bin look'im that fella there!' and he points at this fellow from Hall's Creek, 'That fella there! Him rubbish fella! Him bull-shit! Him not bilong this country! Him f—k-all nothin!'

Well, you weren't allowed to laugh. It's the Official Land Claim Court Hearing. But John Toohey sort've screwed his face around a bit and gave a bit of a cough and straightened his glasses. The other officials are busting a gut not to smile. As for the lady with the ear-phones on, well they nearly jumped off her head! It wasn't that Roy was trying to shock anybody. He wasn't trying to be nasty-mouthed, or crude. He was just telling the truth straight out; in the only way he knew.

Anyway, then Toohey asked Roy a few questions. And Roy told him straight that he had never seen that fellow from Hall's Creek in his country before. He told it in his own way but he got the message across. Judge Toohey soon woke up to it that this fellow from Hall's Creek was just pulling a swiftie; trying it on for what he could screw out of the system. He got nothing. The upshot of it all was that Limmen Bight was declared an Aboriginal Reserve. Up till that time it had simply been Crown Land.

Over time all the old historic names were changed to Aboriginal ones; Elsey Station became Jolkmilkin, Rose River Mission became Numbulah, Delissaville became Belyuen, Beswick became Bamyili and so on. The one that got to me was when they changed Gove to Nhulunbuy. Gove was named in honour of Flight

Lieutenant Gove, the first Australian pilot to be killed over Australian territory by the Japs during the war. He was shot down over towards Milimgimbi. There is a memorial cairn to him at Gove airstrip.

The missions at Roper River and Rose River, or Ngukurr and Numbulwah as they are known today, did a very fine job on very limited resources up until the time they were taken over by the government. They had some very dedicated people there, living on the smell of an oil-rag and doing the work because they loved the people and wanted to help them a bit towards being self-sufficient. When the church was running Roper River Mission it had a saw-mill and a cattle project and big gardens. They encouraged the people to work and they were busy and happy and healthy and took pride in themselves. The mission did a much better job of things than the government did when it took over. Then the spirit seemed to go out of the place. The saw-mill closed down and the gardens went to rack and ruin. The people started moving away to the Katherine and Darwin.

Ngukkur went downhill. The white staff that came there were among the stirrers causing me a lot of trouble. Young things, straight from the city, and here they were, telling me how I should be treating my Aboriginals! Most of them just fresh out of ASOPA! They would tell me, 'Look! These are tribal lands. You've got no right to be here! The Aboriginals don't need a white-fellow running cattle on their lands. It's their country. You should piss off!' If I tried talking to them they would start quoting Professor Elkin[2] at me as though he was God Almighty; '.............Oh! But Professor Elkin says................' I would tell them, 'I've been living and working with Aboriginals all my life! How long did your Professor Elkin spend up in these parts trying to make a go of things?'

And when it came to alcohol, weren't these people the world's worst! There was a lovely waterhole on the Wilton where they liked to go for picnics. It was on Urapunga and within the No Alcohol zone. I told them they were very welcome to come there and have a swim and boil up the billy, but no alcohol. Oh! Wasn't I the bloody worst in the world!

At the same time I was having a rough time with wire-cutting. I would get cattle mustered and put in paddocks ready for trucking next day, and, come morning you would find that during the night someone would have come in and cut the fences or chucked the gates down and let your cattle go. You had to pretty-well watch them twenty-four hours a day once you had got them in the yards ready to truck otherwise they'd be lost to you and you'd have to start mustering all over again. There was absolutely nothing you could do about it. You felt you were fighting a losing battle.

Or I would be getting ready to muster and some young town black, always an outsider, never any of the Urapunga blacks, would front up and he'd tell me, 'You can't muster up that Wilton Valley way. We're gunna have a big ceremony there. You keep away! We don't want you nosing round our ceremony grounds.' I would say to him, 'Look! I don't go anywhere near your ceremony grounds. I steer clear of them. Always have! But I've got to get my cattle mustered.'

The same thing would happen time after time. They would tell me I was mustering on sacred sites. Well, Duncan had been very careful right from the word Go to point out all the sacred sites to me and I was always scrupulous about them. I respect any man for what he believes. But not when they start telling me that some bit of a log or old stump is sacred because Auntie-bilong-'im scratched her backside there back in the 1950s, or some tommy-rot. They would pull this kind of stunt to annoy me all the time.

While Old Duncan Yappanala was alive the situation was manageable. Any problem with these outsiders from Ngukkur or from town and I only had to mention them to Duncan and he would up them good and proper. But in the end the poor old bugger succumbed to cancer. He'd been my right hand man all through the years; always there at my side. I couldn't have done it without him. I hated to see him end his days like that. He deserved better. A very decent, honest man, and a very good, loyal friend to me.

Today you are flat out to get Aborigines to work on the stations. They seem to just want to head into town and pick up their dole. They get as far as Mataranka or Katherine and when they are stone motherless broke and buggered up with the grog they drift off home and wait till the next dole day. It is terrible to think what the Aboriginal race has come to. I know there are white fellows that do the same thing, but I particularly notice it in the Aborigines, knowing how happy they used to be in the old days on Urapunga, always laughing, always singing at night, getting great satisfaction out of the work they did. They thrived on it. And took pride in the job. I am sure the problem is the result of the government giving them dough they don't have to work for. No man feels pride in himself unless he has to work for what he gets. Grog and easy-money have knocked the guts out of the Aboriginal people

The young girls are just as bad. One day, during wet season time, I was working over at the yards, and this young gin was standing there with a piccaninny in her arms. I thought she might have wanted me to tell the hospital at Ngukkur that the little baby was sick. She said, 'Hey! Maluka! You like this baby?' I said, 'Oh, Yes. He's a nice little fellow. What's up with him?' She said, 'Him orright. You like take this baby? You can keep him.' I still didn't catch on. I said, 'What's wrong with him? Is he sick, or something?' She said, 'Oh, him all-time humbug! Young-girl don't like look after baby all time! Him too much humbug!' She was giving him away! As though he was a puppy or a kitten! I told her, 'Humbug nothing! You get back up that bloody camp and you look after him properly!'

When I told old Doreen, she said, 'I get a stick and I flog her! I flog her proper! Them young girls got look after them piccaninny!' She was shaking her poor old head about it, knocked sideways at how the young people were turning out.

But, I don't know! Once they had got the taste for that alcohol and sitting on their backsides doing nothing, they seemed to go to the pack. The good feeling seemed to go out of the place. You didn't hear the singing and click-sticks coming from up in the camp of a night-time any more. The old spirit was gone. Some of the older ones started dying off and they didn't get the big ceremonies of the old times. The younger ones didn't seem to have any respect for them anymore, and, a few this month and a few next, they started packing into their cars and moving away into Mataranka and Katherine, or up to Darwin. Anywhere would do, as long as it was handy to the dole-office and the pubs.

These were a few of the hassles we had on Urapunga towards the end. And once you got these stirrers coming up from down south causing trouble there is little incentive for white people to stay in the north. You were wondering all the time how long you would be able to run your place the way you needed to. It was sticking out a mile; with so much stacked against you, if you didn't get out you would end up walking away with nothing. The writing was on the wall.

Both my boys, Peter and David, grew up loving the Territory. When they were at school they'd come over for the holidays, and after they left school they both wanted to come back to the Territory to work. But I remembered what my father had said about young fellows knocking about a bit and working under a boss to get a bit of experience. So Peter, the eldest, after he finished at Gatton College, went as a stockman over on Legune, on the Territory-West Australian border. David, the youngest, was on Nutwood Downs for four years and ended up running the camp.

But with all the land-claiming and alchohol problems and fence-cutting and other issues, things seemed to be going from bad to worse all the time. It was one thing after another and it never seemed to come to an end. Both the boys were getting to that stage where they were starting to think about the future. They asked me if I ever gave any thought to selling up and getting to hell away from it all. They reckoned the good feeling had gone out of the Territory and that they would be better off moving back to Queensland and getting a bit of land away from it all. They wanted me to get out, too, while the going was good. They came to me one night and put it to me; 'Hey, Old Fella!' – they always call me Old Fella – 'How about we get to hell out of this and all move back to Queensland!' They said they were both thinking about getting settled down somewhere without all the problems that were developing in the Territory.

I said to them, 'I'm not just giving everything away after all years I've put in. I built the place up from nothing. But I'll put it on the market.' What I meant was, more or less just to test the waters to see how it would go. I thought it would take years to sell. I went up and saw a stock agent in Darwin, Dave Loveridge. I said, 'I've got a job for you. The boys aren't happy here any more, with all the alcohol problems and land-claiming that's been going on. They want to move back Queensland way.'

He said, 'Hang on! You're not selling! You're not leaving after all the work you've put in down there! God! Don't give that place away! You've got everything there; the beautiful river; beautiful homestead; beautiful cattle.' It has got to be something when the agent tries to talk you out of putting your place on the market. But I told him that with all the problems that were developing I could see nothing but trouble in the years to come. In the end he said, 'Oh, well. I'll make a few inquiries then.'

It couldn't have been a week later that he rang and said, 'I'm flying down today with a client. He wants to have a look at the place as part of a tourist and cattle venture.' And they came down, and flew around the place. Had a look at the river. Stayed the night.' And the next day he rang me up from Darwin, and he said, 'Can you come up and sign.' Just like that.

I felt, that's it! My world has come to an end! It was as though I was losing everything in life that made any sense to me.

Towards the end I was there on my own. The boys had gone. They were back in Queensland chasing properties. The night I left, I went up to the camp and saw all the old blacks. The old ladies, they were wailing, and saying, 'Maluka! Don't go! Urapunga home bilong you! We like you stop here!' Tears were rolling down their faces. I had tears in my own eyes! And when I drove away I didn't go back to the house. Too many memories. Instead, I went over and camped on the river. The Roper had been part of my life for so long. I listened to the splashes out in the dark that could have been salties or freshies, the flying-foxes, the water running over the rocks at the bar, all the night noises in the bush. I thought to myself, 'No. I won't go back in the morning. I'll just head off down the track.'

Those days on Urapunga were the happiest of my life, but I knew it was no use looking back. You have always got to look to the future, to the years to come.

1 The irony of this story is that those who 'hadn't been invited' and 'knew nothing about it' were some of the most famous drovers who ever took stock across the infamous Murranji track, and who had become legends in their own lifetimes for their fortitude, skill and courage.

2 Professor Adolphus Peter Elkin, CMG; 1891 – 1979; anthropologist. President of the Society for the Protection of Native Races 1933 -1962. A noted authority on the religion of the Australian Aborigines.

sixteen...

'AN EYE TO THE FUTURE'

Return to Tabletop; Cattle-Raising Around the World

And so we shifted back to Queensland. Peter and his wife Leeann are in partnership at Tabletop with me now and have more or less taken over. They have Katherine and John, both very clever kids. Young John was giving me a hand speying some cows recently. He's about twelve. He said, 'Grandad! Can you come and have a look if this is the right bit I'm cutting out!' He's learning on the job.

We're close to the market in Townsville. There's one cattle boat which comes in to Townsville, the *Danny F* that loads fifteen thousand head of cattle for the trade with Egypt. It's all pens. All air-conditioned! Fourteen decks, all cooled! When you see a mob of a thousand head strung out across a flat, well, it's a lot of cattle. But fifteen thousand on one ship! I believe on one trip they had a loss of three head. Three! You can get three killed in a yard in a day when you're mustering!

My second son David, and his wife Michelle, they're on Railview, out at Prairie. Their cattle go in to Cloncurry. There's a story about this Yank once, reading the *North Queensland Register*. He sees the heading, '3000 head of cattle into the Curry'. He says, 'Hell! That sure is some curry! Even in Texas we don't make 'em that big!' In the 'Curry they are cleared and trucked up to Darwin.

David and Michelle's boy, Samuel, goes to Churchie, down in Brisbane. I went down to Townsville to meet him off the plane when he came home for the first lot of holidays. I said to him, 'G'day Sam. How's it going?' He told me, sort've mournfully, 'It's a long way from Railview.' Sam was once bitten by a king brown. There was an edging of stones around the outside border of the lawn at Railview. He was balancing around on these and the snake got him on the foot. Luckily both David and Michelle were up inside the house. A financial adviser who came round every twelve months just happened to be there at the time going over the books with them. Normally David would have been out mustering somewhere. They heard young Sammy give a scream and they raced down. They grabbed him and put him on the kitchen table and washed the bite and bound his leg as tight as they could – which is the correct procedure these days; the venom travels in the lymph not the blood-stream – and raced him into Prairie.

The police officer in Prairie was a trained medic. He had been a hospital nurse before he took on police work. They raced him out to Hughenden. The Hughenden ambulance met them along the road but they could see the town in the distance so they didn't want to stop. Sam was losing consciousness and his eyes were rolling back in his head. They thought they were losing him. Every moment was precious and they reckoned they'd lose time changing vehicles so they just kept going.

Ray's son, David, with his son Sam. The steer had been 'poddied' or hand-fed as a calf and was so tame it could be ridden.

As soon as they got to the hospital they ripped the antivenene into him. Meanwhile the staff there had been on to a doctor down in Bendigo, a Dr. McCormack – the specialist in venomous snake-bite all over Australia. He was giving them them directions by phone. The sister told David and Michelle that everything that could be done was being done and that all they could do was just to go outside and wait.

Meanwhile one of their neighbours back at Prairie had phoned us and we're racing out to be there with them. And after a long while, they came out and said, 'Well, we've managed to save him but it was touch and go!' His blood had started to coagulate. He was in the critical stage in Intensive Care all through the night. Every half an hour they had to take a urine sample and test it. They kept him in hospital for three days in case of any reaction. It was a good few weeks before that foot healed up and it was nasty and inflamed for a long time.

David and Michelle also have little Anna. They run her in to school in Prairie each day, about seven or eight ks. They had another little girl but they lost her. Alexandra had cerebral palsy from birth, and she took a very bad turn one morning at the homestead. They raced her into the hospital in Hughenden but they weren't able to save her.

Losing Alex was very hard on young Sam. The two of them had been great mates. Sammy had one of those battery-powered cars, like a Jeep, and he would put Alex in it, and drive all around the flat and over to the yards, with Alex sitting up beside him. After she passed away he said sorrowfully, 'I won't be able to take Alex driving anymore, will I?' He had always been very good to her. He would wheel her all round in her wheel-chair and you would hear them laughing together all the time.

Alex was a flower-girl at her Auntie Mary's wedding at the Anglican Church in Home Hill, and Sammy was page-boy. Alex looked like a little princess. Sam wheeled her down the aisle behind the bride. You would never think she was handicapped to look at her. She was eight, just turning nine when she died. It was a terribly sad time, but, still, life has to go on.

Ray and Betty Fryer in the garden at Tabletop.

Diane, our daughter, is married to Bill Alford. They have Rainsby out at Aramac. Bill is a great man for horses; all the time buying and breaking-in and he's got good mares he puts to quality stallions. Bill was from Grass Hut, Mingela way, originally. He was an All Souls' boy too, but he ran away, like me! And like me, Bill will tell you, he just wanted to get on with stock work. You'd go a long way to find a better man.

Diane and Bill's boys Timothy and John, both go to Souls. In Year Ten the school allows them to bring their own swags, and they are taken out to some of the cattle properties around the district; Hillgrove, not far out of the Towers, up the Burdekin; and Toomba, owned by an old boy of the school, Ernest Bassingwaite, and to Fletchervale, Chris Allingham's place. They camp out and do a bit of work in the cattle yards; about four boys at a time; not a big group of kids that are going to muck up. At All Souls the swag is part of the school gear. It might be the only school in Australia where a swag is on the list of Requirements that parents have to provide when their boys start. The school takes the boys down to the Burdekin camping and to places like Malanda and Cairns to learn cattle-judging.

The younger two in Diane and Bill's family are Scottie and Fiona who do School of the Air at home. They had a bad scare with Fiona when she had an asthma attack one night. Diane raced her into Aramac, about an hour and a quarter's drive. Fiona was turning blue by the time Diane got her there but they put her on to oxygen straight away and the Flying Doctor took her down to Rocky.

Scottie is dying to get away to Souls. He said to his Dad, 'Tim and John are at Souls! Why can't I go!' Bill said to him, 'Whoa! Hold on there, Mate! I'm flat out keeping up with the fees as it is! You'll get your turn when the time comes!' Bill and Diane have had a rough time in the drought, agisting their bullocks away and just maintaining their breeders. I drive out almost weekly with loads of feed, or drums of molasses, to try to keep the breeders going on both Railview and Rainsby.

Feeding the horses at Tabletop.

I help with all three properties, with the mustering and branding. I ride around the paddocks noticing what needs doing, though these days I keep one of those note-books that the Stock and Station agents send out at Christmas in my pocket to jot down if I notice a patch of rubber-vine or lantana that needs spraying, or a fence is down. If I don't write it down I might forget it!

I have a couple of projects on the go here at Tabletop. There is a big granite monolith across the creek from the homestead and Mother used to tell us, 'When I die that is where you can bury me.' So that is where both she and Dad are buried. I am putting a new fence around it with a chain between the posts to try to keep it a bit nice. When I step off the planet that is where I would like to end up. It is a very peaceful, beautiful spot with the mountains all around and birds and trees. I want to be buried in my swag. None of this cutting down rain-forest trees to waste on coffins for me. I asked my cousin Terry Lyons, who is a Catholic priest, if it would be legal to be buried in a swag. He said, 'Yes. It would be OK. And when the time comes we'll just roll you up in it and lay you down beside the grave. And when the "Ashes to ashes, dust to dust" bit comes, I'll just give you a bit of a shove with my foot and in you'll go!'

I also have it in mind to erect a monument at the junction of the three main stock-routes that used to come down out of the Gulf near Dalrymple Crossing, in honour of the old-time drovers who did those trips. They are mostly dead and gone now and I would like to set up a big granite boulder with a brass plaque with their names on it.

I have always liked to be on the go, so after the kids were all settled I bought myself a round-the-world ticket. I went to Bombay, then to Bahrain, then in to Kuwait – that fellow who invaded Kuwait, Saddam Hussein, he must have been coming down the road the day I was getting out; we cut it that fine. Then I had a good look around Cairo. They seem to mainly eat camel. You see long lines of them coming down to a big camel market. To slaughter them they just rip a knife into their jugular and wait until they fall over.

From Cairo I went down to Kenya and had a look round and then on down into Zimbabwe. Good cattle country there, but, at the airport they gave me a bit of a hard time. They took my passport off of me and said it wasn't legal. I said to them, 'Look, Mate! What are you coming at! I've been in seventeen different countries with that passport. Of course it's legal.'

They wouldn't have that. I've been told I look a bit like old Ian Smith, the Rhodesian Prime Minister, so they might have had it in for me for that. They wanted five hundred American dollars to give me my passport back. They marched me out to this bloody tin shed out the back and shoved me in. I thought to myself, 'Christ! I'm not letting them lock that bloody door on me!' So I shoved it open and just at that moment this fellow walks past, and I thought to myself, 'If that's not an Aussie I'll eat my bloody hat!' There was something about him; the way he walked or something; you could tell by the look of him. Maybe he had a can of Foster's in his hand! But I called out to him, 'Hey, Mate! Can you get on to the embassy and get someone out here to sort this lot out!' And he did! But, gee, it was touch and go there for a bit! And when I got my passport back, they'd scratched out my name and altered it, and the date of birth and everything. Scratched it out and written someone else's in! The lady from the embassy sorted it all out, and she said to me, 'Don't go doing your block or they'll slap you under lock and key as soon as look at you!'

So then I continued down on to South Africa. The amount of cattle and wildlife they can run on properties there is unreal! Then back to Europe and England and to the States. I'd been to Calgary a few times – and Qantas asked me if I would like act as a tour leader taking groups of people over to the Calgary Stampede. I did four trips for them.

I had a look at the King Ranch and some other places in Idaho and in the northern part of South Dakota, but, well, everything is feed-lotting. They pull them off their mothers at about seven months and shove them in these feed-lots. One feed-lot there had thirty-odd thousand head in it. And big semi-trailers like cement mixers come through full of grain and they just auger it out into big troughs. And a chap is sitting there in the office at a computer and he's poking buttons and all the grain is going into big silos. They've got it down to a fine art. If they can't turn off a beast in a certain number of days they're losing money because of all the grain that's going into them.

The properties seem to be small and controlled. The husband and wife and the kids get into their flash cowboy outfits, chaps and all, and they have all these pretty ponies, and they go out for the day and then they all come home at night. Very nice people, extremely hospitable. But I got a couple of young fellows from there a job over here up in the Gulf. They stuck it for a couple of months but then they gave it away. They couldn't understand how we do it, with the size of the places and everything. I said to them, 'Well, you do your best and it works out, eh!'

I went right round the world looking at how they raise cattle in different countries. But I'll tell you what! You'll go a long way before you'll better an Aussie on the job! An Aussie stockman, Mate! You can't beat him! There's no better man!

Afterword...

RETURN TO URAPUNGA
OCTOBER 2003

In October, 2003, at the invitation of a remnant group of Aboriginal elders of the Rittarangu tribe, Ray returned to Urapunga to discuss with them their idea of his returning to Urapunga to get the property back on its feet as a working cattle station. The elders hoped that the young people of the tribe who had drifted away to Mataranka, Katherine and Darwin would then have a reason to come back to their tribal lands to job opportunites and a meaningful and healthy life-style for them and their children. In this they had the backing of ATSIC, the Aboriginal and Torrres Strait Islander Investment Commission.

The head teacher of Urapunga School, Charlotte Thompson, had on behalf of the elders, approached the Commission with a written proposal that members of the Commission should visit Urapunga to see for themselves the opportunities such a scheme would provide and to discuss how it could be put into action. A team from ATSIC came and preliminary investigations and discussions took place. Agreement was reached that what was vital to the implementation of the concept was a project leader, someone with expertise and practical experience in running a cattle station in the Top End's difficult conditions, and also an understanding of and empathy with the tradtional owners, their spiritual relationship to the land and to one another, their history and their culture. In the words of Doreen Yappanala, the widow of Duncan Yappanala, Ray's staunch Aboriginal off-sider and friend of many years, what was needed was 'that old Boss-man, Ray Fryer, him come back again.'

Urapunga was handed over by the Commonwealth government to the traditional owners, the Ngalakgan people, in 1996, following a land claim made by them under the Aboriginal Land Rights Act. Since that time the station, its homestead, cattle-yards, abattoir, sheds, work-shops and air-strip had been allowed to fall into a state of neglect. The cattle had gone. As Ray said, 'They sold the cattle the week after I left. Mustered and sold the bloody lot!' Before making a decision about whether the concept of getting the property up and running again for the benefit of the Aboriginal owners was feasible or not, Ray wanted to see for himself what sort of state the place was in. At the hand-over ceremony, in May, 2002, Galarrwau Yunupingu, the chairman of the Northern Land Council, had said 'the conversion to inalienable freehold title provides the Ngalakgan people with a host of options...which could include tourism, buffalo safari hunting, and pastoral

Ray & friends with whom he returned to Urapunga to attend meetings with the Rittarangu Community Elders.
left to right
Ray Fryer
Estelle Moody
Bluey Bostock
Marion Houldsworth
& Bluey Ellis.

Leaving Tabletop, October 2003.

operations.' Ray needed to decide for himself how viable any of these 'options' were.

He was accompanied on the trip north by four concerned and interested friends; two 'Blueys' – Bluey Ellis and Bluey Bostock, Estelle Moody, the widow of Les Moody, manager of Anthony's Lagoon, and the present writer, Marion Houldsworth. Ray's greatest reservation, he told us, was that he had doubts about whether the young people of the tribe had the will to make the scheme work. He told us, 'Urapunga was supposed to have been given back to the people as tribal hunting lands, but a group of young fellows went up there into the Wilton valley a while back in a vehicle and they got big rain that night and couldn't get back. And it's not that far to bloody walk; about seven miles. We used to walk it all the time! Anyway, big panic on! And you wouldn't believe it, but the government sent a helicopter out from Katherine, a couple of hundred miles and God knows what expense, to bring them back! A seven mile walk! Traditional hunting grounds! I don't think they've thrown a bloody spear on the place since they got it!' He drove a few miles in deep thought, then added, 'Unless the young blokes have got their hearts set on building the place up into some sort of enterprise it will come to nothing. You've got to be willing to get stuck into things and put your back into them to make them work!'

After the fourteen hundred mile drive from Tabletop through drought-stricken Western Queensland, across the Barkly and up the Bitumen before heading two hundred miles east on the Arnhem Highway from Mataranka, it was a key moment when at last we made the crossing of the historic bar at the Roper, the wheels of the Toyota wheels axle-deep in sparkling water, the river-bank luxuriant with magnificent paperbarks and pandanus, just as Ray had described. Further along the road we passed his celebrated Alcohol Free Zone sign, and when five buffaloes lumbered out of the timber it seemed that Ray's account of his days on the Roper was coming to life before our eyes. But there the similarity ended.

At the abandoned homestead, we found contract bull-shooter Scottie Burke, Ray's buffalo-hunting mate of former years, who had once 'laughed all the bloody way home' when they staked three tyres and had to walk. Scottie was camped behind an abandoned stockman's cottage overlooking the river. The cottage had previously been Rod Ansell's, of 'Crocodile Dundee' fame. Perhaps signalling sympathy for what awaited Ray, Scottie greeted him, 'G'day, Cattle King!'

The homestead and gardens at Urapunga in a state of dereliction. The 'Wilton Hilton' sign welcomed visitors who flew in to Urapunga from airstrips all over Australia.

By this time I had been working with Ray on the tapes and materials for this book for fifteen months and had formed a clear image of Urapunga station in my mind. But all preconceptions had now to be scrapped. Reality was about to kick in. And reality took some coming to grips with.

First, there was the silence. I have lived on stations; Caberfeidh and Stainburn Downs at Aramac, Chatsworth at Duchess, Banka Banka at Tennant Creek, and Hooker Creek, an Aboriginal Welfare cattle project on the edge of the Tanami desert. A working station has a sense of vitality. Orders are shouted, cattle bellow, horses stamp. Dust rises; dogs bark; chooks scratch about; children laugh and windmills clank and click. There is a sense of purpose, of meaningful work being got on with. Instead, at the deserted Urapunga homestead, there was only a brooding silence and the screechings of corellas along the river, and crows, sardonic in the morning heat.

Ray led the way to show us around. The establishment was much vaster than I had imagined – homestead, workshops, equipment sheds, blocks of accommodation units, the original school, all in a state of complete dereliction. Of the botanic-gardens-like setting of the homestead nothing remained. The 'Wilton Hilton' sign that had signalled hospitality to all comers, hung drunkenly from the skeleton arm of a dead poinciana. Dessicated lawns crunched to dirt as we passed. I glanced at Ray, wondering how any man could come to terms with seeing all he had worked for, literally turned to dust. Ray, looking thoughtful, slapped a white-anted stump and remarked, 'That would have been the henna tree I was telling you about,' adding, 'This was where I had my ornamental well.' The stone basin was choked with debris. 'I had crotons, those splashy red and gold ones, all around here,' he said, then, staring reflectively at the relics of garden beds, 'They were full of ferns, y'know.'

Inside the homestead we instinctively lowered our voices. Walls, ceilings and floors were filthy. Doors hung from cupboards, overhead fans sagged, windows, louvres and tiles had been smashed. Anything that could be broken had been broken. 'Young buggers!' said Ray, without particular rancour, 'I don't know why, but they will walk miles to smash glass.' In the kitchen the oven stood rusted, its days of providing 'good plain tucker, and plenty of it' long gone. In the radio room I thought of the many calls that had gone out on the air-waves for help; for Sammy after the shooting; for the Flying Padre after Stan Norgren's death, for sick children, for women in childbirth. The examination table which Ray had installed for the Air Med doctors lay buckled. Someone had defecated against it. In the main lounge room, the 'thirty by twenty' that Ray had been so proud of, scattered dung showed where cattle had camped. Ray had made the bricks and built this home with his own hands. Now, pushing his hat to the back of his head, his only comment was, 'Y'know! With a good pressure hose, it wouldn't take more than a couple of weeks to get this all cleaned up. A couple of thousand bucks in paint and glass and electrics and she'd be OK again'. It has got to be a gift in a man not to know when he is beaten.

In one of the flagstones on the verandah a fossilized fern was partly obscured by a drift of dead leaves. When we stopped to admire it Ray grinned, 'Yeah! I caught just about everybody with that! I made a slab and printed the fern into it while it was wet.' We laughed and it crossed my mind that without intending to, Ray will have perpetuated for millennia to come, not only his sense of humour but his boundless enthusiasm for whatever task he sets his hand to.

At the far end of the derelict garden was a concrete slab littered with shards of fibrolite in the midst of which stood a bereft-looking enamelled stove. It was the remains of the 'nice little place' that Ray had built for Stan the Saddler to spend his declining years. Close by was the school which Ray had built for the Aboriginal children; louvres broken, wall-panels smashed in. Dry leaves rattled through the classroom, ablution block, toilets and laundry, where every morning the old ladies had collected the children's clothes and boiled them in the abandoned coppers.

On the top rail of the horse-yards were five saddles, cracked with exposure. 'See that one,' said Ray, 'That's one that Stan made. A bloody shame to see it like that!' 'Take it back with you!' I urged. 'For Stan's sake! Take it to Tabletop!' But, no! Honest as the sun at noon, Ray would not consider it. 'It wouldn't be the right thing to do,' was all he said. Speculatively, I considered the deteriorating saddle. But even I could see that it was not the sort of thing that could be smuggled on board an already over-loaded vehicle.

Ray Fryer and Doreen Duncan at Doreen's home on Urapunga. Both Ray and Doreen would like to see Urapunga restored to a working cattle station to benefit the tradtional land owners & the tribe.

Ray seemed to have greatest difficulty coming to terms with the state of the abattoir. He had invested a huge amount of money into it to save Urapunga in the cattle crash. Now it was derelict, the yards choked with weeds. A black wattle had established itself in the ramp. Inside the main building, our voices echoed. Ray detailed, with remembered pride, the procedures of slaughtering, butchering and freezing; how the cattle had come up, been brain-shot individually, dropped through the trap-door, hung and bled. Now the heavy meat-hooks were rusted into position on the steel track along which 'twenty to thirty a day' had swung towards the waiting boners and slushies. On the wall had been graffitied an anatomically correct depiction of female genitals ready for coition, captioned, 'ngardiz boy himself with all his broffer was here'. Others,

'Timmy' and 'Fabian the Zlarer' had added 'always here – drinking beer'.

By now we were trudging behind Ray in discouraged silence. It was all too depressing. With my family I had survived Darwin's Cyclone Tracy in 1974. The feeling of being powerless in the face of overwhelming odds was the same.

Then there was the the air-strip. The 'forty-two hundred foot' runway which Ray had cleared with the 'little old petrol Fergie' was cracked and eroded. Along its length regrowth suckers sprouted and new timber encroached at both ends. Ray rubbed his head in exasperation; 'I don't know!' he exploded, 'The government's given them a bloody grader and bull-dozer, and look! They can't even keep the air-strip open!' The landing-strip at Urapunga, to which the Air Med plane had come on its monthly visits and to which 'as many as seventeen planes a day' had come, now has A.L.A status only; 'Pilots land at their own discretion'. Ray said, 'The Department of Civil Aviation told them if they didn't chop the trees out of the approach to the air-strip they were going to close it. So do you know what they did! They got a contractor in Katherine to come out and do the work for them! They wouldn't think of doing it them-bloody-selves! So a couple of fellows came out from Katherine with chain-saws and cleared a bit of the timber away. But it grew back and now the air-strip is closed. That's just the way they are. It doesn't seem to worry them. They're given the equipment but they haven't got any energy! They can't seem to get on and do things! So much for the tourism and safari-hunting that Galurrway Yunupingu was on about!'

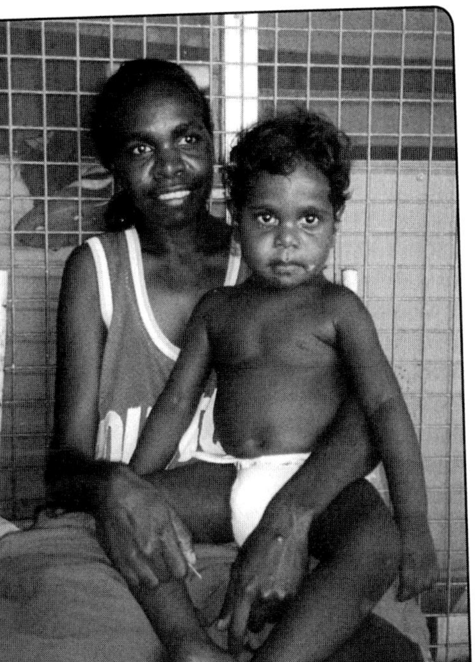

The face of the future.

We were by this time coming to the climax of our visit, Ray's impending meeting with the tribal elders. The 'camp up over the ridge', turned out to be a drive rather than a walk. 'Camp' is a misnomer. In reality the 'camp' is a township, or would be, if the people had not drifted away. There were several streets of pleasant cottages, but most had the locked and barred look of abandonment. Each had its own area of ground, some with a few trees, mangoes, poincianas or showy boungainvillea. By the side of the access road was a massively impressive power-house surrounded by a high steel fence. Nearby was a modern supermarket surrounded by palm-trees. It was boarded up.

At the school, an L-shaped building with wide verandahs, nine tiny children in red singlets, were playing on the lawn. I thought they might be a pre-school group. But no, that *was* the school! Inside, bright-coloured activity boards were set out in readiness for lessons. Ray and the Head Teacher, Charlotte Thompson, greeted one another like old friends. They had had many phone conversations about the proposition the elders were about to make to him. The four teachers shared an air-conditioned, carpeted staff-room. Having, in the 1960s, taught forty-three children aged from three to sixteen in a cement-floored ex-army hut at Delissaville, I thought how far Aboriginal education had come in the meantime. The children were pleased to have visitors and were eager to hear their own voices on my tape-recorder. They spoke beautifully and then showed us a special corner where they had set out a display for their Asian Studies course.

Next we visited Doreen Duncan on the verandah of her home. The bondedness between Doreen and Ray was immediately apparent. Ray couldn't keep the delighted grin off his face. Doreen, tiny yet indomitable, was deeply moved by Ray's arrival. It was Doreen who had seen that the task of restoring Urapunga to productivity could only be done by a man of Ray's calibre, and it was she who had initiated the appeal to the Northern Land Council to ask him to return. She had realized that it was no task for a mere do-gooder; that it would take someone with with Ray's experience in the cattle industry, his understanding of the people, his upright character, and, above all, his no-nonsense attitude to alcohol to get the job done. To the casual outsider she might appear a little old lady of no consequence but Doreen Duncan had the mind of a Boadicea ready to sound the battle-horn. Last of the old people of the old way, her enemies were the insidious forces of alcohol, drug addiction and apathy among the coming generations of her people.

She lamented, 'All my piccaninny! All my son! They sit around all day getting on the grog. And that drug! They sniff the petrol! Oh, Maluka! Them old-day long-you good time! All happy night-time. Click the sticks. Make the dance. All finish now!' She seized Ray's arm as though by his very presence he could make the old, meaningful times come again. 'These young fellas! They lazy! Should be break-in horses, go mustering! Learn things! Be proper men! You come back, Maluka! You come back! You and me, we fix 'em!'

While she spoke, a pleasant young woman, perhaps Doreen's grand-daughter, or great-grand-daughter, with a strikingly handsome toddler in a disposable nappy on her lap, listened with something between sympathy and embarrassment in her eyes. Educated and self-possessed, it was impossible to imagine her with face painted, breasts bared, stamping barefoot by firelight in the corroborees of yesteryear.

I felt I was witnessing the last throes of an era that has gone and cannot return. Ray, more phlegmatic, does not deal in negatives. There was a job to be done. If he was asked to do it, he would do it. He had come to attend these meetings. Attend he would. At the school this evening! No bloody messing about! Everybody had to show up! 'And!' he told us emphatically, as, having shaken hands all round and taken our leave, we drove back to our camp at the Crocodile Dundee cottage, 'I would want it on paper. All legally signed and sealed. A properly drawn up agreement with the Northern Land Council.' Already, in his mind's eye, he was getting this project up and running.

Ray, in his early-seventies, is just hitting his stride. His dynamism is that of a man half his age. If anybody can infuse new life-force into Urapunga, to re-establish it as the valuable resource to the traditional owners and to the Northern Territory economy which it is capable of being, and, importantly, restore to the young people of the Ngalakgan tribe a new belief in themselves and their future, it will be Ray Fryer. He knows and loves the land. He knows and loves the people. If it can be done, he will do it. Bloody oath! Yes!

Ray is a man who likes a challenge.

APPENDIX A

Extract from Report by Charles Todd, Esquire, on the Construction and Completion of the Overland Telegraph Line

January 1, 1873

SURVEY OF THE ROPER

Before leaving the Roper I gave Captain Lawrie instructions to take a complete set of soundings in the Roper, from its mouth up to the landing, to buoy and beacon the bar end channel, placing substantial beacons across its north, and where required on the south bank, between the bar and the river entrance; to mark by beacons, lopped trees, or otherwise, the position of all rocks and shallows in the river; to plot, on a general plan of the river, the deep water channel, and depth of water at low water springs; and to keep a record of the rise and fall of the tide, a tide board being fixed at the landing. This appeared to me the most profitable way in which I could employ the *Young Australian* (sic). I have not yet received Captain Lawrie's report but I understand he has carried out my instructions with much intelligence and zeal. From a telegram received from him, dated August last, he says that the upper river had fallen considerably, but there was little or no difference in the depth of water below Garden Reach, and that there on the bar, there is a foot more water than is shown on the chart, so that the river, in the driest season, is navigable for vessels drawing twelve feet for forty miles; above that there are two pinches I have before mentioned, in the Omeo, and three island reaches, where there is not more than ten or eleven feet, which are the chief obstacles to navigation higher up the river. The channel however could be easily deepened by dredging at these points were there any necessity for it.

STOCK LEFT AT THE ROPER

The following quantity of stock and plant were left at the Roper landing, by Mr Patterson, most of which will be available for carting the iron poles next season, viz;-

Stock	174 horses.
	325 bullocks
Plant and Equipment	16 horse wagons
	4 spring drays
	17 bullock wagons
	13 bullock drays
	32 saddles, harness, etc.

It is interesting to note that the 'iron poles', some of the redundant ones of which Ray made use of in beginning work on building the homestead at Urapunga, were in use in the construction of the Overland Telegraph line as early as 1873. Noting the numbers of wagons and drays used on' the line' it is easier to understand Ray's statement that there were 'any number' of old wagon-wheels lying around.

APPENDIX B

The Loss of the Young Australia – Extract from *Via Torres Strait*, by Ian Nicholson

Construction of the Overland Telegraph line between Adelaide and Darwin in the period 1870- 72 to connect with the submarine cable being laid from the latter port to Banjowangie in Java, called for considerable shipping support. While three cable-laying vessels came down from Singapore to work on the undersea link, there was a long haul from South Australia, eastward via Torres Strait, with surveyors, labourers, building supplies, stores and provisions, etc, for the northern half of the overland route. Some cargo was brought by sailing ship but steamships such as the *Bengal, Dolphin, Omeo* and *Young Australia* were also involved.

The auxiliary screw steamer *Omeo* was probably one of the best known and most frequently seen passenger and supply ships on this run. She was chartered in 1870 by Darwent and Dalwood for the northern section of the telegraph, and first passed through the Straits on about 1st September. The firm ran into difficulties because of the wet season, but pushed the line as far south as Katherine before going broke. When the contract was cancelled in May, 1871, the South Australian Government took over the task, including the *Omeo* charter. Leaving Melbourne in August 1871 she led a flotilla of four sailing vessels north through Torres Strait to Port Darwin with 100 men, 170 horses, and five hundred bullocks as well as countless telegraph poles, etc.

Soon after the steamship's return to Adelaide there was an urgent call for further supplies and help. Charles Todd, Superintendent of Telegraphs, embarked on the *Omeo* and on this trip. She was accompanied by the *Tararua* and P.S. (Paddle Steamer) *Young Australia*. On clearing Booby Island they steered for the mouth of the Roper River to discharge their cargo at the Leichhardt Depot, sixty miles upstream...but the *Young Australia* unfortunately struck a rock in the river and sank. The Young Australia, with a gross tonnage of just 93 tons, had been one of the smallest steamers to make such a voyage via the Straits.

Read in conjunction with Charles Todd's assertion in his Report to the South Australian Government of the day (Appendix A) that he had given Mr. Lawrie, possibly the captain of the Young Australia, instructions to chart the course of the Roper from its mouth to 'the Landing' – the Roper Bar of Ray's story – as 'the most profitable way to employ the Young Australian (sic)', one can but surmise that it was in the course of this programme of mapping 'the rocks ands shallows' of the river that the Young Australia was wrecked, rather than during an attempt to begin the return journey, the inference being that the vessel had been left there in order to be of service to the newly established Overland Telegraph supply depot.

APPENDIX C

Extract from the Northern Territory News, August 5, 1999

Original Crocodile Dundee killed in NT shoot-out

Police in Darwin have confirmed that a man who shot a police officer who died yesterday was a former Territorian of the Year and the original Crocodile Dundee, Rodney Ansell.

Ansell fired at two police officrs and a civilian near a road block on the Stuart Highway in Darwin's rural area, before being killed in return fire.

Assistant Police Commissioner John Daulby says the firearms he used were not registered to Ansell, and Ansell did not have a firearms licence.

Ansell was 44, and had been living at Urapunga Station in the Roper River area, west of Katherine.

Ansell, who was said to have inspired the movie Crocodile Dundee, was the 1988 Territorian of the Year.

In 1992 he was convicted of cattle duffing.

'Crocodile Dundee' having assumed something of an iconic status in Australian thinking, it comes as almost a confirmation of our sense of national identity that such characters exist not only in Hollywood movies but in real life, in the 'The Territory'.

APPENDIX D

The Handing Over Of Urapunga To The Ngulakkan People

NGUKURR NEWS

Number 29, May 2002

Ngukurr News
Published by South East Arnhem Collaborative Research Project with assistance from Ngukurr CEC
Enquiries: 89786476

Reporters
Daphne Daniels, Selma Hall, John Bern & Kate Senior

Views expressed in Ngukurr News are not necessarily those of SEALCP

ŒUrapunga always was and always will be Aboriginal landØ

Extract from John Ah Kit's message to the Urapunga hand-over.

The official hand over of Urapunga Station on the 17th May was an event that the Ngalakgan people had been waiting 30 years for.

Hannah Duncan, Doreen Ponto, Samson Ponto, Dawson Daniels, David Daniels and Sheena Roy accepted the Title Deeds for Urapunga from the Federal Attorney General Daryl Williams.

John Ah Kit, Member for Arnhem sent this message:

[Congratulations to the traditional owners of Urapunga Station, the Ngalakgan people of the Roper River Region on the recent return of their homelands by the Land Commissioner Justice Olney. Due to parliamentary business I was unable to attend the ceremony and I am sorry I wasn't there to be part of history for the Ngalakan people.

I wish the families of the traditional owners all the best and look forward to catching up with them on my future trips to the area[]

Some members of the official party at the Urapunga Hand-over. From left to right are:

Nigel Scullion, Senator for the NT, Len Kiley, Member for Sanderson, who was representing John Ah Kit, The Hon Daryl Williams, the Federal Attorney General and Galarrwuy Yunupingu, the Chair of the Northern Land Council

It is thought-provoking to consider that during his recent visit to Urapunga Ray found the station to be in a derelict condition, most of the Aboriginal people having left to live in Katherine or Darwin. There were nine children only in the school. Urapunga was no longer a viable cattle station. Some of the older men and women still living there approached Ray with a proposition that he return and help them to get Urapunga on its feet again. Although now in his early-seventies, such is Ray's interest in Urapunga and its people, that he is seriously considering returning to do so.

ABOUT THE AUTHOR

Cattleman Ray Fryer and writer Marion Houldsworth at Mt. Isa, on the return from Urapunga, October, 2003

Queensland born Marion Houldswoth was educated at Blackheath College, Charters Towers, Rockhampton Girls' Grammer School and the University of Queensland. She taught for many years in New Guinea.

She has published four previous titles on North Queensland and her special interest is the history of Queensland and the Northern Territory. With grandchildren in Townsville, the UK and France, she commutes regularly around the traps, but North Queensland is still 'home'.

Also by Marion:

Barefoot Through the Bindies, 2002

Hearts Bright with Hope: A Grammer School Diary, 1948-51

The Morning Side of the Hill: A Townsville Childhood, 1939-45

The Immigrant Boy: A Townsville Boyhood, 1912-18

BIBLIOGRAPHY

Byerly, Frederick, (Editor) *The Complete Jardine Expedition Journals*, JW Buxton, Brisbane, 1867. Facsimile edition Corkwood Press, Adelaide, 1994

Berndt, Ronald and Catherine; *The World of the First Australians, Aboriginal Traditional Life, Past and Present*. Aboriginal Studies Press, Canberra, 1992

Buchanan, Bobbie. *Keep the Branding Iron Hot*. Central Queensland University Press, Rockhampton, 2002

Durack, Mary, *Kings in Grass Castles*, Constable and Company, London, 1957

Gibson-Wilde, Dorothy and Bruce, *A Pattern of Pubs, Hotels of Townsville 1864-1914*, James Cook University, 1988

Gibson-Wilde, Dorothy; *Gateway to a Golden Land*, James Cook University Press, 1984

Hill, Ernestine, *The Territory*, Angus and Robertson, Sydney, 1951

Hooper, Colin; *Angor to Zillmanton, Stories of North Queensland's deserted towns*, Merino, Brisbane, 1998.

James, Francis; *That's why We're Here; A Pictorial History of All Souls and St Gabriel's School*, Mimosa Press, Charter Towers, 1988

Leichhardt, Ludwig, *Journal of an Overland Expedition in Australia*, T and W Boone, London, 1847. -Facsimile edition, Corkwood Press, 1996

Lyons, Father Terry; *The Illusive Evans; A Family History* (unpublished)

Messel, H et al; *Surveys of Tidal River Systems in the Northern Territory of Australia, and their Crocodile Populations*. Pergamon Press, Sydney, 1980.

Miller, Lillian Ada; Harrison Printing, Toowoomba. 1999 (2nd. Ed.) *The Border and Beyond*

Nicholson, Ian; *Via Torres Strait, A Maritime History of the Torres Strait Route and the Ships' Post Office at Booby Island*. Roebuck Society Publication, Sunstrip Print, Nambour, Q. 1996

Plowman, R.B. *The Man from Oodnadatta*, Shoestring Press, Wangaratta, 1992

Northern Territory Medical Services, Darwin, 1968, *Leprosy in Northern Territory Aborigines*

Reynolds, Henry; *The Other Side of the Frontier, Aboriginal Resistance to the European Invasion of Australia*, James Cook University Press, 1981

Walker, Richard and Helen; *Curtin's Cowboys, Australia's Secret Bush Commandos*, Allan and Unwin, Sydney, 1986

Journals and Other Publications

ABC News Online, August 5th 1999

Marcus Casey, *Daily Telegraph*, 6th October 2002, Should the Predator be Protected?

Deakin University Research Paper, *Ngandi Life in the Early Days* Told by Sam Thompson. Recorded by Cherry Daniels and Ross Thompson, Translated from Ngandi and re-told in English by Cherry Daniels

Smith, Tim; Centre for Asia Pacific Arts, Canberra, 1993, *Nineteenth Century Photography in the Northern Territory.*

Land Rights News – June 2002

Whitehead, P.J. and Stephenson; P.J; James Cook University Press, 1998; *Lava Rise Ridges of the Toomba Basalt Flow*, North Queensland.

INDEX

T

U

V

W

Y

Z